CONTENTS

DESIRE AND DOUBT

Giovanni Battista Piranesi, S. Maria del Priorato, Rome, Italy, 1764–66
(Photograph by Author)

This one is for Catherine

FOREWORD

On the subway the other day I watched a composer jot
down individual notes, then erase them, jot down other
notes, assemble them into phrases, then weave the phrases
into fields of passages and movements. Had he looked
up across the aisle, he might have seen me engaged in a
similar procedure, writing the words you are now reading.

I have always considered that design and writing
share these similar modes of production and performance, both of which involve for me the three steps Walter
Benjamin cited for work on prose: 'a musical stage when
it is composed, an architectonic one when it is built, and
a textile one when it is woven'.

Even more than the English word 'compose', the
German word that Benjamin uses – *komponiert* – expresses
the tectonic attribute of components, *komponenten*, and
thus the act of placing them together in a series, which
requires a building up, a weaving together. 'Bits and pieces',
in the words of Lawrence Weiner's aphorism, 'put together
to present a semblance of a whole'. Which is what every
cultural artefact (whether a piece of music, an essay, a
building, a novel, a film) is – indeed, it's what all narrative,
all identity, all ideology, all and every culture is (as any
anthropologist could tell us).

This is one way to understand the title of this book.
Tectonic because of the components, the 'bits and the pieces'
of our culture. *Acts of* because the putting 'together to present' is a form of cultural performance. *Desire and Doubt*
because it is only 'a semblance of a whole' that gets fabricated.

This building up, which aims to fabricate the semblance of a complete whole, is what Alain Badiou means
when he says that the subject is a *configuration* that exceeds its situation. And what Max Frisch means when

he says an individual 'is a sum of various possibilities' that goes beyond specific biography. ('Only the variations reveal the common centre', he said in 1964, sounding a lot like he could be describing current ideas about parametrics). Individual identities, at whatever cultural scale, are always contingent, and are neither reducible to their component parts nor complete as fixed wholes.

In Benjamin's writing the weave is never so total that the individual components are no longer evident, nor so unwoven (even at his most *Arcades Project* fragmentary) that the components remain totally isolated from each other. This is as true in eighteenth-century novels like Sterne's *Tristram Shandy* and Diderot's *Jacques the Fatalist*, as it is in nineteenth-century novels like Dickens' *Bleak House* and Zola's *Germinal*, in last century's Beckett's *Company* and Frisch's *Gantenbein*, or in this century's McCarthy's *The Road* and Robison's *Why Did I Ever*. A few favourites that taught me a few things about design and writing: how figures merge into and emerge from a woven field, how the seemingly continuous text (nineteenth-century 'realism') is revealed as built up of discontinuous bits, and how the most fragmentary text (eighteenth- or twentieth-century or this century's 'experimentation') is revealed as developing through a continuous reweaving.

Transforming the parameters of the bits (whether musical or literary or tectonic components), as well as the parameters of how they are assembled and woven together and apart, is how poignancy is developed in cultural artefacts. This is what is at stake in these various and varied forms of formal play through the centuries. Architects and critics all too often forget the poignancy and play that architecture is capable of, because they think architecture is a vessel in which life happens, rather than a performance of life itself, of the culture of life, of how we as a culture think life in and through architecture. For many reasons it seems easier for people to find poignancy in literature or film than in buildings. This is why even as the oldest art form, architecture can still learn from other performative media, especially the youngest, cinema.

I have never understood the distinction made between these types of cultural production – considering how radical Coltrane's reweaving of the typology of a show tune like *My Favorite Things* is – which is why the essays on art, cartoons, food, music became for me a parallel way to explore modes of evocative engagement in a wide range of cultural artefacts – of which architecture is one of many. The themes that link those forms of cultural artefact and the cultural artefacts produced by Shigeru Ban, Gianlorenzo Bernini, Giulio Romano, Louis Kahn, Rem Koolhaas, Greg Lynn, Ludwig Mies van der Rohe, Luigi Moretti, Andrea Palladio and Giovanni Battista Piranesi are investigated in the longer essays on narrative, mutability, identity and hybridity. Perceiving the parallels between diverse modalities of the world is what I learned most of all, in different ways, from Gregory Bateson and Gordon Lish, both of whom never underestimated the deep relations between formal and social meaning.

For me the most engaging work in any media in any century are those sentient artefacts that appear to consider their condition and circumstance before us and in relation to us, simultaneously 'out loud' and *sotto voce*, visibly enacting their process of thought, the process of thought that has been tectonically woven into them, so that we might consider along with them and through them – even and especially so we might consider alternative formations.

Of course, forewords are really back-words views on what has already been written, so I have placed the most recent essay first as a way of indicating how the development of these performative readings has set the stage for one of my current projects: a series of close readings of a few such sentient buildings through a few centuries.

Now, if I have arranged the subsequent essays in this book in relation to the three categories (Tectonic, Acts of, Desire and Doubt), they might equally well have been arranged in many alternative manners, in other fields of association, production and performance. Arranged, say, according to when they were written (which isn't always the same as when they were first delivered in conferences or when they were subsequently published). For example, quite different types of essays were written around the same time: 'Tectonic Acts of Desire and Doubt: What Kahn Wants to Be' was written around the time I was writing 'Identity and the Discourse of Politics in Architecture'. 'John Coltrane's Sample and Scratch' was written around the time I was writing 'Why Architecture is Neither Here nor There'. Each one could be a lens to view the other, certainly they were mutually influential.

Their composition would be even better understood not just in relation to each other, but by extending this field in relation to the architectural designs I was working on at the same time – those designs that were building up emergent identities through components (*A/Partments, Neighbor Hood Acts* and *Rates of Exchange*) during the writing of 'Tectonics' and 'Identity', and those designs that were reworking typology through hybrid sample and scratch reweavings (*Urbia* and *Guest/Host House*) during the writing of 'Coltrane' and 'Here nor There'. In every case the writing inflected the design and the design inflected the writing. Each of these designs involved selecting certain tectonic figures and media components to build up, weave and transform together from one spatial scene to the next, enacting the parameters of the diverse social fields (low, middle, high) in which these projects were situated. Tectonic actors of desire and doubt. The work of every essay and every design project for me has been to enact this desire for, and doubt about, both the parts and the whole, in both the formal and the social sense.

So although the graphic format of this series is not conducive to my more image-intensive project essays, their presence is interwoven in the texts included here. As is the presence of everyone who assisted in the development of these themes in the design: the clients, the builders, all those in the office, each of whom in their own way assisted in working through these issues in research and material form. There are too many to name here, but special mention goes to William Arbizu, Reid Balthaser, Andrew Blocha, Cathy De Almeida, Michael Hargens, Madhavi Jandhyala,

Damon Lau, Nicholas Locke, Eduardo McIntosh, Alvar Mensana, Muchan Park, Younjin Park, Andrew Parsegian, Doug Pfeifer, Adam Phillips, Luc Wilson, Brian Ziska and, above all, to Jason Vigneri-Beane and Aaron White, for years of sustained engagement.

In other words, the fact that every subject is a configuration that exceeds its situation is also the reason for acknowledgements.

Thus these written and designed artefacts existed in the wider design field, so thanks to the university deans and chairs who established a field of dialogue in the context of which these ideas were engaged: at Columbia (Bernard Tschumi, Mark Wigley), Cornell (Kent Kleinman, Dagmar Richter), Harvard (Rafael Moneo), Iowa State (Robert Segrest), Northwestern (Nancy Troy), Parsons The New School for Design (Kent Kleinman, Paul Goldberger, William Morrish, Peter Wheelwright), Pratt Institute (Anthony Cardonna, Evan Douglis, Tom Hanrahan), University of California at Los Angeles (Sylvia Lavin), University of Illinois at Chicago (Stanley Tigerman), and to all my engaged students for whom and with whom these matters became a moment of exploration.

Still further, thanks to those who extended the discussions into and through wider publication: first and foremost *Assemblage*, which established an extraordinary forum at a crucial juncture in architecture thanks to editors K. Michael Hayes, Catherine Ingraham and Alicia Kennedy, and to the project and review editors and editorial board for years of discussion and debate (Stan Allen, Beatriz Colomina, Mario Gandelsonas, Sanford Kwinter, Robert McAnulty, Sarah Whiting, Mark Wigley). And to Cynthia Davidson, who through *ANY* and *Log* has extended the debate through decades as well, thanks to her and to her guest editors Ben van Berkel, Caroline Bos and Mitchell Schwarzer. And thanks to those responsible for the other publications collected here: Philip Anzalone, Fareed Armaly, Stella Betts, Bridget Borders, Richard Burdett, Stephen Cairns, Irene Chang, Jeffrey Inaba, Jeffrey Kipnis, David Leven, Bernard Tschumi, John Whiteman.

Further still, thanks to the Graham Foundation for Advanced Studies in the Fine Arts, who funded the initial development of these writings, as well as probably funding, through the decades, most of the individuals, institutions and enterprises mentioned here, keeping alive research in architecture.

Close in to this occasion: thanks to Brett Steele, who started this series precisely to keep vital written discourse in architecture, to Thomas Weaver, so attuned to the word and the image, and to Pamela Johnston, for her careful and thoughtful attention to the text. William Arbizu (along with Nicholas Locke) contributed to the development of the initial design ideas for the book, coinciding with many of the modes of Wayne Daly's incisive design for the series. Thanks also to William Whitaker and Nancy Thorne of the Architectural Archive at the University of Pennsylvania.

Closer now, thanks to those not yet named who in various ways helped manifest these various considerations: Michael Bell, Guido Beltramini, Francesco Benelli, Paul Byard, Byongsoo Cho, Bill Bywater, Gwen Chovanec, Donna Cohen, Pat Cohen, Bruce Ferguson, Rosalie Genevro, Laurie Hawkinson, Sue Henderson, Brian Hofland, Jeffrey Johnson, David Joselit, Phil Kupritz, David Lewis, Carter Manny, Scott Marble, Robert H. Mayer, Joanna Merwood-Salisbury, Jorge Otero-Pailos, Christopher Phillips, Anne Rieselbach, Jonsara Ruth, David M Saltzman, Elisabeth Sussman, Enrique Walker, Brian Wallis and George Wheeler.

Closer still:

To Ira, architect, and Lenore, artist, who gave me eyes to see, and the value of seeing and making things to see.

To Max, now no longer ten, nor the other ages he was in those times when I invoked his insightful presence in my writing in my life then as now.

And to Catherine, to whom this book is dedicated, there from the start of these writings, for our life composed built woven together with architecture with words.

TECTONIC

FABRICATORS

Let's try this statement on for size (or scale): all architects are fabricators.

In both senses of the term. In the sense of those who make things *and* make up things. As in the legal definition: 'to make up with the intent to deceive'. As in the fact that all architects make real the imaginary, make up imaginary worlds in order that they can be constructed, that they fabricate reality … with the intent to what? To deceive or to conceive? That we as architects rather than receive reality as is, de-conceive one reality and conceive of another, in the manner and matter of fabrication?

The definitions of fabrication range between all these states: 1. To make by art or skill and labour, construct; 2. To make by assembling parts or sections; 3. To devise or invent (a legend, lie, etc.); 4. To fake or forge. But doesn't this define the very act of architecture as well: a skilled assembly of parts and sections, with the intent to devise and invent, to forge anew, a new (as of yet) still fictive reality in advance of it being constructed into the world? Reality is indeed parametrically mutable: by adjusting the parameters of parts or sections of reality we can fabricate anew[1]. This is the ineluctable oscillating play – between the parameters of the received reality (the documentary mode) and the parametric fabrication of a re-conceived reality (the fictional mode) – that is architecture.

Now this goes against the received story we often like to tell ourselves: that we architects are engaged in the real manner and matter of real construction, except of course in periods when architects play with matter and manner as in Mannerism. Something someone like Giulio Romano does when, with a nod and a wink, he fabricates, in both senses of the term, a triglyph as if it were slipping down from its 'crucial' position in the entablature of his 1534 Palazzo Te courtyard. Even if, or especially because, a triglyph is just a faked beam end, a fabrication of the legendary wooden origin-myth of classical architecture. Or as in Luigi Moretti's 'fake' rustication of his 1947–50 Casa Il Girasole. But what makes Moretti's rustication fake? Given that it is real stone, developed parametrically along the diverse range of material and cultural parameters of its identity – as picturesque landscape elements, rusticated blocks, fluted surface, classic figural statuary, modernist thin cladding – a transformative performance not only of the historical biography of stone in architecture, but also of Moretti's own autobiography as an architect.

At Casa Il Girasole, Moretti reveals stone in its then real factual constructive condition as a form of veneer, in contrast to the deceiving stucco-over-brick 'rustication' Bramante devised 450 years earlier for the *piano rustico* of his 1501 Palazzo Caprini. Contrary to certain received notions of architectural authenticity, this fabrication was already a performative material mode in the High Renaissance, given that the architects of the Cinquecento were imitating the rustication of the ancients, putting on a fictive front – frontin', as it may be said on the street today, fake playing. This stuccoed fabrication of 'rustication' (and other attributes of classical antiquity) reduced, as Christoph Frommel notes, 'the costs of construction considerably and made the possibilities of a direct imitation of the ancients very inviting for patrons of reduced financial means. Without this economical technique, Bramante's direct successors – not just Raphael, Peruzzi and Giulio Romano, but also Jacopo Sansovino, Sanmicheli and Palladio – would never have been able to achieve some of their most important works.'[2] Thus it can be said that the very production of the Renaissance in fact depended on this wholesale full-scale fabrication.

Speaking of Palladio: standing in front of his 1565 Palazzo Valmarana in Vicenza, Guido Beltramini, Director of the Palladio Centre, said to me that this was his favourite, because it 'has all this nervous energy', and

Luigi Moretti, Casa Il Girasole, Rome, Italy 1949-53 (Photograph by Author)

Antonio Lafrery, Palazzo Caprini and Palazzo Stati Maccarani, 1549

directing my attention to the mezzanine window cut out in the middle of the top entablature, said that here Palladio 'lets us know this joke'. Now jokes and fabrications are what we expect from Giulio Romano not Andrea Palladio, particularly as – to cite chapter and verse, chapter XX line 10 in Book I of his 1570 *Quattro Libri*, in the section entitled 'On Abuses' – Palladio rails against any fabrication of any building element that diminishes its primary purpose, which according to him is 'to appear to produce the effect for which they were put there, which is to make the structure … look secure and stable'.[3] The equivocal choice of words is telling – 'appear', 'effect', 'make the structure look' – but appearance, affect, fabricated structure are, as Renaissance historians tell us, some of the main modalities of the Cinquecento, which was a matter and manner of representation rather than reality. But then again this is no more or less fabricated than the applied 'columns' of Roman antiquity, applied as they were all over amphitheatres and temples and triumphal arches, or the applied bronze-bling columns on the facade of Mies's Seagram Building. So these forms of double fabrications go way back. And in fact at Palazzo Valmarana, Palladio abuses the standard forms of security and stability in three radical ways. First, by the aforementioned window cut right out of the primary horizontal structure that is the entablature. Second, by pushing the giant composite order into the building facade so much that it cuts into *and* through the lower implied entablature to such an extant that the cut is revealed by the top edge of this cornice sticking out past the pilaster, brutally destroying any sense of the horizontal distribution of load at that level. And third, there is the really shocking 'oh no he didn't' moment: the removal of the giant order from the ends of the facade – at exactly the points that classically would demand the most support, security and stability – so that the edges of the building are left to lone caryatids perched on single-storey secondary pilasters to hold up the visual load now weakened even more than by Giulio Romano's slipped triglyph.

This nervous built fabric of a facade relates to the degree of creative nervousness Palladio most likely felt in his imaginary 'reconstruction' of antiquity, particularly in the illustrations he provided for Daniele Barbaro's 1556 publication of Vitruvius, wherein he makes up, fakes, forges, invents, fabricates parts of buildings (such as the use of the giant order for a private house) that have no reference or justification in Vitruvius, but which he will then use in his own work to reconceive the very form of the villa and the palazzo. And in the case of Palazzo Valmarana he reinvents his own received transmission of contemporary Roman palazzo design. He transfers and transforms the Bramante Palazzo Caprini model – of the rusticated ground level and the use of orders in the *piano nobile* that he adhered to in his earlier 1552 Palazzo Porto – from the social fabric of Rome to that of Vicenza, by expanding the orders across levels, representing (with some still nervous leftover Porto traces of rustication and those single-storey *piano nobile* secondary columns) that the nobles there occupied both the ground level and the *piano nobile*. All those tectonic elements – columns, entablatures, rustication – which even in Bramante's palazzo were faked depth, Palladio now develops as multiple superimposed layers collapsed into a radical surface relief yet still maintains the legibility and interaction of the separate layers – which certainly has made many an architect and historian nervous since.

This kind of superimposed pictorial and tectonic layering had already been suggested on the exteriors and interiors of Giulio Romano's Palazzo Te, and by now it has been demonstrated that Palladio took a lot from Giulio Romano, a lot more than had generally been assumed, and not just credit for the Palazzo Thiene commission (which was in fact Giulio Romano's design and for which Palladio was the local on-site assistant). In his 1546 Basilica, Palladio was also inspired, as Beltramini and Howard Burns have noted, by the elastic and adaptable serliana system that Giulio Romano developed in a radically iterative and responsive manner in the renovations at San Benedetto Po of 1540. The serliana – that motif so associated with Palladio that it is mistakenly labelled the Palladian Window

Andrea Palladio, elevation of Palazzo Valmarana, *I Quattro libri dell'architettura*
(Venice: Domenico de' Franceschi, 1570), Book II, Ch. III, p. 17

Andrea Palladio, Palazzo Valmarana, Vicenza, Italy 1565 (Photograph by Author)

(originated in fact by Bramante, promoted subsequently by Serlio) – is all too often described as an arch with flanking rectangular openings. In fact it should really be understood as a mutant figure, a hybridising of the two structural forms to the point of endangering the actual structural stability of both – the arch interrupting the top chord of the trabeated rectangular frame, the rectangular frame removing the arch sides – were it not for the crucial column supports that arrive at this precarious moment of interface to save both from mutual collapse. Which in Andrea Palladio's use in the Basilica creates the effect of an extraordinary if repetitive diaphanous screen, syncopating major and minor order, with its notable compression at the corners.

What Giulio Romano developed (in the 1520s and 1530s at Palazzo Te and in 1540 at San Benedetto Po), and what Palladio borrowed from him in part, is not the repetitive serial use of certain motifs, but what has been claimed as the very definition of parametric design: iterative systems that are able to adapt and respond in a motivated manner to internal and external forces. Parametric systems have been a main wave of exploration, in name or approach, for the past two decades, although it turns out that in 1950 Luigi Moretti referred to the design use of parameters right from his editorial send-off in the first issue of his journal *Spazio*, and by 1952 was calling for an *'architettura parametrica'*, even before he was pioneering the use of computers in his 1960–65 design for the Watergate complex. As for Giulio Romano, Burns has noted his extensive use of responsive hybrid systems: 'Further combinations of arched and trabeated solutions, like the serliana, always elastic, expressive and adaptable to irregular or pre-existing facades, are ever present in his work',[4] which is particularly evident in his radically iterative play on Bramante's Belvedere through compression and expansion in the lateral façade at San Benedetto Po.

Having now measured and digitally modelled and animated Giulio Romano's Palazzo Stati Maccarani (known to many solely as the site of the best coffee in Rome,

Sant'Eustachio Il Caffè), I can say that it turns out that Giulio Romano was operating parametrically even in the early 1520s. In this palazzo he developed a series of tectonic elements in the *piano rustico*, *piano nobile* and attic storeys, which transform along a set of parameters horizontally in each of the three exposed facades and vertically up through the building levels. The latter transformation begins to radically shift and mutate the strict class division of *rustico* retail and *nobile* residential of Bramante's Palazzo Caprini, remixing the mixed-use palazzo in ways that resonate with the rise of the merchant and middle class in this period, as already indicated by Frommel's assessment of the shift in patronage at this time.

These themes of parametric and performative muta-bility are evident throughout Giulio Romano's work, from the buildings to the decorative arts to the tapestries to the frescos to the drawings. In the same period as his design of Palazzo Stati Maccarani, Giulio Romano is preparing his infamous etchings for *I modi* (*The Positions*), a collection of representations of erotic couplings paired with smutty sonnets from leading author and cultural figure Pietro Aretino, which as Bette Talvacchia has noted was scandal-ous not for its smuttiness but for its expression of the mu-tual desire of both sexes in the exchange.[5] Indeed, what are Kama Sutra-like manuals – move her leg now here, move his arm now there – but a form of relational paramet-ric positionings? Yet in Giulio Romano's case these itera-tions of relational and interactive body components or building components are not merely a formal parametrics, but a parametrics of identity. A social parametrics, address-ing and enacting the social and psychological transforma-tion of class and gender relations in his time.

Lest anyone think I'm trying to fabricate a justification from the past, rather than a provocation for the future, I would concur with Manfredo Tafuri that the past is only useful when used not to settle but rather to unsettle the present and future – just as the possibility of new paramet-ric and performative techniques of analysis and fabrication should unsettle our understanding of the past. So let's get

Andrea Palladio, Basilica (Palazzo della Ragione), Vicenza, Italy, 1546–49
(Photograph by Author)

Giulio Romano, San Benedetto Po, Polirone, Italy, 1540–47 (Photograph: Brian Lee)

back to the future of architecture then, the fabricated future of full-scale fabrication. Recently Eduardo McIntosh wrote, incisively, to tell me:

They have been sending me to these software workshops, where companies go and brag in front of other companies about how they use ___ to make the new hotness. From ___ to ___ to some small unknown offices, the project is: make a homogeneous skin out of different panels. If you want to be cool your claim should be like ___'s team: 'We made this skin with 1 trillion panels and no panel is the same' – so I don't know, for a moment I thought that maybe it was cooler to make a more interesting form with exactly the same panel. The other topic is curves: 'We evaluate curves to make sure they are good curves' – for a moment I thought I was with my high school buddies in Ecuador. And continuity, everything has to be continuous here.

As Eduardo's 'for a moment' suggests: continuous or discontinuous, curved or straight, all different *or* all same, these should not be our exclusive choices in this still new century. In regard to parametric design, if anyone were asked to explain some important situation with the question 'what are the parameters here?', the meaningful answer would never be a trillion gradient responses, but a very limited set of relational and consequential actions (and reactions and interactions). As any other performative medium teaches us, some of these actions and reactions and interactions would logically sequence the events in question and some would cause a surprising turn of events. What parametric fabrication promises today is the ability not just to indiscriminately slide the software slider bar or CNC mill or waterjet contour cutter back and forth in an infinite gradient, but instead to track certain sets of parameters. Exploring the parameters of social and cultural identity through the exploration of formal identities. And if we take the word fabrication even further back to its root as 'fabric', it is still amazing to realise that all the definitions, beyond the first ones regarding cloth, have everything to do with the conceptual and material and social sense of architecture and urbanism, everything to do with the complex, underlying structure of what we make and what we make up: 1. Framework, structure: the fabric of society; 2. A building, edifice; 3. The method of construction; 4. The act of constructing, esp. of a church building; 5. The maintenance of such a building. Even the petrography definition refers to the *'spatial arrangement* and *orientation* of the *constituents'* of a rock, a definition that if understood in the material and political meaning of constituents could parametrically refer as well to the fabrication of the city, to a skilful and responsively adaptive assembly of parts and sections, with the intent to devise and invent, to forge a new urban fabric.

So let's imagine new spatial arrangements and orientations of our tectonic and cultural constituents, investigating and instigating the fabrication of those underlying structural assumptions of our seemingly 'secure and stable' social and built fabric. Let's fabricate social relations – at every scale.

NOTES

Forthcoming in Phillip Anzalone and Bridget Borders (eds.), *Full-Scale* (New York: Columbia University Graduate School of Architecture, Planning and Preservation).

1. For a discussion of the fabricated assembly of ideology and culture as 'Bits & Pieces Put Together to Present a Semblance of a Whole', and its manifestation in and through social space, see the Foreword in this volume and Mark Rakatansky, 'A/Partments', *Assemblage* 35 (1998), 48–61.

2. Christoph Luitpold Frommel, 'Living *all'antica*: Palaces and Villas from Brunelleschi to Bramante', in Henry

A. Millon, ed., *Italian Renaissance Architecture: from Brunelleschi to Michelangelo* (London: Thames and Hudson, 1976), 195.

3. Andrea Palladio, *The Four Books on Architecture*, trans. Robert Tavernor and Robert Schofield, (Cambridge MA: MIT Press, 1997), 56.

4. Howard Burns, '*"Quelle cose antique e moderne belle de Roma"*: Giulio Romano, The Theatre and the Antique', in *Giulio Romano*, ed. Manfredo Tafuri (Cambridge: Cambridge University Press, 1998), 141.

5. Bette Talvacchia, *Taking Positions: On the Erotic in Renaissance Culture* (Princeton: Princeton University Press, 1999).

TECTONIC ACTS OF DESIRE AND DOUBT (1945–1980): WHAT KAHN WANTS TO BE

And.

Not or. Acts of desire *and* doubt. Because if there's desire, there's doubt.

And vice versa.

If there is *some* doubt, then there has to be *some* desire – desire for something else – that is causing that doubt. This is because desire, as Jacques Lacan observed, is the difference that results when you subtract need from demand. The demand, say, for the attention of love – to use Slavoj Žižek's example of the cry of the infant – is never satisfied by just the functional satisfaction of the need, say, for milk: 'Thus desire is neither the appetite for satisfaction, nor the demand for love, but the difference that results from the subtraction of the first from the second, the phenomenon of their splitting.'[1]

But, if you prefer the words of architects to those of psychoanalysts or theorists, then here's Louis Kahn, circa 1968, on the economies of desire and need: 'Need is so many bananas. Need is a ham sandwich. But desire is insatiable and you cannot ever know what it is.'[2]

Or here, circa 1969: 'Down deep, man only trusts desire, not need. Need is just so many bananas as far as I'm concerned. Desire is the entire strength of man's striving to live.'[3] Or here, circa 1972: 'Desire is insatiable, and it is the root of dissension. It is opening up the avenues where desire can be felt.'[4]

When Kahn, to use that more famous example, asks Brick 'what it wants', or asks a railroad station 'what it wants to be', this is because the desire or the identity of a brick, or of a railroad station, is not given – is never given. This desire, this identity, always has to be constructed, has to be fabricated. In this game of ventriloquism, the responses that Kahn ascribes to the brick or to the train station always express some lack or some excess: Brick 'wants an arch', but arches, Kahn replies to Brick, are 'difficult to make, they cost more money, I think you can use concrete across your opening'. And when the railroad station seems to tell Kahn that it 'wants to be a street', Kahn replies it can only be a 'meeting of contours englazed'.[5]

The particular identity crises to which Kahn refers in these examples are crises that are related, of course, to the oscillating social, economic and political identity crises of that time, that time being the period following World War II, and to the concurrent crises within architecture: between collective identification and individual expressionism, between modernist desire and mannerist doubt.

I

I will refer to many kinds of acts here, some of which will be tectonic acts. I'll put this another way: the tectonic acts of desire and doubt that I will refer to here are only the precipitate of many other acts of desire and doubt – political, ideological, social, biographical, formal, institutional, disciplinary. It is impossible to separate these issues from each other, but it is also impossible to imagine that these issues will ever neatly line up or synthesise or resolve, without some lack or some excess.

It is not a particularly productive task for the historian or the critic or the theorist to *resolve tensions* or to *choose sides* or to *predict styles* or to *make heroes*. What the historian or the critic or the theorist *can* do is to draw on the past, to illuminate its complexity. And this illumination will inevitably speak to the present, it might even illuminate the complexity of the present, if it does so by productively leaving – as Manfredo Tafuri suggested in his final book – 'the problems of the past living and unresolved, unsettling our present'.[6]

If there is a political dimension to the practices of history or criticism or theory, then it is this: it is the extent to which one's practice attempts to disturb or, conversely, to shore up the present – to disturb or to shore up our way of knowing the present, the way the present represents itself (and the past) to itself. Any historical or critical or theoretical representation will make some attempt, or some complex of conflicted attempts, in the directions of disturbance and shoring up, whether one seems to desire this or not.

So: what is your desire?

And between what needs and what demands – ideological, disciplinary, institutional, psychological – is this desire of yours oscillating?

Whatever your (or my) desire may be, there is no historical or critical or theoretical method that can resolve the tensions of the past or, for that matter, those of the present. And likewise, whatever your (or my) desire may be, there is no historical or critical or theoretical method that can entirely and thoroughly disrupt the attempts of the past or the present to present themselves as resolved.

This oscillation between attempts at resolution and at disruption is the crisis of identity as well as its very form and formation. It is the very contingency of identity, as Ernesto Laclau notes, which social practices try to conceal by continually developing seemingly fixed and stable cultural identities.[7] But eventually any identity, any acts of identification, will be revealed in its performance to have fractures and instabilities, 'distortions and excesses that point at its precarious and contingent constitution'.[8] Cultural practices that seek to challenge past identities do so as often by intensifying and exaggerating the principles of that identity as by challenging them. Any success in breaking down prior identities will in turn also fail, as rather than undoing identity, new identities will develop in turn to fill in the lack: 'Failure will trigger new acts of identification … which attempt (vainly) to master those destructuring effects… This is why there is a permanent and alternating movement whereby the lack is rejected and invoked, articulated and annulled, included and excluded.'[9]

In some of the more engaging work of Kahn, and in a number of other contemporaneous architects, the new identities constructed simultaneously enact this oscillation between a desired identity, its failure, and a complex new identity that results. And yet, either in other contemporary work or in later work by these same architects, these tectonic enactments of desire and doubt will also fail, giving rise to new identities that will result in more formulaic symbolisations and stylisations of these previously enacted tectonic tensions.

It would be pointless, however, to lament these new identities as some form of failure or decline or degeneration – they are merely further attempts for stable identities. They too will fail, and their failures will lead to other attempts, other architectures, other histories, other criticisms, other theories.

It would be equally pointless to suggest that these rarefied 'high-art' enactments or symbolisations are pure expressions of the zeitgeist in some definitive way – they merely put into play certain tensions of their time. One could just as productively analyse the 'commercial' architecture of a given time to see these tensions and complexities at play, even if – some might suggest – in a less refined, more confused and consequently more overt, way.

II

Let me give one such example of confusion and tension. When I was a student in architecture school, circa 1980, I was taken on one of those class field-trips that one is always taken on in architecture school, a field-trip to see the (then) new 'Levi's Plaza', the corporate headquarters in San Francisco of Levi Strauss & Co (manufacturer of 'blue jeans' and other fashionable attire) designed by the firm of Hellmuth, Obata, and Kassabaum, a building complex that represented the early stages of HOK's fashionable but belated move from their tepid 'late modern' identity-phase into their tepid 'postmodern' identity-phase, a complex done up not with bricks but with brick veneer, in order, it was claimed by HOK (or at least by the Project Designer who gave us the tour) to be 'contextual' – contextual that is, in a neighbourhood of masonry warehouses soon to be replaced by corporate headquarters aspiring to emulate the masonry warehouses that would no longer be there when they, the corporate headquarters, got done emulating and replacing them.

Now this brick veneer had been applied to long horizontal precast concrete panels and these concrete panels in turn had been hung in such a manner that the half-bricks of each panel were (and undoubtedly still are) separated from each other by an expansion joint of what seemed like (at the very least) an inch. When another student asked if this (at the very least) inch between the veneered bricks on the panels – in particular between the veneered half-bricks on these panels – didn't defeat the supposed effect of the brick, the response from the Project Designer at HOK's San Francisco office – HOK being then (and undoubtedly still are now) surely among the five largest architectural firms in the world – said with all seriousness and no little degree of irritation was:

'We wanted to be true to the panels.'

In my desirous and doubtful current identity as Public Speaker, I guess it is now time for me to say:

'That reminds me of a joke.'

The joke I am reminded of is a tectonic joke. It is the only tectonic joke I know. It is a joke, by the way, that I first heard in architecture school the same year as that field-trip. It is a joke that finds the identity of its humour in the very desire and doubt of that Kahn morality tale I mentioned earlier, that identity crisis of Kahn and of his brick, one of those discussions that Kahn, it seems, liked to have with inanimate objects.

Here is the joke.

It goes like this:

'Louis Kahn asked a brick what it wanted to be, and it said: "Veneer".'

However cynical this joke might sound to you – and certainly it represents, among other things, the cynicism of students, already tired from all that is past and has passed – it represents now, as it represented in Kahn's time, the real constructional condition of brick, at least in the United States: for institutional buildings of the scale at which Kahn was working, it was not possible to use brick in a load-bearing capacity.

In terms of the questions of identity and its failure, of desire and its doubt, it is no use mourning this condition, either with manic mourning for the ubiquity of simulacra – 'It's all veneer!' – or with melancholic mourning for some lost past – 'There was a time when a brick was a brick, when bricks bore the loads of our lives!' No use mourning – given that one of the originary uses of brick was precisely as a facing material. And no use mourning because it is not necessary to choose between the seemingly 'stable' identity of load-bearing, or brick's 'failure' as veneer. It is merely a condition to examine, to explore, to investigate, to address, to play with – which Kahn did, both to greater and to lesser effect.

I said it was not possible to use brick in a load-bearing capacity, but of course, what I should say is that it was not commercially practical, which, in most cases, certainly in all of Kahn's cases, amounts to the same thing. It was precisely this seeming failure in this particular historical period, this doubt regarding modernism, that circulated around this sort of identity – this identity of the material realm – which triggered Kahn's very desire for this particular material: this material that he could evoke, in a historicist way, but never use in a purely functional and unproblematic way. Because of 'need' you see, which may be just that quantitative 'so many bananas' as Kahn said, but it is Kahn himself, in that same year circa 1972, who tells Brick: 'arches are difficult to make, they cost more money, I think you can use concrete across your opening'.

The (expression of the) individual identity of that brick, or of that architect, has to come to terms with needs and desires and demands outside itself, with its place in

the collective identity: the concrete element is, as Kahn
said, circa 1973, the 'restraining member which keeps
the arch from pushing out. It brings it back into the wall.
I call it a composite order. I recognise in which way the
concrete is helping brick to be used again. Brick has within
it its own death, because it is not resourceful enough.'[10]
This restraining and ordering of individual architectural
identity was conceived by Kahn as not unlike the restraining and ordering enacted by society itself, as for example
when Kahn said the same year, that 'the plan is a *society*
of rooms in whatever may be their duty and in what way
they supplement the duty of others …'[11]

III

'You could build the entire idea of a society of man',
Kahn said, circa 1968, 'by just thinking of the brick structure which can be built.'[12] Let's let this last statement stand
as is (or was), but with the slight addition of one phrase:
'and cannot be built'. Not *or*. By this I mean both the brick
structure – or any other material(ist) identity – that can
and cannot be built in any historical period, *as well as* the
'entire idea' of a society that can *and* cannot be built in any
historical period.

Even the phrase 'historical period' leads me to the
problem of identity and its so-called stability or instability.
Or, as it is often stated in the terms of a certain sort of art
history: stable period following instable period, instable
following stable. And yet, it should be common knowledge
by now that one can find instabilities in what appears to be
stable (the very seeds of its so-called degeneration) as well
as stabilities, or attempts at stabilities, in what appears to
be instable.

For example, it is often assumed that postmodernism
established itself as a definitive break from modernism
by proposing identities and concerns that were completely
absent from that earlier period. But the identities that
postmodernism in architecture would claim for itself –

contextualism, historicism, fragmentation – are already latent within modernism, as becomes most evident in this period following World War II. In the United States, for example, there was a sense of new possibility and progress – including the new possibilities of global empire, which would manifest themselves through expansionism and imperialism – as well as a sense of restriction, through the social and cultural xenophobias of McCarthyism and Cold War (identity) politics. In architecture these tensions circulated around fears of collectivism, with its totalitarian overtones, and fears that individual caprice would destroy common values and traditions – thus the oscillation one sees between identification with collective contextualism and identification with individual expressionism. These tensions and many others were expressed architecturally from the level of urban design to that of tectonic detail.

The 'emergence' of postmodernism in architecture occurred when these tensions no longer seemed much like tensions, when they seemed to reflect little more than the arbitrariness of any stylistic choice. And yet this postmodern identification with the failure, or the arbitrariness, of any stable design identification will in its turn fail, as we are now witnessing, as new 'stable' identities are being sought, or rather constructed, before our eyes.

Here is an example, one out of many: the current focus in contemporary practice on tectonics as a form of comforting stability – (precious) tectonic details as ends in and of themselves, rather than as a means of critical thought. Details without doubt. Tectonics (and Craft and Material) as Truth.

IV

But first, let's go back and locate some past desire and doubt in tectonic detail in the hopes of illuminating the present situation. Let's go back, say, to the ambivalence of the 'Miesian corner', which begins to appear most dramatically in his project for the Illinois Institute of Technology

Library and Administration Building around the end of the war, circa 1944. Here one finds a wavering between a destruction and an intensification of the corner, of the identity of the corner. While prior examples of modernist glass corners had already begun to problematise the corner, as they allowed its occupation by material that was not load-bearing, those examples still maintained a continuous wrapping condition of the facade. But Mies van der Rohe, in extending this break the entire vertical length of the building – at the IIT Chemistry Building (1945), or at the Seagram Building (1954–58) – unhinged each facade in a way that is at least as, if not more, disruptive than the veneered effect of those contemporaneous non-structural I-beams welded to the surface of his buildings. Once freed, these facades would develop into the detached walls and screens not only of Kahn, but also of Edward Durrell Stone and eventually of Charles Moore and Robert Venturi and Denise Scott Brown. While the form from Mies to Venturi and Scott Brown changes significantly, the underlying ambivalence of identity changes only in character – from the *sotto voce* disquiet of the former to the billboard anxiety of the latter.

Veneer again, you see.

Because, of course, the wall in its modernist (non-load-bearing, free-facade, free-plan) condition inevitably becomes so free in the phenomenon of its splitting, its splitting of need and demand (Lacan again), that the architect finds it difficult to keep it from floating free of the building (as facing, as surface, as veneer).

But – and this is an important but – notice that even as Moore and Venturi and Scott Brown attempt to demonstrate as well as manifest the failure of one aspect of modernism's project of abstraction (in other words, modernism's own attempt to manifest the failure of traditional identity), they do not entirely return their walls and screens to their traditional (classical and vernacular) referents – they still abstract those references. Not as totally as Peter Eisenman would *attempt* to abstract these referents and, equally, by necessity, would fail – Eisenman still referencing his walls and screens to the traditional structural frame.

Both sides, in other words, are unable either to align themselves completely or to remove themselves completely from
their traditional identities.

Thus, while the postwar period may be characterised
as almost-but-not-quite beyond (modernist) belief, the postmodern period might be characterised as beyond-and-thus-
almost-but-not-quite back to (traditional) belief.

Here again one might say that, circa 1945, it was Mies's
turn toward – desire toward – the classical and the symmetrical that caused the doubt that materialised in the
disruption of the corner, a doubt that obviously was not
desired in his earlier asymmetrical modernism that maintained the corner.

Or vice versa.

Maybe having materialised, and made tectonic, his
doubt at (and of) the corner, Mies felt the desire to attempt
to contain the violence of this rupture through the obvious,
'time-honoured' means of classical symmetry.

Thankfully we know that these questions of origins,
these questions of the originary design moment, cannot
and will not be resolved. And need not be: Mies's corner,
as I stated earlier, both destroys and intensifies the identity
of the corner.

V

This now leads us back to Kahn, to the identity crises of
Kahn, as he oscillates between seeking historicist stabilities
(the symbols of the arch, the circle, the brick, the room, the
assembly of rooms) and manifesting the inability of any
of these 'stabilities' to stabilise in a definitive manner.

Thus, the Richards Laboratory Building, 1957–65:
where what might have been a uniformly gridded simple
volume develops complex particularisations and negotiations horizontally and vertically through the precast structural frame, as well as through the shifting of the fenestra-
tion, offices bays, the stair and exhaust towers. And where
the thinness of the brick veneer is made visible at the tops

Louis Kahn, United States Consulate, Luanda, Angola, 1959–62, Louis I. Kahn Collection, University of Pennsylvania and the Pennsylvania Historical and Museum Commission

Louis Kahn, Library, Phillips Exeter Academy, Exeter, New Hampshire, 1965–72, Louis I. Kahn Collection, University of Pennsylvania and the Pennsylvania Historical and Museum Commission

Venturi and Scott Brown, Flint House, Greenville, Delaware, 1978–80,
The Architectural Archives, University of Pennsylvania by the gift of Robert Venturi
and Denise Scott Brown (Photograph: Matt Wargo)

Peter Eisenman, House II, Hardwick, Vermont, 1969–70
(Photograph: Norman McGrath)

of the concrete stair towers and in the split in the corners of the Biology Building tower.

Or the Salk Institute, 1959–65: where the programmatic division of labour creates an architectural division – where the condition of the study, 'the architecture of the oak table and the rug', in Kahn's words, circa 1960, is seen as exceeding the laboratory space, 'the architecture of air cleanliness and area adjustability',[13] creating a split between the study towers and the laboratory that must be bridged. And where the view of this prime real estate causes an exceeding of the axial space of the study (but not of the laboratory). And where the wood infill in the study does not quite fill in the concrete frame, creating a rift that must be glazed.

Or the Dominican Motherhouse of Saint Catherine de Ricci, 1965–69: where the individually regularised blocks of the refectory, school, chapel and entrance are 'haphazardly' skewed.

Or the Exeter Library, 1965–72: where the traditionally regularised facade, a 17ft-deep brick 'veneer' – a planar surface: empty openings along its top, split at its corners – wraps around the structural concrete core, yet another of Kahn's ruins wrapping around a building: 'though it is only seventeen feet wide [sic]', Kahn said, circa 1972, 'it's fully a brick building, and there is fully a concrete building inside of it...'[14]

Or the Kimbell Art Museum, 1966–72: where the difference between the cycloid shell and the infill walls, between, that is, the Roman ideal and the stressing (in both senses of this term: the emphasis and the deformation) of this classical ideal, creates a rift that must be glazed.

It might even be said that Kahn's process is homologous to the very tectonic and structural acts of the structural system of so many of his buildings. I am referring to his use of *prestressed* and *post-tensioned* – two words that work well here – concrete: a structural and constructional system in which the possibility of deformation is allowed to materialise in order to *attempt* to control this deformation in and through the process of its tectonic construction.

While this structural deformation is often concealed at the end of the constructional process yet 'remembered' in and by the structural system, the deformation of Kahn's idealised conceptual structure is often 'remembered' and not only allowed to remain in view, but accentuated in a mannerist way.

'The internal life of the structure', Kahn said, circa 1972, 'is one in which the strains are held in check.'[15] In this desire Kahn can be seen to share something more with medieval morality plays than merely his use of 'personified abstractions'.[16] The characters Everyman and Goods and Discretion and Mischief and Death in morality plays are analogous to Kahn's characters of Brick and Order and School and Silence and Light. According to literary critic Jonathan Dollimore, the traditional morality play also allows strains to be revealed, only to keep them in check:

The formal coherence of the morality play reflected the coherence of the metaphysical doctrine which was its principal subject. Disorder and suffering are finally rendered meaningful through faith in, and experience of, a providential order... The best morality plays are anything but flatly didactic: they confront, experientially, some of the deepest religious paradoxes. Nevertheless they are paradoxes that are articulated through, and contained by, the same formal pattern: human kind exists in the shadow of original sin; we fall, suffer, and eventually repent; there is usually a relapse, incurring despair, before a secure recovery to redemption.[17]

Dollimore demonstrates that this desire for resolution, for stability, in the morality plays will fail, and thus lead to later Jacobean tragedy, in which:

Coherence comes to reside in the sharpness of definition given to metaphysical and social dislocation, not in the aesthetic, religious or didactic resolution of it ... contradictory accounts of experience are forced into 'misalignment', the tension which this generates being

a way of getting us to confront the problematic and contradictory nature of society itself.[18]

For Kahn these strains – the tensions 'of society itself', as Dollimore says – may be revealed, but they should not remain 'problematic and contradictory'. 'Order', Kahn said circa 1955, 'supports integration'.[19]

At least, this was what Kahn attempted, even if what resulted is a sometimes contradictory programmatic and tectonic play of desire and doubt in Kahn's institutions: 'It is an indication of the tentative nature of things, the question of the institution', Kahn said, circa 1968 (certainly a year for the questioning of institutions): '... the questioning of the institutions will bring about a much purer translation of our institutions, and even bring about those we yet can't see or feel'.[20]

Questioning of institutions, yes, for innovation even, but mostly for purification, for integration, for wholeness. Kahn's desire for the latter is so strong that even in his 'poem' to Scarpa, Kahn felt compelled to keep the potential strain of Scarpa's separate elements in check, insisting on 'the wholeness of inseparable elements' that 'manifest the wholeness of "Form"'.[21]

Both Kahn's architecture and his writing circulate around this struggle, around this sense of strain and of resolution, of possibility and of loss, of innovation and of nostalgia, of particularisation and of (monumentalised) unity, of letting the institution 'become what it wants to be' and that becoming always with some aspect lacking or in excess.

VI

Lack and excess: 'I thought of the beauty of ruins', Kahn said, circa 1961, '... the absence of frames ... of things which nothing lives behind ... and so I thought of wrapping ruins around buildings.'[22] The building is not sufficient *in*, as the expression goes, and *of* itself. The doubt of this insufficiency triggers the desire for the supplement of the building within the building, or perhaps one should say the building without the building – in the sense of its symbolic function being beyond, outside of, in the lack of, in the excess of, its use-function. 'A building built', Kahn said, circa 1963, 'is in bondage of use… Isn't it true that a building being built is of more interest than one that is finished? A building that has become a ruin is again free from the bondage of use.'[23]

Free from the bondage of use: oh, how convenient that would be for a historical period seeking to evoke history without evoking its bondages, seeking, that is, a new identity out of that failure that was the failure of historical identity in modernism. It sounds like such a wonderful dream, this freedom from the bondage of use, like so much of Kahn's dreamy talks and writings and interviews – the great mass of it all now collected in those weighty volumes which are quoted reverentially by historians and critics and theorists with very little critical reflection or contextualisation. But of course it is a dream, and if there is any modification to be attempted on this bondage then that modification would have to be enacted from within that bondage, rather than symbolised from without. This is why, with rare exceptions, this additive supplement from without – rather than an attempt to find and address the supplement (the lack or excess) within – almost always becomes the occasion for diagrammatic symbolic abstraction, for screens and ruins.

Screens and ruins. Or to use Kahn's word, circa 1973: shield: 'I wanted to make the shield out of paper, though concrete was the more logical material … I wanted to express the fact that the concrete was not asked to do any work, that it was able to stand up like a piece of paper when you bend it.'[24] Something that would have the kind of 'architectural identity',[25] to use Kahn's phrase, lacking in the screens and *brise-soleils* of Edward Durrell Stone and all those other embassy architects. Kahn wanted to close in, to make architectural, what he considered to be the ephemeral quality, but not the condition itself, of the screen. From screen to shield: perhaps it is not surprising then, and even most appropriate, that the first instance of this shielding function, the United States Consulate

Louis Kahn, Richards Medical Research Building, Philadelphia, Pennsylvania, 1957–65 (Photograph: John Ebstel, Courtesy of Keith De Lellis Gallery)

Louis Kahn, Kimbell Art Museum, Fort Worth, Texas, 1966–72
(Photograph: Grant Mudford)

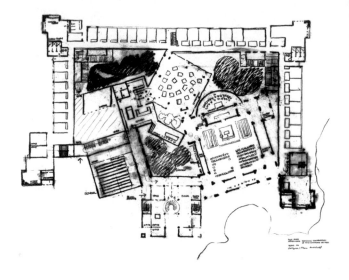

Louis Kahn, Dominican Motherhouse, Media, Pennsylvania, 1965–69,
Louis I. Kahn Collection, University of Pennsylvania
and the Pennsylvania Historical and Museum Commission

Louis Kahn, Sher-e-Bangla Nagar, Dhaka, Bangladesh, 1962–1983,
The Architectural Archives, University of Pennsylvania
(Photograph: Nurer Ramhan Khan)

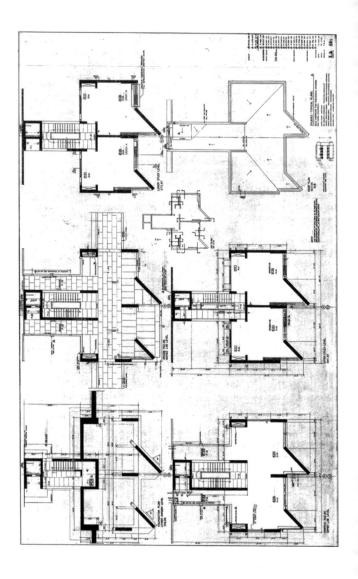

Louis Kahn, Salk Institute for Biological Studies, 1959–65, La Jolla, California, Plan LA-18s (1965), Louis I. Kahn Collection, University of Pennsylvania and the Pennsylvania Historical and Museum Commission

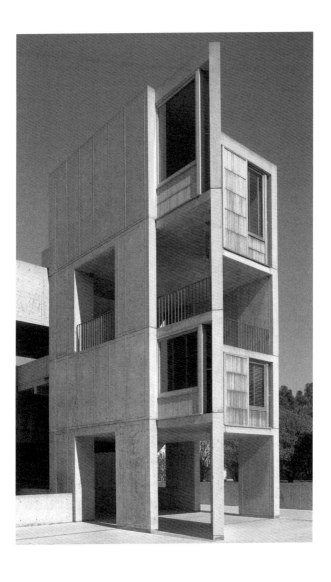

Louis Kahn, Salk Institute for Biological Studies, 1959–65, La Jolla, California
(Photograph: Grant Mudford)

in Luanda, 1959–62, falls just within the end of what has been called the 'heyday', circa 1954–60, of the US embassy building programme. 'Better embassies mean better business',[26] is how one interest group, the American Embassy Association, put it. Succinctly.

VII

From screen to shield, protecting whatever was deemed to need protection, whether the US Consulate in Luanda, the India Institute of Management (modelled upon the Harvard Business School), or Sher-e-Bangla Nagar, the capital complex in Dhaka, Bangladesh. But all of Kahn's shields had holes: symbolic cutouts of pure geometric figures. And when a singular set of geometric figures and identities will not stabilise, then the figures and identities will multiply: what starts in Dhaka as a careful, albeit formalistic, play of variations in the brick hostels (various filling ins and emptyings of the circle motif), ends up in the concrete National Assembly Building as an arbitrary piling up of cutout shapes, an erratic game of mix n' match, a desperate attempt at symbolic evocation in the face of the failure of evocation.

In the face of failure, in the facing of the facade: because now, at Dhaka, unlike its earlier role as restraining member in the 'composite order of brick and concrete', there is nothing to restrain the concrete – in what Kahn once again called a composite order (of concrete and marble) – as those inconsequential lines of marble, mere cover-ups of the concrete pour joints that bear no relation to those cutouts, make so evident.

While there is beginning to emerge some critical work within the field of art history on this postwar period, regarding the exportation of US ideology through the visual arts,[27] there is much that needs to be said in relation to architecture beyond the necessary but obvious examples of embassies, as this exportation included, among other things, the broadcasts of talks by prominent architects on the official propaganda airwaves of the Voice of America, prominent architects, that is, like Louis Kahn, whose talk 'Form and Design' was broadcast out to the free, as the expression goes, and unfree world, circa 1960.[28] As it happens, Tafuri is one of the few historians to comment on the 'marketable' identity of Kahn's architecture:

Kahn's architecture proved highly exportable. Pushed aside in the United States, he found that his celebrative approach was highly pertinent to the developing countries. Like another great interpreter of American institutions, Daniel Hudson Burnham, Kahn likewise was to see his own mythic imperial symbols realised outside the United States, as consolation prizes handed over to countries where it had designs for expansion.[29]

So it should not be too surprising, then, that Kahn's most diagrammatic work might appear in a third world country, and in this regard Kahn's remarks, delivered in India, might reveal some additional information about the symbolic meaning of one of his favourite diagrammatic symbols, the circle. When a student at the Indian Institute of Management, in reference to the circular openings in the building's 'porches', asked 'What are the holes for?', the response from Kahn – Kahn being at that time among the five most prominent architects in the world – was:

'To make accurate spitting possible.'[30]

However cynical this response might sound – and certainly it represents, among other things, the cynicism of architects, in this case an architect just days away from his death by heart attack in Penn Station, on his way back to Philadelphia from India, tired from all that had passed – it represents now, as it represented in Kahn's time, the real constructional condition of symbols. It is not possible to construct or to use (old or new) symbols in a load-bearing capacity – they will not bear the load of a definitive identity, as even the most seemingly stable Big Symbols, say, the Cross, have undergone structural failures, identity crises,

Louis Kahn, Sher-e-Bangla Nagar, Dhaka, Bangladesh, 1962–83, The Architectural
Archives, University of Pennsylvania (Photograph: Nurer Ramhan Khan)

Louis Kahn, Library, Phillips Exeter Academy, Exeter, New Hampshire, 1965–72
(Photograph: Grant Mudford)

Reformations and Counter-Reformations. One seeks out
a symbol for assurance, for stability, the stability of self-
evidency, the stability of timelessness, but then there
always comes that kind of question, that kind of 'What
are the holes for?' kind of question:

**His [Kahn's] architectural works are intent on bringing
back a collective memory. In this Kahn has revealed himself to be profoundly American, expressing the never-sat-
isfied need to equip himself with secure historical points
of reference. It is an old traditional need of Americans
to recognise themselves as a people in symbols that resist
the wear and change of history. But the process can only
be tautological: the new bases for architecture set up
by Kahn are every bit as artificial as the myths and institutions in which he put his trust.**[31]

One of the myths that circulates around Kahn is that
he is supposed to have resurrected some comforting
archaic depth of presence, yet what surfaces in this process
of resurrection is the disquiet of surface, the surface, that is,
of symbol – which perhaps suggests some further linkages
and relations between Kahn and Venturi and Scott Brown.

VIII

My point here is not to simplify the complex sensitivities
and insensitivities of Kahn in the third world, which would
require its own case study, but merely to state that the diagrammatic crudeness of some of his third-world symbolisms
exposes certain diagrammatic and crude symbolisings that
reappear in his work in the United States. This is, in part, the
problem of veneer, the problem of the institutional, physical,
political and social tectonics of veneer, beyond the crudeness
(but not just in the technical sense) of, say, the slate facade
panels of his Erdman Dormitory.

Let me compare one of Kahn's more sophisticated
enactments with one of his cruder symbolisations, as they

appear simultaneously in his library at the Phillips Exeter Academy. As for the former I am referring to the exterior walls of the building, those traditionally regularised and veneered outer walls that, as I already mentioned, rift at the corners. What I want to talk about is the interior condition of these exterior walls, or rather, the relations between their interior and exterior conditions, as exemplified in the relations between the study carrel and the wall.

'The carrel', Kahn said, circa 1972, 'is the room within a room.'[32] But here at Exeter it is the relationship between this room-within-a-room and the wall that is unique. First, the carrel and window are not separate elements: the casework of the window is transformed into the casework of the carrel. Or, if you prefer, vice versa. Second, the condition of the carrel has caused a rift in the window, and thus there becomes the 'individual' window for the study carrel and the 'collective' window for the general reading area. Third, this individual window (and thus the interior of the carrel) is pushed out toward the exterior (as your thoughts are as you read and work in the carrel) while the collective window is pushed in toward the interior (toward the collective reading area). Fourth, the individual carrel is not for a single individual – 'The windows should be made particular to suit a student who wants to be alone even when he is with others'[33] – the individual is already with others, or at least another, as the carrels are for a *pair* of individuals: alone with another, alone with others.

Thus, the contingency of the carrel and the window is worked and worked until an accumulation of metonymic relations circulating between and within them – inside/outside, subject/object, use/structure, private/public, individual/collective, body/architecture, wall/room, surface (window)/volume (carrel) – are drawn forth, and most importantly, are shown, enacted, as already enfolded. What results is the development of a complex tectonic articulation and figuration that is not merely the simple addition of the two original figures: window and carrel.

Kahn goes on to vary this figuration from floor to floor, even if in a vertical hierarchy complicit with Kahn's

Louis Kahn, Library, Phillips Exeter Academy, Exeter, New Hampshire, 1965–72
(Photograph: Edward Brodzinsky)

Louis Kahn, Library, Phillips Exeter Academy, Exeter, New Hampshire, 1965–72
(Photograph: Edward Brodzinsky)

ideological notions of social and metaphysical hierarchy: 'The windows are larger at the top and smaller at the bottom…', he said, circa 1972, 'They form a graduation of forces that come down with little force, where the forces are dancing like angels, to the bottom, where they are grunting.'[34] This is the sort of hierarchy one could imagine inscribed in built form as in the mind of a college preparatory school – the angels at the top, the grunts at the bottom – and then, as we might expect from Kahn post-Richards Laboratory, this figuration is regularising and repeating floor by floor rather than allowing individual and idiosyncratic differences within or between floors. Whatever strains are allowed to be revealed are consequently held in check.

This complex tectonic articulation is in extreme contrast with the simplistic relation between the library's circular cutouts in the concrete wall of the central space (itself as empty and emptied out as the circle). The meaning of these circles? 'To make accurate spitting possible?' (Highly doubtful that would have been his answer had the Exeter students asked). The barrier of this opening, which thankfully is not just a railing, at least maintains some of the library theme by being a bookcase and display area, which is more than can be said for the circular cutouts at the Indian Institute of Management (although it is also the case that this entire Ahmedabad complex enacts an extraordinary interwoven range of sequenced openings and passages, constantly creating interactions between intimate and institutional scales). But at Exeter, there is hardly any struggle between these two bondages of use (structural bracing and barrier-case), almost no tectonic articulations, almost no (subtle and detailed) workings (as with the study carrels) of the metonymic contingencies: just cut and fill.

Here is one test of tectonic articulation: does the presence or absence of any given architectural element conceptually and structurally affect any other given element? Does, in other words, one element *respond* to or *affect* a response from any contingent element?

For the central space of the Exeter Library, the wall remains unaffected by the presence of the barrier-case –

whereas the exterior wall of the library is conceptually and structurally affected by the presence of the carrel, although only at the level of infill (all greater strains are held in check). The circle of the central space is just a leftover, a leftover from earlier design schemes, a leftover from the earlier time when Kahn desired the building to be composed of brick arches, but before the time of the doubts of limited building budgets and building committees began.

It must be emphasised that these conditions, the cutout on the one hand and the wall/carrel on the other, indicate two radically different ways of working and their differences mark the poles of Kahn's operation. Is it not interesting that in the very same building there are moments of simplistic, even bombastic, symbolism *as well as* moments in which simple means are used to develop subtle, complex enactments? There is no point in attempting to synthesise *this* confusion of the architect. Why allow each aspect of the building its own free and easy rationale without regard for the tension between aspects? While this is surely the way most architects design (and write), why should this be the way of the historian or critic or theorist? Why be the architect's agent? Why not use the terms of one aspect to push against, to illuminate, to affect the potentials and limits of some other aspect of the building? Why not examine the convergences and divergences, the range of the affiliations, of the various aspects of a work?

But what is wrong, you might well ask, with synthesising this pairing of the cutout and the wall/carrel? Is it not, to use Tafuri's formulation, the utopian *sphere* of idealised geometries and the worldly *labyrinth* of compromised contingencies? Well, *if* Kahn was aware of the radical disjunction of this pairing, he did not, at Exeter, directly enact it (as, say, Giovanni Battista Piranesi did in his abrupt erasure of the iconographic imagery on the back of the altar and throughout the church complex at Santa Maria del Priorato – an enactment of the disjunction of the object to itself, radically transforming the syntactic and semantic relations of tectonic character).[35] These two aspects at Exeter Library are not constructed in such a way as to

Louis Kahn, Indian Institute of Management, Ahmedabad, India, 1962–74
(Photograph by Author)

Louis Kahn, Library, Phillips Exeter Academy, Exeter, New Hampshire,
1965–72, Section, ca. May 1966, Louis I. Kahn Collection, The University of
Pennsylvania and the Pennsylvania Historical and Museum Commission

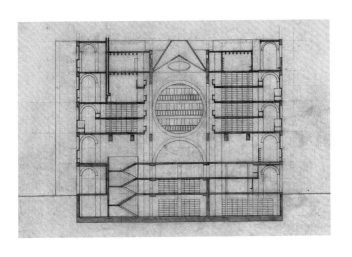

Louis Kahn, Library, Phillips Exeter Academy, Exeter, New Hampshire,
1965–72, Section, ca. November 10, 1966 Louis I. Kahn Collection, The University of
Pennsylvania and the Pennsylvania Historical and Museum Commission

directly address their relations at all, either their radical disjunction or their continuity or their reversals or their mediation of the difference of each identity to the other.

A juxtaposition does not a relationship – or a synthesis – make.

My point about the potentially radical disjunction of these operations is this: there is a difference, a tectonic difference, between an identity *symbolised* through abstract means, and an identity whose symbolism is being *enacted* through tectonic means.

This difference is the difference between metaphor and metonymy: metaphor as a form of substitution from some other place, and metonymy as a form of association based not on some other place, but on the very place (or some aspect of the place, or what is contiguous to the place) of the object in question.[36]

Kahn's circle at Exeter is an imported metaphor for, as Kahn says, circa 1972, 'a connecting architecture', for what he desired that central and empty space to be: '… a free, unobligating room'.[37] Free from obligations – oh, that dreamy talk again: how convenient that would be for a historical period seeking to evoke some idealised history of room typologies without evoking their obligations. But this central space does not enact any direct sense of connectivity other than the questionably obvious connectivity of the stereotypical atrium space. It does not enact any direct sense of connectivity precisely because it attempts to be free and unobligating, free, that is, from the bondages of its obligating uses: the uses of the reference desk, the uses of the circulation desk, the uses of the card file (now, of course, in the form of the computer). The attempt to empty this central space, in other words, is not radical enough to affect (or to make an architectural opportunity of) these institutional obligations.

Whereas the wall and the study carrel at Exeter – which could be, and most often are in most libraries, nothing more than 'just' an unconnective collection of carrel, window and wall – tectonically enact a sense of connection and interrelation by virtue of the metonymic relations of *their interrelated obligating uses* being first conceived of, and then drawn out, in and through the architecture. Christian Metz's observations regarding contiguity and metonymy in film can be extended here to architecture: that one element may have proximity to another element does not necessarily guarantee – generate, develop, enact – a metonymic effect.[38] There are plenty of study carrels next to plenty of windows in plenty of libraries, but that does not mean that their metonymic relations have been addressed or operated on in the architecture of those libraries, those windows, those carrels.

Metaphor in architecture thus emerges as a form of doubt or a form of fear of the object, the doubt or fear of materialist identity, the fear that the object does not have sufficient meaning *in* and *around* itself. Which is why the metaphoric architects of recent time, say Venturi and Scott Brown, have been more concerned with diagrammatic architectural symbols than with tectonic enactments. The architect's doubt of the material realm causes the architect not to take seriously the construction of the building as a site of doubt, as a site where one could find that doubt within, rather than in spite of, the tectonics of the object. The failure of the cynical postmodern architectural identity (of the cutout column or the thin historicist quote) has led to its seeming opposite: a romanticism for a truthful and stable tectonic identity that has resulted in a fetishisation of materials and details, which, in the end, is just another way of avoiding materialist identity, precisely by substituting the use of fetishised high or low materials for the very questioning of material identity, precisely by substituting the use of fetishised constructional details for the very questioning of the social artifice of material construction.

I have stated this elsewhere with regard to the architectural construct of social and psychological and tectonic events, but let me state it again here with particular regard to the latter: every event, as it is constructed through an architecture, is already its own representation.[39] So then one might reveal it as such, construct it as such, in the gesture of its gesture, in the construct of its gesture, in the contingency and oscillation of identity and its failure.

TECTONIC ACTS OF DESIRE AND DOUBT

The same might be said of the tectonics of historiographic or critical or theoretical events and studies, as they are constructed through oral or written presentations in, say, just to give an example (or two): annual professional meetings and their publication in journals.

And speaking again of identity and its failure, it is necessary to say that Kahn, of course, is not important *in and of himself*, which is why, had I the time and space I do not now have here, I would need to relate Kahn's tectonic acts of desire and doubt with the tectonic acts of desire and doubt to some other architects of his time – architects such as Luigi Moretti and Carlo Scarpa – in order to develop a certain tension: not a dualistic or a dialectical tension, but a triadic tension. Why these three architects? (I could easily have picked three others.) Because of the present, of course, because of (the identities of) certain contemporary architectural practices, certain practices that reference the look of Kahn, Moretti and Scarpa without working their critical capabilities: certain precious craftisms that could be referred to as neo-Scarpisms, certain disjunctive formalisms that could be referred to as neo-Morettisms, certain normalising institutionalisms that could be referred to as neo-Kahnisms. It would be pointless to lament these new identities as failures, as degenerations of some previous Masters, as the seeds of these degenerations, as always, may be found in the so-called Masters themselves, when they become self-satisfied in their own internalised expressions. Like Brick, the architect who does not engage (internally) in relation to the externalised collective order, and vice versa, 'has within', to use Kahn's words, her or his 'own death'.

So I will end here, with this question:

What do you want Kahn to be?

Because every historian, critic or theorist who attempts to work on, or think through, Kahn and his architecture and his writing will repeat the same process of ventriloquism: they – we – will all ask of Kahn, as Kahn did of the brick, what Kahn wants to be.

And Scully's Kahn, Tafuri's Kahn, Frampton's Kahn, your Kahn, my Kahn will not give the same answers.

How could they?

But neither will each of these Kahns give entirely different answers.

How could they?

Which leaves us, all of us, neither with the total failure and indeterminacy of no identity for Kahn, nor with some stable and objective identity of the true Kahn, but with our own (morality) tales, our own disturbances and shorings up of the present, our own dialogues with the inanimate 'facts' of the past – with all their identities and failures of identities – that we, like Kahn with his brick, must animate, must piece together in the tectonics of disciplinary research and presentation and representation, in our own constructed acts of desire and doubt.

Originally presented at the Annual Meeting of the Society of Architectural Historians, April 1995, and published in *ANY* 14 (special issue: *Tectonics Unbound,* edited by Mitchell Schwarzer, 1996), 36–43.

TECTONIC ACTS OF DESIRE AND DOUBT

NOTES

1. Jacques Lacan, *Écrits: A Selection* (New York: Norton, 1977), 287. Slavoj Žižek's example is from his *Tarrying with the Negative: Kant, Hegel, and the Critique of Ideology* (Durham: Duke University Press, 1983), 120.

2. Richard Saul Wurman, ed., *What Will Be Has Always Been: The Words of Louis I Kahn* (New York: Rizzoli, 1986), 'Lecture, Drexel (University) Architectural Society', 29.

3. Wurman, *What Will Be Has Always Been*, 'Lecture, University of Cincinnati', 76.

4. Wurman, *What Will Be Has Always Been*, 'Architecture and Human Agreement, Lecture at University of Virginia', 135.

5. The brick example is taken from Wurman, *What Will Be Has Always Been*, 152. The train station example is from 'Order Is' in Vincent Scully, *Louis I. Kahn* (New York: Braziller, 1962), 113.

6. Manfredo Tafuri, *Ricerca del Rinascimento: principi, città, architetti* (Turin: Einaudi, 1992), xxi; English edition, *Interpreting the Renaissance: Princes, Cities, Architects* trans Daniel Sherer (Yale University Press, 1996), xxix.

7. Ernesto Laclau, 'Introduction', in *The Making of Political Identities*, ed. Laclau (New York: Verso, 1994), 1–5.

8. Ernesto Laclau and Lilian Zac, 'Minding the Gap: The Subject of Politics' in *The Making of Political Identities*, 32.

9. Ibid., 33. For a more extensive discussion of the question of identity and architecture, see 'Identity and the Discourse of Politics in Contemporary Architecture' in this volume.

10. Wurman, *What Will Be Has Always Been*, 'Interview with John W. Cook and Heinrich Klotz, from Conversations with Architects', 196.

11. Wurman, *What Will Be Has Always Been*, 'A Conversation with William Jordy', 237.

12. Wurman, *What Will Be Has Always Been*, 'Interview, VIA magazine', 49.

13. 'Form and Design', from Scully, *Louis I. Kahn*, 119–200.

14. Wurman, *What Will Be Has Always Been*, 'Comments on the Library, Phillips Exeter Academy', 178.

15. Ibid., 181.

16. David Bevington, *From Mankind to Marlowe: Growth of Structure in the Popular Drama of Stuart England* (Cambridge: Harvard University Press, 1962), 792.

17. Jonathan Dollimore, *Radical Tragedy: Religion, Ideology and Power in the Drama of Shakespeare and his Contemporaries*, 2nd ed. (Durham: Duke University Press, 1989), 38–39.

18. Ibid., 39.

19. 'Order Is' from Scully, *Louis I. Kahn*, 114.

20. Wurman, *What Will Be Has Always Been*, 'The Institutions of Man, Lecture at Princeton University', 21.

21. Wurman, *What Will Be Has Always Been*, 'In the Work of Carlo Scarpa', 324.

22. Quoted in David B. Brownlee and David G DeLong, *Louis I. Kahn: In the Realm of Architecture* (New York: Rizzoli, 1992), 70.

23. 'Remarks', *Perspecta* 9/10 (1965), 330.

24. Wurman, *What Will Be Has Always Been*, 'From a conversation with Richard Saul Wurman', 232.

25. Wurman, *What Will Be Has Always Been*, 'Interview with John W Cook and Heinrich Klotz, from Conversations with Architects', 197.

26. Jane C. Loeffler, 'The Architecture of Diplomacy: Heyday of the United States Embassy-Building Program, 1954–1960', *Journal of the Society of Architectural Historians* XLIX:3 (September 1990), 252.

27. See, for example, *Reconstructing Modernism: Art in New York, Paris, and Montreal 1945–1964*, ed. Serge Guilbaut (Cambridge MA: MIT Press, 1990) and Alan Sekula, 'The Traffic in Photographs' in *Modernism and Modernity*, ed. Benjamin H.D. Buchloh, Serge Guilbaut and David Solkin (Halifax: Nova Scotia College of Art and Design, 1983), 121–59.

28. Scully, *Louis I. Kahn*, 71.

29. Manfredo Tafuri and Francesco Dal Co, *Modern Architecture* (New York: Abrams, 1979), 407.

30. Wurman, *What Will Be Has Always Been*, 'Louis Kahn Defends – Indian Institute of Management', 252.

31. Tafuri and Dal Co, *Modern Architecture*, 403.

32. Wurman, *What Will Be Has Always Been*, 'Comments on the Library, Phillips Exeter Academy, Exeter, New Hampshire', 180.

33. Quoted in Brownlee and DeLong, *Louis I. Kahn: In the Realm of Architecture*, 129.

34. Wurman, *What Will Be Has Always Been*, 'Comments on the Library, Phillips Exeter Academy, Exeter, New Hampshire', 178.

35. Manfredo Tafuri, *The Sphere and the Labyrinth* (Cambridge MA: MIT Press, 1990), 48–9.

36. When I say metonymy, I am referring to forms of contingent displacements that draw out (metaphorical) meaning, and not to the simple substitution of part for whole that more properly belongs to that sub-division of metonymy known as synecdoche.

37. Wurman, *What Will Be Has Always Been*, 'Comments on the Library, Phillips Exeter Academy, Exeter, New Hampshire', 180, 181.

38. Christian Metz, *The Imaginary Signifier: Psychoanalysis and the Cinema* (Bloomington: Indiana University Press, 1982).

39. See Mark Rakatansky, 'Transformational Constructions' (for example: *Adult Day*) *Assemblage* 19 (1992), 6–31.

ENVELOPE PLEASE

Let's say the building envelope is a kind of map, that it maps
the dialogues between public and private, inclusions and
exclusions, insides and outsides, programmes and contexts.

Now a map of course isn't – can't be, can never be –
the whole territory. You can't totally collapse the two together, but neither can you keep them totally separate. In
order to make any map, some attributes, some *things*, have
to be left out of (excluded from) whatever territory is being
mapped, while some other attributes, some things, have
to be not only included but exaggerated. What gets into the
map, as Gregory Bateson said, is difference within sameness, the difference that makes a difference to whom(so)
ever is making the map.

We all know how difficult it is just to map even one
thing rigorously, but nothing means anything unless it's
in relation to something else. As Bateson said, it doesn't
take one to know one, it takes *two* to know one. So mappings need to respond to, to dialogue with, other mappings
to draw forth the character of their mapping. When things
encounter each other, rub against each other, engage each
other, what you would hope for is a performance of interaction and relations, discussion and debate, not just pure
juxtaposition (separation), nor pure blending (collapse).

The question then is not just what might be mapped
in and by the building envelope, but does the envelope show
itself to be in the act of mapping, does it perform this mapping before us, is it performative? Not just as yet another
building envelope claiming to be performative just because
someone predetermined some insular energy or structural
or formal calculations back inside the office computer – so
that we can't see the building envelope thinking through its
predetermined actions, can't see it considering before

our eyes its considerations and determinations, never see it in the midst of interactions between these various envelopings of the public and private, inclusions and exclusions, insides and outsides, programmes and contexts. To be performative what needs to be enacted is not actions, but interactions. As one famous actor said, when asked the secret of acting: 'Acting? Acting? Never act. Only react'. It's so clear when you watch extraordinary actors, how it's only the bad actors that 'express', that act out some insular single motive and emotion. Characters only emerge through their reaction and response to other characters and situations and settings. Which is why even with monologues, the best ones, whether tragic or comic, are always dialogues with the others in yourself. It is through this simultaneous collapse and separation of characters each to the other that the differential character of characters is drawn forth.

So I would say: if it takes two to know one, it takes *three* (not two) to tango. Three is the minimum number – if you want to move beyond simple binary juxtapositions and oppositions into more complex and poignant relations.

You can know this like you know the back of your own hand if you take a look at the back of your hand to see how the montage of veins, muscles, tendons, bones, joints, ligaments, bursa, nerves and nails appear as inflective and inflected systems, emerging and disappearing, coincident and non-coincident. All of which bring complex differential articulations to that enveloping that is your skin.

Imagine: structural, infrastructural, programmatic, typological, ideological, informational, material mappings appearing in architecture as inflective and inflected systems, emerging and disappearing, coincident and non-coincident – what an architecture that would be! It's in the tracking of *how* each of these mappings inflect and influence one another that these performances become interesting: neither collapsing into each other, nor remaining entirely separate – cross-indexing and cross-determining while remaining each legibly vivid and evocative.

Architects could thus be playing with the coincidence and non-coincidence of the envelope to the various and

Govard Bidloo, *Ontleding des menschelyken lichaams* (Amsterdam: By de weduwe
van Joannes van Someren, de erfgenaamen van Joannes van Dyk, Hendrik en de
weduwe van Dirk Boom, 1690)

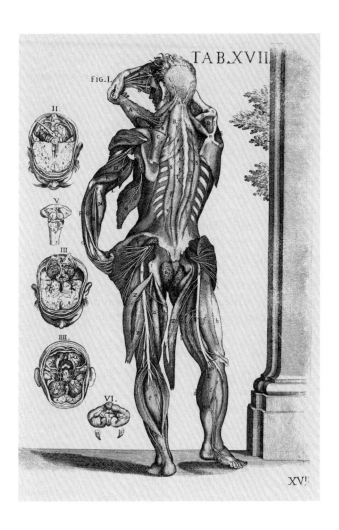

Pietro da Cortona, *Tabulae anatomicae a celeberrimo pictore Petro Berrettino Cortonensi Delineatae* (Rome: Fausto Amideo, 1741)

varying public and private attributes of site, programme, iconography, structure and material. Coincidence in both senses of the word: correlation *and* happenstance, co-determination *and* re-determination.

Thus rather than deciding whether our buildings are supposed to be *either* open *or* closed, inside-out or outside-in, in attention or distracted, we can let them be on the verge of, in the midst of, thinking out loud about their decisions. In the midst of mapping the differential ranging between decisions, between regimes, between states – its social exchange enacted right there before our eyes.

So let's open up the envelope, but not announce the winner just yet. Or if we announce this year's winner, know that there will be another winning envelope next year, and the year after, and the year after that. Let's open up the building envelope and pull out what's in, in what's out, but let's leave the envelope with that look of anticipation, that look of being on the verge, of being in the midst of these interactions, like Bernini's sculptures where the lips are parted – in that social exchange – in the midst of speaking.

Originally published in Bernard Tschumi and Irene Cheng (eds.), *The State of Architecture at the Beginning of the 21st Century* (New York: Monacelli Press, 2004), 76.

ACTS OF

SPATIAL NARRATIVES

There is no mute architecture. All architects, all buildings 'tell stories' with varying degrees of consciousness. Architecture is permeated with narratives because it is constituted within a field of discourses and economies (formal, psychological and ideological), to any one aspect of which it cannot be reduced, from any one aspect of which it cannot be removed.

If we examine any type of domestic architecture for example, we will find already inscribed *within* the architecture a complex array of mentalities and practices[1] concerning the relations between genders, between parents and children, between 'inside' and 'outside', between what is supposed to be 'public' and 'private', between what is supposed to be seen, smelled or heard and what is not, and so forth. The hierarchy and degree of definition of spaces, their relative size and location, and the sub-architectural apparatuses of each space (furniture, appliances, media devices) – all of these are defined by and in turn give definition to the social and psychological narratives that influence the behaviours (encouraged, allowed, discouraged or forbidden) associated with each space. The elements of this field are polyvalent: each aspect will be influenced by mentalities and practices already established (perhaps even already in decline) and newly emerging (perhaps not even fully articulated) – and thus each of these aspects will conflict with, reinforce, or ignore the other aspects.[2]

Yet to speak of narrative strategies in architecture plunges one immediately into difficulty. Between those who would insist upon (or call for) the intrinsic nature of a 'non-rhetorical' architecture (claiming that a brick is just a brick, a wall just a wall, a room just a room, that stone and steel, metal studs and gypsum board cannot or should not 'speak') and those all too eager to 'add meaning' to buildings through the 'telling of fables', there seems barely enough space to suggest another position.[3] The seemingly opposed positions of a 'non-rhetorical' architecture and a 'story-telling' architecture converge in their belief that rhetorical meaning does not reside in buildings other than in the most general sense, either as a 'timeless expression' of classical (or vernacular) ideals or as a 'zeitgeist expression.' Both of these positions posit that if architecture could tell a story, that story would need to be designed *into* the 'mute' and empty vessel of architecture as an *additive* feature.[4]

But rather than conceiving of narrative architecture as arising from an addition of a singular story-line, it would be critically more constructive to speak in the plural, of narratives – of exposing and reworking certain repressed narratives within the field of discourses and economies already at work in architecture.

I

Before proceeding further it will be necessary to address the so-called linear structures of both narrative and temporality, as these related issues inevitably arise as arguments that are supposed to keep narrative wholly distinct from architecture. There is still a tendency to conceive of narrative in terms of conventions that were assumed to operate in nineteenth-century realist fiction – a linear development from origin to end. And thus any strategy that opposes the 'naturalness' of these assumed conventions is thought to be 'anti-narrative'.

There are two problems with this view. On the one hand, recent literary theory has shown that the conventions of realism operate in much more complex and indeterminate ways than had been previously thought: beginnings do not constitute definitive origins, development is never seamlessly continuous (as transitions are inevitably disjunctive), endings do not provide definite closure.[5] And while it has been claimed that a book (unlike a building)

Starts and Stops Instantly at Your Touch

not studied the mechanism, tested it, used a little patience and followed well-worked-out rules for its operation.

I am quite sure that when somebody told your grandmother that finer, and more even, and perfect stitches could be taken in cloth with a needle set in a strange machine operated by a wheel and belt, than she could make by hand, that *she too, said that this new sewing machine "won't work"*—and it probably took some time for her to be convinced.

But you to-day know the perfection of sewing machine work, and

'The office building is a *house* of work of organisation of clarity of economy.'
Ludwig Mies van der Rohe, 1923

functional...

can exert total control over its sequential unfolding, there are in fact no definitively linear readings. Each time we re-read a book we encounter aspects or relations between aspects that we remembered differently or not at all. Our attentions and inattentions are different with each passage through a book. The hegemonic claims of 'conventional' narrative for naturalism and stability attempt to mask these disjunctions, as Roland Barthes noted:

… our society takes the greatest pains to conjure away the coding of the narrative situation: there is no counting the number of narrational devices which seek to naturalise the subsequent narrative by feigning to make it the outcome of some natural circumstance and thus, as it were, 'disin-augurating' it… The reluctance to declare its codes char-acterises bourgeois society and the mass culture issuing from it: both demand signs which do not look like signs.[6]

On the other hand, 'anti-narrative' strategies (montage, meta-narrative, and so forth) always continue to narrate, cannot avoid narrating – even as they problematise and resist certain conventional practices precisely in order to reveal the seams of narrative, to reveal how narrative is constructed from a discontinuous series of effects. 'Anti-narrative' strategies, in other words, are not non-narrative.

It is within this struggle, between the inability to nar-rate in a seamless and definitive manner and the inability not to narrate, that narrative is constituted. This is the way, as it were, that narrative narrates, within this field of disability and ability.

There has been a similar misunderstanding with regard to the temporal dimension of architecture. It is commonly claimed that temporality does not exist *within* architecture (the way it supposedly exists within – and thus make possible – literary narrative), that buildings are 'frozen in time', that temporality exists only in the experi-ence of a building through time. Given these claims it is not surprising to find the current interest in 'processional' buildings and building complexes that appear to be the only architecture to develop a linear 'narrative' with a 'proper' beginning, middle and end (Giuseppi Terragni's Danteum project, Giacomo da Vignola's Villa Lante and the Sacra Monti are frequently cited examples). My previous comments regarding narrative extend to procession in architecture: that is, on the one hand, all so-called processional architecture operates in much more complex and indeterminate ways than is generally assumed,[7] and on the other hand, all architecture is processional (in other words, cannot be non-processional).

When I say that all architecture is processional, I mean that whether a building maintains the conventional relationships between spatial units for a given institutional type or attempts to disrupt such conventions, in both cases the subject will experience a procession through the various units of institutional space: from street to lobby, to stairs or elevators, to other lobbies or reception spaces or corridors or rooms, to other anterooms or corridors or rooms, and so forth. Even in the unlikely case that one's route through a building would differ each time, it would always be a sequence through a series of spaces. This is not merely an arbitrary procession along a 'neutral' continuum that has been characterised as 'public' at one end and as 'private' at the other.[8] We need only imagine a typical procession through the various spaces of a domicile, an office or a governmental building, to be aware not only how each space is deeply saturated with a complex field of social and psychological narratives, but also how the effects of these narratives accrue (not necessarily in a unified way) in the procession from space to space.

Thus one could argue that the most significant temporal dimension of architecture is not given by the physical experience of moving through a building, but rather by the temporality of institutional practices inscribed in architectural space. Our understanding of the (seemingly stable) types of institutional space (the domicile, the office, the school, the museum, and so forth), is such that, once we experience these types, we need not physically traverse a given building to have a sense of the temporal dimension

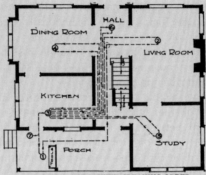

DIAGRAM 1—UNPLANNED CLEANING ORDER

Method.—Worker gets tools from tool closet (1), and walks down hall and begins on living room (2) ; returns with trash to kitchen (3), and walks to dining room (4) ; after cleaning it, again returns to kitchen with trash, and proceeds to clean the study (5) ; she walks back to kitchen again, and last cleans hall (6), ending by bringing back tools and last refuse to kitchen again, before taking the final walk back to tool closet (1). This is not an exaggeration, but the method used by a so-called "good worker."

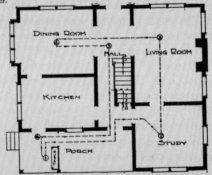

DIAGRAM 2—PLANNED CLEANING ORDER

Method.—Worker gets tools from tool closet (1), and proceeds direct to study (2) ; from study through door to parlor (3) ; across parlor hallway to dining room (4) ; she then begins at upper end of hallway (5), and cleans its length back to the door opening on rear porch, carrying all waste and tools back directly to service porch (6). Note that this method eliminates *all tracking to kitchen* and results in about two-thirds less unnecessary steps and walking.

adaptable…

of inhabitation likely to be found there. Even before we enter a domicile in our culture, whether it is a suburban tract house or an 'open' loft, we know the forms of inhabitation that we can expect to find: the processional ordering and temporal use of the spaces, and thus the temporal and spatial ordering of the institutional rituals that take place there. But perhaps it is in the relationship between these two temporalities (the temporality of physical procession and the temporality of institutional practices) that the temporal dimension of architecture is best described.

II

Thus I will be arguing that *the ways in which human subjects are constituted and managed in institutional space* may provide one of the more productive themes for a narrative architecture.[9] In fact, all designed space functions as institutional space.[10] Institutions are the principal sites through which ideologies work, and thus, as in the case of ideologies (and conventional narrative, as Barthes noted) it is in the interest of institutions to effect (or at least give the illusion of) stable conditions. And like narrative, both institutions and ideologies are constructs – they are neither natural, nor universal, nor timeless, but artificial structures created through shifting historical circumstances. They are both a discontinuous series of effects working within a field of ability and disability. The function of ideology, as Slavoj Žižek notes, 'is not to offer us a point of escape from our reality but to offer us the social reality itself as an escape from some traumatic, real kernel'. It is the very inconsistency of the social field, the impossibility of its seamless constitution, its gaps and residues, that ideology has to mask, conceal, screen.[11] And it is in such gaps – at the level of the subject, the institutional programme, the building, the site, and so forth – that certain critical architectural narratives might emerge.

The institutional programme is one professional mask that architecture wears in the service of ideologies.

Generally the ideological and social shifts that have affected (given rise to, been barriers to) architectural shifts in
the built form of institutions have been given little attention
by architectural historians and critics in favour of a variety
of formal analyses. However it is difficult to comprehend
the shift in western domestic space – from generalised
spaces in earlier centuries to the subsequent development
of specialised rooms – unless this shift is read in relation
to the history of domestic mentalities and practices: shifts
in the concepts of family, gender, privacy, hygiene, the place
of the child (and servants and non-family) in the house, the
relationship of the family to the 'outside' society, relations
between classes, as well as the partial transfer of education and moralisation from the religious to the secular and
familial domain.[12] Similarly, a number of developments in
domestic, other institutional, and urban spaces beginning
in the eighteenth century can be related to the 'need' of the
State for the surveillance and management of social space
(the policing of the social body) instigated by a 'concern'
for hygiene. Beyond the official stated intentions, these
hygienic programmes involved the 'surveillance, analysis,
intervention and modification' of populations as a means
of providing finer and more adequate control mechanisms,
as well as the maintenance of bodies as usable labour.[13]

But there are also moments when seemingly contradictory ideologies coalesce. One such moment, as Michel
Foucault has pointed out, is that of the French Revolution-
aries' embrace of Jeremy Bentham's Panopticon project as
an instrumental model for a 'transparent' society, which
they linked to the Rousseauian vision of a totally unob-
structed collective communication that would eradicate
the darkness where injustice and unhappiness breeds.[14]
Yet even in Rousseau it is already clear that this transparency is not to be equally distributed: Rousseau's desire for
people to be able to look freely into each other's hearts was
not, for him, a matter of abolishing social differences, but
merely a way to give the 'sense' of social fraternity in order
to maintain the existing social order.[15] These contradictions, within and between ideologies, would become visible

WEDNESDAY

6:00– 6:30	Rise and dress; start water heater
6:30– 7:00	Prepare breakfast
7:00– 7:30	BREAKFAST
7:30– 8:30	Wash dishes; inspect icebox; plan meals; start lunch
8:30– 9:00	Make beds; light cleaning
9:00–12:00	Ironing
12:00– 1:00	LUNCH
1:00– 2:00	Finish ironing; put away clothes
2:00– 3:00	Wash dishes; straighten kitchen
3:00– 4:00	*Rest period*
4:00– 5:00	Market; walk
5:30– 6:00	Prepare supper
6:00– 7:00	SUPPER
7:00– 7:30	Wash dishes

THURSDAY

6:00– 6:30	Rise and dress; start water heater
6:30– 7:00	Prepare breakfast
7:00– 7:30	BREAKFAST
7:30– 8:30	Wash dishes; straighten kitchen; plan meals
8:30– 9:00	Make beds
9:00–11:30	Bedrooms and closets cleaned
11:30–12:00	*Rest period*
12:00– 1:00	LUNCH
1:00– 2:00	Wash dishes; prepare vegetables toward supper
2:00– 3:30	Upstairs windows cleaned (Up and down stairs windows alternately each week)
3:30– 4:00	Silver polished
4:00– 5:30	*Rest period*
5:30– 6:00	Prepare supper
6:00– 7:00	SUPPER
7:00– 7:30	Wash dishes

FRIDAY

6:00– 6:30	Rise and dress; start heater
6:30– 7:00	Prepare breakfast
7:00– 7:30	BREAKFAST
7:30– 8:30	Wash dishes; straighten kitchen; plan meals

flexible...

in the architectural form of the Panopticon, which is not
specifically a prison (being equally useful for hospitals, fac-
tories or schools), or even a building type. The Panopticon
is a system of management – an instrument for the control
of the visible and the invisible, for the control of bodies, of
power. The theme of instrumental transparency in architecture, which the Panopticon exemplifies, circulates around
the problems of management, of the illumination of some
darknesses and the preservation of other darknesses, of
efficient communication and productive labour, and of the
maintenance of the physical and moral 'health' of the 'social
body'. This theme will return again and again: in the social
hygiene movements, in the infiltration of Taylorism and
Scientific Management into the workplace and the home,[16]
in many of the urban proposals and architectural polemics of the modern movement.[17] What is often constituted
as, or presented under the guise of, progressive reform or
democratisation or social health, harbours the technologies of management and surveillance either as its means
or its ends.[18] A more recent manifestation of instrumental
transparency can be found in the 'open office' system
(which has been referred to as a 'managerial tool'), where a
shift away from earlier forms of the spatial repressiveness
of hierarchisation and compartmentalisation of the subject
in the office environment would just result in other forms
of hierarchisation and compartmentalisation – as well as in
the increased lack of privacy that came with an increased
efficiency of institutional management and surveillance.[19]

III

It should be clear however that architecture cannot control
behaviour in some absolute manner. Architecture partici-
pates in the managing of subjects because its own structuring is not dissimilar, at many levels, to the structuring of
the programmes/institutions that it 'houses' – in terms, for
example, of the organisation, hierarchisation and systematisation of order, activities, behaviour, movement and

visibility. One could examine how the obsessive rationality – obsessive to the point of irrationality – of both architecture and institution is woven through and through the space of, say, the office: from the regularised architectonic systems of structure, to the hierarchical 'space-planning' of subjects (managers, staff and visitors), to the standardised body registers of office practices (under the 'rigours' of ergonomic 'science'), right down to the compartmentalisation of subjects and objects via various filing systems. These systems exemplify the capillary action of Foucault's 'microtechnologies of power', the 'circulation of effects of power through progressively finer channels, gaining access to individuals themselves, to their bodies, their gestures and all their daily actions'.[20] It is in this manner that architecture functions both *as and under authority*. Architecture both structures and is structured by institutions.[21] It is a commonly held notion of our 'postmodern' time that different programmes can inhabit the same space because programmes are completely independent from architectural spatiality. But it is the similarity, not the disparity, between institutional structures, and between the structure of institutions and architecture, that allows for this interchangeability of inhabitation and management.

From the preceding discussion it should also be clear that the play of ideologies in architectural form is so complex that it would be pointless to expect a unitary ideology to be reflected in a building (even at the moment it is actualised as a design project or in built form). The conceptual gaps and temporal lags between ideologies and built forms are analogous to the gaps and lags between ideologies and 'material' conditions.[22] To trace this ideological drama one would need to examine how the object, in Manfredo Tafuri's words, 'reaches compromises with regard to the world and what conditions permit its existence' and thus what conditions govern its relationship to production and use.[23]

It would be equally pointless to imagine that any architectural project could be reduced, either in analysis or design, to a definitive map that could account for all the forces at play, to a totalising diagram of formal, psychological and

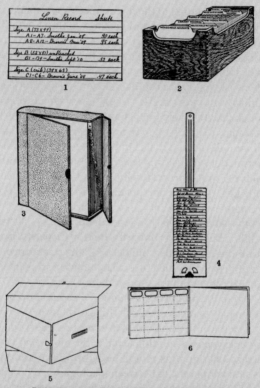

BUSINESSLIKE EQUIPMENT FOR THE HOME

(1) Sample Card from the Home Record Cabinet
(2) The Time and Worry Saving Home Record Cabinet
(3) A Vertical Letter File for Receipts
(4) A Tickler Which Reminds the Busy Housewife
(5) A Vertical Filing Envelope for Saving Large Clippings
(6) A Book of Handy Labels for Home Use

elegant…

social relations. The convergence of discourses and economies at the nexus of subject, space, site or programme provides an opportunity not to resurrect an ultimate truth-
value of 'Site' or 'Programme', but to utilise each force
against itself, against the other forces, and against the
entire project. The nostalgia of current 'contextualism' can
be interrogated by architecturally utilising past or present
aspects of the context to simultaneously problematise the
object by the site and the site by the object. The naive
problem-solving of 1960s behaviourialism can be similarly
interrogated by architecturally utilising the programme
to question certain institutional practices. In all cases, any
representation of these forces will always be one of many
possible representations.

IV

Thus far I have been discussing some of the ways subjects
are constituted and managed in institutional space. To demonstrate the deep pervasiveness of these structurings and
mechanisms it will be necessary first to examine how they
are involved in a kind of repressed architectural unconscious, and second, how the examination of this architectural unconscious reveals certain gaps and inconsistencies
within the social field from which critical narratives and
strategies might emerge.

    The architectural project, like the social field, is never
without some slippage, some gap, some residue that cannot
be sheltered, institutionalised, concealed. In fact, one definition of architecture could be *the management of what can and
cannot be 'concealed'*. One could speak, in this light, of many
things that refuse to remain concealed: anomalous behaviours, sexuality, certain odours,[24] domestic violence (in the
broadest sense), displaced social groups, and so on – as well
as the social and institutional ideologies and mechanisms
that attempt to manage the visibility of their own as well
as others' practices. Yet it is because all that is supposed
to be concealed refuses to remain concealed that it must

be managed through the constant presentation of certain conventions of architectural order and propriety.[25]

Unheimlich is one word that has been used to refer to that which refuses to remain concealed. As several writers have noted, Sigmund Freud, in his essay 'The Uncanny', puzzles over the strange confluence of meaning between two words that should have entirely opposite meanings – on the one hand *heimlich* (the canny, the homely) and on the other hand *unheimlich* (the uncanny, the unhomely). In the beginning of the essay, Freud says that the '… German word *unheimlich* is obviously the opposite of *heimlich*, *heimisch*, meaning "familiar", "native", "belonging to the home"; and we are tempted to conclude that what is "uncanny" is frightening precisely because it is *not* known and familiar.' In the course of the essay another meaning of *heimlich* is revealed: that which is '… concealed, kept from sight, so that others do not get to know about it … to behave *heimlich*, as though there were something to conceal … *heimlich* places (which good manners oblige us to conceal)'. Thus the 'uncanny is in reality nothing new or foreign, but something familiar and old-established in the mind which has been estranged only by the process of repression'. It is through this understanding that the force of Friedrich Schelling's definition of *unheimlich* as 'the name for everything that ought to have remained … hidden and secret and has become visible' becomes evident to Freud. The *unheimlich*, far from being the opposite and outside of the *heimlich*, *is* the *heimlich* – it is what is already inside, the homely that returns as the unhomely.[26]

Let me go further with this already established elucidation. First, it is worth noting that it is not only in the German language that words related to the concept of home reveal an uncanny meaning. For example, the English verb 'to dwell' is derived from the Middle English *dwellen* (from the Old English *dwellan*), which means 'to lead astray, hinder', and is akin to the Middle Dutch *dwellen*, which means 'to stun', and the Old High German *twellan* and the Old Norse *dvelja*, which mean 'to delay, to deceive' – which in turn are all derived from the Indo-European base **dh(e) wel-*, which means 'to mislead, to deceive, to obscure, to

CONTENTS

[xi]

productive…

make dull.'[27] And for the Sakalava, a tribe in Madagascar, among whom 'no one would refuse another entrance into his house *unless he were hoarding or hiding something*', the word *mody*, which means 'at home' or 'heading home', also means 'to pretend what one is not'.[28]

It is precisely the uncanny connotations of dwelling that Martin Heidegger repressed in favour of more *heimlich* ones (in his etymological 'derivations' from Old English and High German) in his late essay 'Building Dwelling Thinking'. It is interesting in this light to reconsider one of Heidegger's most famous statements: 'Language is at once the house of Being and the home of human beings.'[29] Heidegger claims that it is our highest 'summons' to try 'to bring dwelling to the fullest of its nature',[30] but fails to acknowledge that this fullness includes both the *heimlich* and *unheimlich*. Such a failure of acknowledgement, Freud suggests, is what causes the *unheimlich* to return.

The *unheimlich* meanings of 'dwelling' suggest what in architecture is 'familiar and old-established' that returns in the uncanny. The very constitution of architecture reveals, to reiterate Žižek's words, a 'traumatic, real kernel'. I am referring to a condition that is not specific either to recent times nor to western cultures but, as the anthropologist Peter J. Wilson notes, is an aspect of all cultures that inhabit 'permanent' dwellings:

When people adopted settlement and domestication as a permanent feature of their lives, they did not impinge directly on their drives of aggression and sexuality, but they did impinge directly on the *conditions of attention*. That is, they impeded their sensory ability to monitor, stimulate and govern these drives. Living behind walls affects the various aspects of attention, and people so affected must respond. This occurs in part by specialising attention, by developing modes of surveillance, supervision and inspection, and by evolving stratagems of evasion and display.[31]

Architecture constructs this evasion and at the same time is in constant flight from acknowledging its part in this construction. This evasion is the trauma of architecture, the 'antagonistic kernel' that always prevents the closure of the architectural field.[32] Thus it should not be so surprising that language returns to us this uncanniness of inhabitation, this duplicity, this doubled concealment. And it should also not be surprising that the mechanisms and conventions masking the trauma of this uncanniness should themselves attempt to remain hidden and repressed so that they, like the ideologies they mask, appear natural, stable, unalterable.

I am suggesting that the constitution and management of subjects through the types, or rather stereotypes, of institutional space, that is, through the *compulsion to repeat* these stereotypes without examination, is one means by which the uncanny returns in architecture. In psychoanalytical terms, as Peter Brooks notes, 'repetition is a way of remembering brought into play when recollection in the intellectual sense is blocked by repression and resistance.'[33] It is not the past as past that is recollected, that is, as 'something belonging to the past … in a bound state':[34] what is repeated is repressed material brought into the present as an active force, as a defence against the direct examination of complex and potentially dangerous psychological relations.

Architecture, for the most part, abandons itself to the unconscious repetition of stereotype – of the house, office, museum, hospital, library, and so forth – to such an extent that few architects think to reexamine the fundamental assumptions implicit within the conventional programme. (As Freud says: 'The patient abandons himself to the compulsion to repeat, which is now replacing the impulse to remember.'[35]) The basic functions of institutional stereotypes – regardless of how their configuration varies from culture to culture or the formal shifts that may occur within a given culture through time – are as *mechanisms of management*, to reinforce 'proper' social and psychological relations, and as *mechanisms of defence*, to guard against potentially dangerous social and psychological relations, that is, all 'that ought to remain hidden and secret'. Architecture, according to Georges Bataille, is the expression of the very soul of society, but 'it is only the ideal soul of enough ideal to force her *to subordinate housekeeping routine to the attainment of the higher ends of personal and family happiness and success.* What shall the homemaker do with her leisure time? Here are some suggestions:

Ten Things to Do in Leisure Time

1.—Take time to read more about her own specialty, as government and state food bulletins, books on household management, child care, house planning, equipment, etc.

2.—Take time for actual correspondence course in homemaking subjects; attend special classes in cooking, food conservation, budget making, which her community may offer.

3.—Take time to interest herself in and understand her husband's business, so that she can aid, sympathize and be a comrade in his work.

4.—Take time to supervise her children's school work, play, friendships; take them to museums, zoos and places of interest on their holidays.

5.—Take time for daily grooming, hygiene and physical exercise.

6.—Take time for reading and making personal thought-out decisions on the problems of life, ethics, immortality, philosophy of life, etc.

7.—Take time for music, art, language, business, hobby or interest beyond housekeping.

8.—Take time to "keep up on" some specialty or pursuit in which she excelled before marriage, or by which she used to earn her living, so that she can relieve herself of some phases of housework for which she is not fitted, and so that, in case of death or disability, she would be more able to take upon herself the burdens of family support, if occasion required.

distinctive…

society, that which has the authority to command and prohibit, that is expressed in architectural compositions properly speaking. Thus great monuments are erected like dykes, opposing the logic and majesty of authority against all disturbing elements: it is in the form of cathedral or palace that Church or State speaks to the multitudes and imposes silence upon them.'[36]

The conservative cry within the architectural discipline to 'remember' and repeat past formal, typological and institutional models with the claim that these models will shore us up, will make us safe and *heimlich*, is thus only the most vocal, *only the most apparent*, indication of this widespread compulsion to repeat. This architectural cry is similar to another current cry – to the 'Great Books' – a claim for connoisseurship as a defence against the critical examination of the classical canon. Such conscious cries for 'remembering' share with obsessional neurosis a 'forgetting' that 'consists mostly of a falling away of the links between various ideas, a failure to draw conclusions, an isolating of certain memories'.[37] This isolating of certain memories – literally in architecture an isolating of elements, institutional forms, 'typologies' and styles from the past – seeks to bring back the past, to repeat what is 'remembered' as pleasurable, as *heimlich*. But, as Jacques Lacan observes, the object is not retrievable, what is recalled is never the object itself: 'The object is encountered and is structured along the path of repetition – to find the object again, to repeat the object. Except, it never is the same object which the subject encounters. In other words, he never ceases generating substitutive objects.'[38]

It is because the past is irretrievable (as only substitutive objects are generated in lieu of that past) and because, most importantly, truly conscious remembering requires a remembering not only of forms but of their repressed significance, that what is recalled in this repetition is repressed trauma.[39] Thus the most significant repetition that these conscious cries for 'remembering' mask is a behavioural repetition – *the resistance to critical analysis* as a mechanism of defence. As Freud states:

The crux of the matter is that the mechanisms of defence against former dangers recur in analysis in the shape of *resistances* to cure. It follows that the ego treats recovery itself as a new danger... The patient now regards the analyst simply as an alien personality who makes disagreeable demands upon him and he behaves towards him exactly like a child who does not like a stranger and has no confidence in him. If the analyst tries to explain to the patient one of the distortions which his defence has produced and to correct it, he meets with a complete lack of comprehension and an imperviousness to valid arguments. We see then that there really *is* a resistance to the discovery of resistances and that the defence mechanisms ... are resistances not only to the bringing of id-contents into consciousness but also to the whole process of analysis and so to cure.[40]

V

Freud, in his discussion of defence mechanisms, states that they are 'in fact, infantilisms' that 'share the fate of so many institutions which struggle to maintain themselves when they have outlived their usefulness'. He continues this passage with a quote from Goethe's *Faust* summarising the potential danger of both defence mechanisms and institutions, '*Vernunft wird Unsinn, Wohltat Plage*'. Reason becomes unreason, kindness torment.[41]

It is, of course, as impossible to escape the framework of institutions as it is to escape the framework of ideology. What is possible is an unending task – the development of abilities to perceive and examine the structuring of institutions, to reveal those conditions where reason becomes unreason, kindness torment. In opening our institutions up to questioning, we reveal their artificial, and therefore alterable, construct. Bertolt Brecht, whose work was based on revealing the changeable character of that which presents itself as familiar and immutable, has already noted the difficulty of breaking into the repetitive cycle of society:

QUESTIONS ON HOUSEHOLD ENGINEERING

II

PLANS AND METHODS FOR DAILY HOUSEWORK

1. Make out a schedule of your present plan of work. Study to see where it can be improved. Try the new schedule two weeks. Revise and try another two weeks, and report.

2. Time yourself for at least a week on the same task, as, washing dishes, peeling potatoes, making beds, or cleaning the bathroom. How long does it take? Do you find the time varying from day to day? Write down two complete "time-studies" on these tasks, showing the first record and the last.

3. "Standardize" some household task so that you can do it every day in an identical manner without much mental attention. Does this not make it seem less difficult?

4. What are your worst "interruptions"? Make a schedule which will take care of them as much as possible.

5. Do the same task with two different tools, and note the difference, or do the same task with two different methods, or do it under two different sets of conditions. Find out the way that seems the best and shortest for your particular case and report.

versatile…

For it seems impossible to alter what has long not been altered. We are always coming on things that are too obvious for us to bother to understand them. What men experience among themselves they think of as 'the' human experience. A child, living in a world of old men, learns how things work there... Even if he realises that the arrangements made for him by 'Providence' are only what has been provided by society, he is bound to see society, that vast collection of beings like himself, as a whole that is greater than the sum of the parts and therefore not in any way to be influenced. Moreover, he would be used to things that could not be influenced; and who mistrusts what he is used to?[42]

Conventions, as representations of that which 'has long not been altered', are blocks both to awareness and to potential change. 'The past', as Freud says, 'is the patient's armoury out of which he fetches his weapons for defending himself against the progress of the analysis, weapons which we must wrest from him one by one'.[43] What are the means by which the defences of the past might be wrest from the patient? To ignore them, to proceed as if they did not exist would, of course, be useless. However paradoxical it might at first appear, it is precisely by utilising the compulsion to repeat against itself – by allowing it to display itself in its principal form (as a resistance to examination) – that progress is gained within the analysis: 'We render it harmless, and even make use of it, by according it the right to assert itself within certain limits... to display before us all the pathogenic impulses hidden in the depths of the patient's mind... Only when it has come to its height can one, with the patient's co-operation, discover the repressed instinctual trends which are feeding the resistance; and only by living them through in this way will the patient be convinced of their existence and their power.'[44] As Brooks observes:

Repetition is both an obstacle to analysis – since the analysand must eventually be led to renunciation of

the attempt to reproduce the past – and the principal dynamic of the cure, since only by way of its symbolic enactment in the present can the history of past desire, its objects and scenarios of fulfilment, be made known, become manifest in the present discourse... The narrative discourse – like the discourse of analysis – must restage the past history of desire as it exercises its pressure toward meaning in the present ... At issue ... is not so much the history of the past, or at least not the history of the past directly, as its present narrative discourse. This is a space of dialogue, struggle, construction.[45]

A restaging of the past history of desire as a construction requires a methodology able to distance itself enough from the past to perceive it as a construct – and therefore not just reproduce it. As Brecht suggests, such a methodology would treat 'social situations as processes, and … regard nothing as existing except in so far as it changes, in other words is in disharmony with itself'.[46] But to create this distance it is necessary to denaturalise, to defamiliarise the past. For Brecht this involved a strategy he termed *Verfremdungseffekt,* most commonly translated as 'alienation effect': 'A representation that alienates is one which allows us to recognise its subject, but at the same time makes it seem unfamiliar', in order to 'free socially conditioned phenomena from that stamp of familiarity which protects them against our grasp today'.[47] As in the psychoanalytical model, this involves a two-fold process: a restaging, a working on the past (on what is repressing and what is repressed), and in this process a swerving, a distancing from any direct repetition in order to allow for analysis and the potential for a different construction. The point is not to reproduce the restrictive nostalgia of memory but to develop the critical possibilities of counter-memory.[48]

Earlier I suggested that it might be possible to pursue an architecture that would be critically productive in the sense of exposing, critiquing, problematising and reworking certain repressed narratives already at work in architecture. Rather than avoid sites of ideological and psychological saturation, such an architecture might draw out some of this saturation. This act of drawing out is one method by which the obsessiveness and irrationality of the 'normal' and 'rational' may be revealed, may 'display before us all the pathogenic impulses' circulating around the repressed doubleness of inhabitation. One could characterise this inhabitation in the terms suggested by Wilson (in the developed modes and stratagems of surveillance, supervision, evasion and display) or in the somewhat more general terms I suggested earlier: the organisation, hierarchisation and systematisation of institutional practices.

The architectural operations addressing these issues could occur not only in the traditional realms of the architect (spaces, walls, windows, doors, and so on), but also at the level of what I have called the 'sub-architectural' – the level of the office desk, or the filing system, or the household cabinet. One might argue that these things have an impact that is at least as immediate, if not more immediate, in terms of the structuring of institutional ideologies, but it is at this level that architects mostly specify out of manufacturers' catalogues or leave to others to select. Even given the task of designing, say, a reception desk, most architects would architecturally repress its obvious social and psychological aspects. Inscribed through and through with a libidinal and ideological economy, the reception desk is a site of institutional desire in the broadest sense – as an apparatus of control, as a site that receives and keeps out, as an implicit participant and frame for the ubiquitous gender and class stereotyping of the 'receptionist' position. Architects are of course not inattentive to these institutional matters of design – on the contrary they occasionally custom-design everything from spaces to furniture. It is just that their 'deepest' attention tends to reside in the *decorative* design of lobby spaces and reception desks and executive desks, rather than designing these spaces and furnishing – or utilising standardised objects – in a critical manner.

VI

The limits of these critical narrative strategies are reached when they become just another way for architects to feign interest in extra-formal issues. What becomes crucial is not the arbitrary or casual evocation of conceptually or politically current concerns but the critical act of selection, processing and reworking these issues – not to further mystify the object, nor to reduce the object to a diagram of social forces, but as a way to expose and examine the whole architectural enterprise. This of course includes the play of form through the architect, which is as much an issue to be explored and problematised as other psychological or social forces, and is thus subject to the same examinations and disjunctions within a narrative operation. In fact the very act of architectural narration is not only not exempt from similar examinations and disjunctions, but requires that such techniques be turned on itself in order to expose the complexity and contingency of its own operations. There is however always a difficult balance between a discourse which fails to examine its own constitution and one that becomes self-consumed in privileging its own constitution, between, one might say, naive realism and unrelenting metafiction.

It only remains in this regard to suggest that the interventions that attempt to expose and problematise institutional narratives might also expose and problematise, rather than merely reproduce, the tedium of an absolutist rationality. In fact, it is from the gaps and slippages of that rationality that these interventions may emerge: 'Something that exceeds the thinkable and opens the possibility of "thinking otherwise" bursts in through comical, incongruous, or paradoxical half-openings of discourse'.[49] As Brecht never tired of pointing out, this involves pleasure – the pleasure 'felt when the rules emerging from this life in society are treated as imperfect and provisional',[50] the pleasure of 'the instability of every circumstance, the joke of contradiction and so forth: all these are ways of enjoying the liveliness of men, things and processes, and they heighten both our capacity for life and our pleasure in it'.[51]

THE *HOW* IN THE HOME

SYMBOLS FOR THE ELEMENTS OF THE MOTION CYCLE

Symbol	*Name*	*Color*
⌐o	Search	Black
⊂o	Find	Gray
→	Select	Light Gray
∩	Grasp	Lake Red
∽	Transport Loaded	Green
9	Position	Blue
#	Assemble	Violet
U	Use	Purple
╫	Dis-assemble	Light Violet
0	Inspect	Burnt Ochre
8	Pre-position for Next Operation	Sky Blue
⌒	Release Load	Carmine Red
⌣	Transport Empty	Olive Green
⌐	Rest for Overcoming Fatigue	Orange
⌒o	Unavoidable Delay	Yellow Ochre
⌐o	Avoidable Delay	Lemon Yellow
ዖ	Plan	Brown

attractive…

However successful these narrative strategies may be at the level of the object, one still needs to acknowledge the limits of architectural practice to directly affect widespread social change, as well as the abilities of the hegemonic culture to absorb critical strategies. As Brecht has noted, 'Capitalism has the power instantly and continuously to transform into a drug the very venom that is spit in its face, and to revel in it.'[52] It is thus always necessary for critical strategies – and this includes the strategies that might emerge from the theoretical positions of this essay – to be constantly reevaluated and renewed.

Having stated certain critical limits of the architectural object I would nevertheless maintain the productiveness of an architectural narrative that is *constituted within and through these limits*. I would therefore disagree with the conclusions that Tafuri has drawn from his many years of analysing the *naiveté* and bitter betrayals of avant-garde utopian dreams and progressive ideologies: 'To the deceptive attempts to give architecture an ideological dress, I shall always prefer the sincerity of those who have the courage to speak of that silent and outdated "purity"; even if this, too, still harbours an ideological inspiration, pathetic in its anachronism.'[53] But what may be, for some, sincerity and courage, for others will be indifference, fatigue, business as usual. At the risk of conveying, again in Tafuri's words, 'impotent and ineffectual myths, which so often serve as illusions that permit the survival of anachronistic 'hopes in design',[54] I would suggest that if we, with our lowered 'postmodern' expectations, can distinguish between direct political action and critical representations, we may be able to practise some means of both resistance and proposition within our work. In acknowledging the ineluctable rhetorical aspects of our field, we might critically examine within the limits of our discipline – in ways that need not be on the one hand totalising or utopian, nor on the other hand conciliatory or reactionary – the complex relationships between architecture and social practices.

Originally published in John Whiteman, Jeffrey Kipnis and Richard Burdett (eds.), *Strategies in Architectural Thinking* (Cambridge, MA: Chicago Institute for Architecture and Urbanism/MIT Press, 1992), 198–221, and *The Harvard Architecture Review* 8 (1992), 102–21.

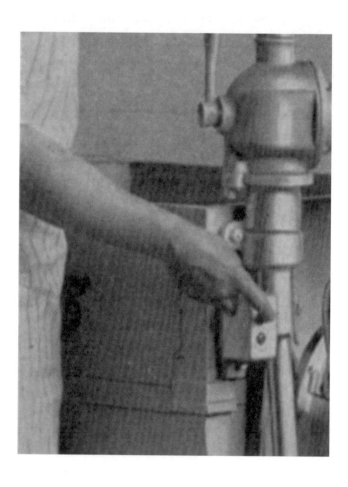

'If this wonderful new 'scientific management' brings such result in other businesses, why couldn't it do the same in my business of home-making.'
Christine Frederick, 1926

TECTONIC ACTS OF DESIRE AND DOUBT

NOTES

Figures of the office systems courtesy of the PLEION Corporation. Additional figures from Christine Frederick, *The New Housekeeping: Efficiency Studies in Home Management* (Garden City: Doubleday, Page and Company, 1915); Christine Frederick, *Household Engineering: Scientific Management in the Home* (Chicago: American School of Home Economics); Christine Frederick, *You and Your Laundry* (New York: The Hurley Machine Co., 1922); Lillian Gilbreth, *The Home-Maker and Her Job* (New York: D. Appleton and Company, 1928).

1. I am referring to both mentalities and practices to avoid collapsing two related but distinct historiographic approaches. Regarding the former, see Jacques Le Goff, 'Mentalities: A History of Ambiguities', in *Constructing the Past: Essays in Historical Methodology*, ed. Jacques Le Goff and Pierre Nora (Cambridge: Cambridge University Press, 1985), 151–65. Regarding the latter, see Michel Foucault, 'History of Systems of Thought', in *Language, Counter-Memory, Practice*, ed. Donald F. Bouchard (Ithaca: Cornell University Press, 1977), 199–204, and Foucault, *The Archaeology of Knowledge* (New York: Pantheon, 1972). On the relations between the two approaches see Lynn Hunt, 'French History in the Last Twenty Years: The Rise and Fall of the *Annales* Paradigm', *Journal of Contemporary History* 21 (1986), 209–24 and Peter Burke, *The French Historical Revolution: The Annales School 1929–89* (Stanford: Stanford University Press, 1990).

2. This multiplicity is further enlarged by several other constitutive elements. Whether a 'new' project or a renovation, the architectural work takes its place within a physical site with its own field of discourses and economies. All these forces are 'filtered' and added to by the attentions and intentions (again at various levels of consciousness) of the architect, the succession of subjects who observe and inhabit the building, and the institutional programmes under which they are managed.

For a discussion of the collision of forces under which architecture is constituted, and the concomitant 'collision' necessary in historical analysis, see Manfredo Tafuri, 'The Historical Project', in *The Sphere and the Labyrinth: Avant-Gardes and Architecture from Piranesi to the 1970s* (Cambridge MA: MIT Press, 1987), 1–21.

3. The confusion that surrounds the term 'narrative architecture' is exemplified in the following attempt at a 'definition' by the editors of *Oz* (the journal of the College of Architecture and Design at Kansas State University) in their 1988 issue dedicated to this topic: 'Many architects have something to say in their architecture, a story to tell. There are a variety of means architects employ in expressing their own, or their client's values, thoughts, wishes, beliefs, and desires. They often communicate a unifying theme elaborated throughout the "plot." Some of the storytellers of our discipline choose to relate the entire story in a single building while others "write" continuing sagas in which each building is a sequel to the last. Others, whether consciously or not, allude to earlier work by masters or to vital vernacular traditions. The architect's tale can be as captivating

and powerful as the writer's. The best narratives give building added meaning and encourage people to become involved with and to cherish works of architecture.'

4. The limits of these positions become quickly apparent if one considers, for example, the matter of the so-called appropriate character for a given institutional type (houses 'homey', museums 'stately', prisons 'foreboding'). Is this character supposed to be understood as an additive feature or as residing in the building?

5. See, for example, Peter Brooks, *Reading for the Plot: Design and Intention in Narrative* (New York: Knopf, 1984); Fredric Jameson, *The Political Unconscious: Narrative as a Socially Symbolic Act* (Ithaca: Cornell University Press, 1981); D.A. Miller, *Narrative and Its Discontents: Problems of Closure in the Traditional Novel* (Princeton: Princeton University Press, 1981); and Edward W. Said *Beginnings: Intention and Method* (Baltimore: Johns Hopkins University Press, 1975).

6. Roland Barthes, 'Introduction to the Structural Analysis of Narratives', *Image–Music–Text* (New York: Hill and Wang, 1977), 116. That certain postmodern practices seek to create signs which only look like signs is merely the flip side of the same coin, merely another attempt to posit a comforting separateness of 'coding' and 'narrative'.

In my use of 'hegemonic' here, I am referring not to a unitary power, but again to a diverse field of discourses and economies. As Ernesto Laclau and Chantal Mouffe (in their *Hegemony* and *Socialist Strategy: Towards a Radical Democratic Practice* (London: Verso, 1985), 142) have noted, 'the hegemonic formation … cannot be referred to the specific logic of a single social force. Every historical bloc – or hegemonic formation – is constructed through regularity in dispersion, and this dispersion includes a proliferation of very diverse elements… The problem of power cannot, therefore, be posed in terms of the search for *the* class or *the* dominant sector which constitutes the centre of a hegemonic formation, given that, by definition, such a centre will always elude us. But it is equally wrong to propose as an alternative, either pluralism or the total diffusion of power within the social, as this would blind the analysis to the presence of nodal points and to the partial concentrations of power existing in every concrete social formation.'

7. So, for example, what is particularly interesting about Terragni's Danteum project is the numerous ways in which a strict linear narrative cannot be maintained, the ways in which gaps, slippages, breaks appear in the project, the ways in which Terragni's stated intentions (and the subject's experiences of the project) lose their linear grip, turn back on themselves, cross paths, dead-end and are subsumed by the problems of translation, not merely from book to building, but from intended (and non-intended) meaning to geometry, from metaphysical architecture to State architecture, and vice versa. Thus understandably linear readings – 'The progression from dense to framed to open – Inferno, Purgatory, Paradise – following a scheme of ascent to the most holy and sacred space leads finally to the room dedicated to the New Roman Empire' (Thomas Schumacher, *The Danteum* (Princeton: Princeton

Architectural Press, 1985), 32) – also cannot be maintained. For example, the Paradise space can be read as more cage-like and less open (with its slitted walls and field of glass columns and trellis) than the Purgatory space. And the room dedicated to the New Roman Empire, the Impero, is a narrow passage that gives no passage, a dead-end that requires the visitor to double-back and pass again through Paradise. One might also ask why Terragni releases his otherwise tight theatrical control in a number of locations: in the opening between Purgatory and Paradise, and in the arcades in Inferno and Purgatory that allow an avoidance of the direct experience of those spaces.

8. In fact, it may be suggested that there is no such thing as pure 'public' or pure 'private' space, considering, for example, the degree to which the interventions of social values (from table manners to sexual manners) have shaped domestic practices.

9. I am using the term 'management' here in a similar manner as Foucault has used the terms 'power' or 'power relations', that is, to refer to *the entire range of its manifestations*, not solely the negative and repressive ones. His definition of the term 'subject', although brief, is also useful here: 'subject to someone else by control and dependence; and tied to his own identity by a conscience or self-knowledge'. (Michel Foucault, 'The Subject and Power', in *Art After Modernism: Rethinking Representation*, ed. Brian Wallis (New York: The Museum of Contemporary Art, and Boston: Godine, 1984), 420.

10. For a discussion of how urban parks are involved in the constitution and

management of subjects, see Galen Cranz, *The Politics of Park Design* (Cambridge MA: MIT Press, 1982).

11. Slavoj Žižek, *The Sublime Object of Ideology* (London: Verso, 1989), 45.

12. See Philippe Ariès, *Centuries of Childhood: A Social History of Family Life* (New York: Vintage, 1962). See also Robin Evans, 'Figures, Doors and Passages', *Architectural Design* (Autumn 1978), 267–78 and his 'The Developed Surface: An Enquiry into the Brief Life of an Eighteenth-Century Drawing Technique', *9H* 8 (1989), 120–47.

13. Michel Foucault, 'The Politics of Health in the Eighteenth Century', in *Power/Knowledge: Selected Interviews and Other Writings 1972–1977*, ed. Colin Gordon (New York: Pantheon, 1980), 166–82. Regarding the effects of hygienic movements on domestic and urban spaces see Georges Teyssot, 'The Disease of the Domicile' in *Assemblage* 6 (1988), 72–97. Regarding other institutional spaces, in addition to Foucault's studies of the clinic, the asylum and the prison, see Anthony Vidler's essays on industry, hospitals and prisons in *The Writing of the Walls: Architectural Theory in the Late Enlightenment* (Princeton: Princeton Architectural Press, 1987) as well as his *Claude-Nicolas Ledoux: Architecture and Social Reform at the End of the Ancien Regime* (Cambridge MA: MIT Press, 1990). See also Robin Evans, T*he Fabrication of Virtue: English Prison Architecture, 1750–1840* (Cambridge: Cambridge University Press, 1982).

14. See Michel Foucault's comments in 'The Eye of Power' in *Power/Knowledge*, 146–65. Foucault refers to the discussion of the theme of social transparency in the writings of Rousseau by Jean Starobinski (see Starobinski, *Jean-Jacques Rousseau:*

Transparency and Obstruction
(Chicago: The University of Chicago
Press, 1988) and *The Invention of
Liberty* (Geneva/New York: Skira/
Rizzoli, 1964; paperback reprint,
1987), 100ff). Also see Jacques-
Alain Miller's extensive reading of
utilitarianism through the body
of Bentham's work in 'Jeremy
Bentham's Panoptic Device',
October 41 (1987), 3–29.

15. Starobinski, *Jean-Jacques Rousseau*,
92–101.

16. On the shifts in practices of
the management of domestic
space, see Barbara Ehrenreich
and Deirdre English, *For Her Own
Good: 150 Years of Experts' Advice
to Women* (Garden City: Anchor,
1978); Dolores Hayden, *The Grand
Domestic Revolution: A History
of Feminist Designs for American
Homes, Neighborhoods, and Cities*
(Cambridge MA: MIT Press, 1981);
and Gwendolyn Wright, *Moralism
and the Model Home: Domestic
Architecture and Cultural Conflict
in Chicago 1873–1913* (Chicago:
University of Chicago Press, 1980).
For a discussion of the ways in
which women's picture magazines
played a mediating link between
the social spheres of 'industrial
production and... domestic
reproduction', reinforcing the
scientific management lessons
of order and efficiency, see Sally
Stein, 'The Graphic Ordering
of Desire: Modernization of A
Middle-Class Women's Magazine,
1914–1939', *Heresies* 18 (1985), 7–16.
For a discussion of Le Corbusier's
embrace of, and subsequent
disillusionment with, Taylorism
see Mary McLeod, 'Architecture or
Revolution: Taylorism, Technocracy,
and Social Change', *Art Journal* 43:2
(Summer 1983), 132–47. Other aspects
of Le Corbusier's work related to

the themes of spatial management
and instrumental transparency are
discussed briefly in Bruce Brice
Taylor, 'Technology, Society, and
Social Control in Le Corbusier's Cité
de Refuge, Paris, 1933', *Oppositions*
15–16 (Winter–Spring 1979), 169–86.
For an extensive reading of the work
of Le Corbusier and Adolf Loos with
regard to the construction of the
subject in the domestic interior see
Beatriz Colomina, 'The Split Wall:
Domestic Voyeurism' in *Sexuality
and Space*, ed. Colomina (New York:
Princeton Architectural Press, 1991).

17. Laszlo Moholy-Nagy's comments
(from his Bauhaus Book, *Painting,
Photography, Film*) contain a
remarkable summary of these
themes: 'Men still kill one another,
they have not understood how
they live, why they live; politicians
fail to observe that the earth is
an entity, yet television (Telehor)
has been invented: the "Far Seer" –
tomorrow we shall be able to look
into the hearts of our fellow-man,
be everywhere and yet alone;
illustrated books, newspapers,
magazines are printed – in millions.
The unambiguousness of the real,
the truth in the everyday situation
is there for all classes. *The hygiene
of the optical, the health of the
visible is slowly filtering through.*'
Laszlo Moholy-Nagy, *Painting,
Photography, Film* (Cambridge MA:
MIT Press, 1969), 38, emphasis in
original text. (The first edition of
this book was published in 1925;
the second edition, from which
this translation was made, was
published two years later). Another
example is Mies van der Rohe's
1923 comments on office buildings
(that appeared alongside his well-
known statement 'Architecture
is the will of the age conceived in
spatial terms') in the first issue

of the avant-garde publication *G*: 'The office building is a *house* of work of organisation of clarity of economy. Bright, wide workrooms, *easy to oversee*, undivided except as the organism of the undertaking is divided. The maximum effect with the minimum expenditure of means.' (From *Programs and Manifestoes on Twentieth-Century Architecture*, ed Ulrich Conrads (Cambridge MA: MIT Press, 1970), 74; the emphasis is mine, although further emphasis could be given to the equation of office and house, as well as to the spatial aspects of work, organisation, clarity, economy and division).

18. As Foucault notes (in 'An Interview with Michel Foucault', in *History of the Present* I (1985), 2): 'As soon as a power infinitely less brutal and less extravagant, less visible and less ponderous than the big monarchical administration became necessary, greater latitudes for the participation in power and in the decision-making process were given to a certain social class. But at the same time and in order to compensate for it, a system of training was elaborated, essentially aimed at other social classes, but also at the new ruling class – for the bourgeoisie has in a way worked upon itself, it has developed its own type of individuals. I do not think that the two phenomena are contradictory: one was the price paid for the other. For a certain bourgeois liberalism to become possible at the level of institutions, it was necessary to have, at the level of what I call 'micro-powers', a much stricter investment in bodies and behaviours. Discipline is the underside of democracy.'

19. This is not to suggest that transparency as such is repressive, even less that we return to earlier forms of cellular management.

20. Foucault, 'The Eye of Power', 151–52.

21. As Denis Hollier notes (in his *Against Architecture: The Writings of Georges Bataille* (Cambridge MA: MIT Press, 1989), 33): 'There is consequently no way to describe a system without resorting to the vocabulary of architecture… Architecture under these conditions is the architructure, the system of systems. The keystone of systematicity in general, it organizes the concord of languages and guarantees universal legibility. The temple of meaning, it dominates and totalizes signifying productions, forcing them all to come down to the same thing, to confirm its noologic system. Architecture is a compulsory loan burdening all of ideology, mortgaging all its differences from the outset.' For a further discussion of architectural metaphor in philosophical thought, see Mark Wigley, 'The Production of Babel, the Translation of Architecture', in *Assemblage* 8 (1989), 7–19. For a discussion of the structuring and counter-structuring of architecture and culture, see Catherine Ingraham, 'Lines and Linearity: Problems in Architectural Theory', in *Drawing/Building/ Text*, ed. Andrea Kahn (New York: Princeton Architectural Press, 1991).

22. By temporal lag between ideologies and built form I am referring, for example, to the time between the height of the 'open classroom' pedagogical movement and the appearances of the first built examples, and to the degree to which these built examples may even have assisted in the movement's decline.

As George Duby notes (in 'Ideologies in social history', in Le Goff and Nora, *Constructing the Past: Essays in Historical Methodology*, 158–59) ideologies indicate changes in 'the lived reality of social organisation … slowly and reluctantly, because they are by nature conservative. They are the locus of a process of adaptation, but this is sometimes very slow and always remains partial. Moreover, in a subtle dialectical process, the weight of ideological representations is sometimes such as to hold back the development of material and political structures …'

23. Tafuri, 'The Historical Project', 17.

24. For a discussion of the relationships of propriety, property and the proper name see Ingraham, 'The Faults of Architecture: Troping the Proper' in *Assemblage* 7 (1988), 7–13.

25. For a discussion of the historical shifts in cultural practices related to various odours, see Alain Corbin, *The Foul and the Fragrant: Odour and the French Social Imagination* (Cambridge MA: Harvard University Press, 1986) and Norbert Elias, *The Civilizing Process: The Development of Manners* (New York: Urizon, 1978).

26. All the quotations in this paragraph are from Sigmund Freud, 'The Uncanny', in Freud, *On Creativity and the Unconscious* (New York: Harpers, 1958), 122–61. For two other discussions on the uncanny in architecture see Vidler, 'The Architecture of the Uncanny: The Unhomely Houses of the Romantic Sublime', in *Assemblage* 3 (1987), 7–29 and Wigley, 'Postmortem Architecture: The Taste of Derrida', *Perspecta* 23 (1987), 156–72.

27. *The Compact Edition of the Oxford English Dictionary* (New York: Oxford University Press, 1971) and the *Webster's New World Dictionary* (New York: William Collins and World Publishing, 1978). I would like to thank James F. Gramata for pointing out this etymology to me.

28. Gillian Feeley-Harnik, 'The Sakalava

House (Madagascar)', *Anthropos* 75 (1980), 580, quoted in Peter J. Wilson, *The Domestication of the Human Species* (New Haven: Yale University Press, 1988), 98. Emphasis in original text.

29. Martin Heidegger, 'Letter on Humanism' in Heidegger, *Basic Writings* (New York: Harper and Row, 1977), 239.

30. Martin Heidegger, 'Building Dwelling Thinking' in Heidegger, *Poetry, Language, Thought* (New York: Harper, 1971), 145–61.

31. Wilson, *The Domestication of the Human Species*, 182. Emphasis in original.

32. Žižek (in *The Sublime Object of Ideology*, 162–64; emphasis in original) is using the term 'the Real' in the Lacanian sense, that is, to refer not to a 'transcendent positive entity', but to an entity, like the Freudian example of the primal parricide, which 'although it does not exist (in the sense of 'really existing', taking place in reality) has a series of properties – it exercises a certain structural causality, it can produce a series of effects in the symbolic reality of subjects.' In fact it is only in a series of effects that this entity is present, but 'always in a distorted, displaced way… Laclau and Mouffe [in *Hegemony and Socialist Strategy*] were the first to develop this idea in its relevance for the social-ideological field in their concept of *antagonism*: antagonism is precisely such an impossible kernel … only to be constructed retroactively, from a series of its effects, as the traumatic point which escapes them; it prevents a closure of the social field'.

For the same reasons as Žižek has noted with regard to the primal parricide, it would be pointless to search for the 'traces' of the built *unheimlich* in 'prehistoric reality, but it must none the less be presupposed if we want to account for the present state of things'. In addition, we should not expect that architecture would need to blatantly and continually enunciate its *unheimlich* side (as it does in the rare example, say, of the panoptic prison) for its effects to be felt. In other words, direct suppression is not the only or principal means of control, as Jacques Lacan notes (in Lacan, 'Television' in *October* 40 (1987), 31–32; emphasis in original): 'Freud didn't say that repression *comes from* suppression: that (to paint a picture) castration is due to what Daddy brandished over his brat playing with his wee-wee: "We'll cut it off, no kidding, if you do it again".' That this enunciation is repressed and masked not only does not take away from its pervasive power, it assures it.

33. Peter Brooks, 'Psychoanalytic constructions and narrative meanings', in *Paragraph*, 7 (1986), 57.

34. Sigmund Freud, *Beyond the Pleasure Principle* (New York: Norton, 1959), 12, 30.

35. Freud, 'Further Recommendations in the Technique of Psychoanalysis: Recollection, Repetition and Working Through' in Freud, *Therapy and Technique* (New York: Collier, 1963), 161.

36. Hollier, *Against Architecture*, 46–47. Bataille continues: 'It is, in fact, obvious that monuments inspire social prudence and often even real fear. The taking of the Bastille is symbolic of this state of things: it is hard to explain this crowd movement other than by the animosity of the people against the monuments that are their real masters.' Hollier commenting on this passage says (49, 55):

'[Architecture's] job … is to serve society to defend itself against that which is its basis only because of its threat… Architecture functions as the fantasy that man identifies with to escape his desire (to escape it is to control it). Man is confined: *conformed* within himself.'

37. Freud, 'Recollection, Repetition and Working Through', 159.

38. Lacan, *The Seminar of Jacques Lacan: Book II, The Ego in Freud's Theory and in the Technique of Psychoanalysis 1954–1955*, ed. Jacques-Alain Miller (New York: Norton, 1988), 100.

39. As Joan Copjec notes (in '*India Song/Son nom de Venise dans Calcutta désert*: The Compulsion to Repeat' in *October* 17 (1981), 42–43): 'The compulsion to repeat is definitely not, according to psychoanalysis … an attempt to return to a previous state of satisfaction; rather it is the return to a trauma, which is conceived, psychoanalytically as it is medicosurgically, as a wound, a break in the protective skin which triggers catastrophe, misfortune through the whole of the organism.'

40. Freud, 'Analysis Terminable and Interminable' in Freud, *Therapy and Technique* (New York: Collier, 1963), 256–58.

41. Ibid., 255–56. Freud continues: 'The adult ego with its greater strength continues to defend itself against dangers which no longer exist in reality and even finds itself impelled to seek out real situations which may serve as a substitute for the original danger, so as to be able to justify its clinging to its habitual modes of reaction. Thus the defensive mechanisms produce an ever-growing alienation from the external world and a permanent enfeeblement of the ego and we can readily understand how they

pave the way for and precipitate the outbreak of neurosis.'

42. Bertolt Brecht, 'A Short Organum for the Theatre', in *Brecht on Theatre*, ed John Willett (New York: Hill and Wang, 1964), 192.

43. Freud, 'Recollection, Repetition and Working Through', 161.

44. Ibid., 164–65.

45. Brooks, 'Psychoanalytic constructions and narrative meanings', 57, 62, 67.

46. Brecht, 'A Short Organum for the Theatre', 193.

47. Ibid., 192.

48. On the concept of counter-memory see Friedrich Nietzsche, 'History in the Service and Disservice of Life' in Nietzsche, *Unmodern Observations*, ed. William Arrowsmith (New Haven: Yale, 1990), 87–145 and Michel Foucault, 'Nietzsche, Genealogy, History', in *Language, Counter-Memory, Practice*, 139–64. It is also interesting in this regard to note Jacques Derrida's comments on architecture and 'memory' (in 'Jacques Derrida in Discussion with Christopher Norris', *Deconstruction in Architecture II* (*AD* Profile 74, London: St Martins, 1989), 73,emphasis in original): 'Now as for architecture, I think that *Deconstruction* comes about – let us carry on using this word to save time – when you have deconstructed some architectural philosophy, some architectural assumptions – for instance, the hegemony of the aesthetic, of beauty, the hegemony of usefulness, of functionality, of living, of dwelling. But then you have to *reinscribe* these motifs in the work. You can't (or you shouldn't) simply dismiss those values of dwelling, functionality, beauty and so on. You have to construct, so to speak, a new space and a new form, to shape a new way of building in which those motifs are reinscribed, having meanwhile lost their hegemony. The inventiveness of powerful architects consists I think in this reinscription, the economy of this reinscription, which also involves some respect for tradition, for memory. Deconstruction is not simply forgetting the past. What has dominated theology or architecture or anything else is still there, in some way, and the inscriptions, the let's say, archive of these deconstructed structures, the *archive* should be as readable as possible, as legible as we can make it.'

49. This is Michel de Certeau's characterisation of the method of investigation of Foucault. De Certeau, *Heterologies: Discourse on the Other* (Minneapolis: University of Minnesota Press, 1986), 194.

50. Brecht, 'A Short Organum for the Theatre', 205.

51. Brecht, 'Appendices to the Short Organum', in *Brecht on Theatre*, 277. Theodor Adorno's critique of Brecht, even given 'its partiality' (Jameson's apt expression (*Aesthetics and Politics* (London: New Left Books, 1977), 209), would be neither the first nor the last to comment on the distance between theory and practice, and the difficult relationship between direct social content and ambiguity, in the work of Brecht. I would suggest that while the danger of social content in an aesthetic work that lacks a degree of ambiguity is overly simplistic didacticism, on the other hand the danger of ambiguity from without, rather than from within, specificity of content is easy and empty seduction (as witnessed by the success of such politically questionable artists as Joseph Beuys and Anselm Kiefer). Closer examination of Adorno's position reveals, again in Jameson's words

(in *Late Marxism: Adorno, or, The Persistence of the Dialectic* (New York: Verso, 1990), 223), a 'subtle appreciation of his great adversary, Brecht', even in the aggressively critical essay 'Commitment' (in *Aesthetics and Politics*, 177–95) but particularly in the more balanced *Aesthetic Theory* (New York: Routledge & Kegan Paul, 1984), 344: 'Still it is Brecht in large measure to whom we owe the growth in the self-consciousness of the art work, for when it is viewed as an element of political praxis its resistance to ideological mystification becomes that much stronger.'

52. Bertolt Brecht, 'Rauschgift', in *Gesammelte Werke* (Frankfurt: Suhrkamp, 1967), vol VIII, 593, quoted in Yve-Alain Bois' essay (on the work of the artist Hans Haacke) 'The Antidote' in *October* 39 (Winter 1986), 143. Bois continues: 'This recuperative power undoubtedly complicates Haacke's preparation of the antidote. His strategy is to convey his awareness of this in the work itself.'

53. Tafuri, *Architecture and Utopia: Design and Capitalist Development* (Cambridge MA: MIT Press, 1976), ix. Also see his *The Sphere and the Labyrinth*.

54. Tafuri, *Architecture and Utopia*, 182.

ROBIN EVANS

This time I will begin where he ends:

If it wasn't for the needless multiplication of the rib, the decorative version of it, they wouldn't have had the intuition of things defined by surfaces first, in which the ribs become subordinate arrangement. That means that the surface becomes structure. A tremendous revolution was made possible by the particular understanding of ornament as we now describe it. It seems to me that such an observation about what seems to be subordinate is always active in techniques or theories. It just indicates a way of looking at buildings. ('Le Corbusier and the Sexual Identity of Architecture')[1]

Anyone who ever met Robin Evans would recognise that gesture – that characteristic gesture of modesty in the last sentence of his last lecture at Columbia University. But it is the prior sentence that reveals the gesture I want to call his immodesty, reveals that his aims as a critic are anything but modest, suggesting, as it does, an entire re-examination of techniques and theories, an entire overturning of the way techniques and theories and buildings have been thought of up to now. This doubled condition, a particularly Evansian condition of one thing enfolded with its seeming opposite, can be seen again, here in a letter to me – the second ellipsis is his – in which he refers to a number of his recent essays:

… the manner of treatment is markedly similar in that an unfamiliar interpretation of a well-known phenomenon is put forward … I hope). In each instance this is done by taking the received opinion of renowned critics as the

touchstone for revision or contradiction (Wölfflin, Wittkower, Panofsky plus others to suit).[2]

But there is a further doubling of modest and immodest intent, or rather, enfolded within what I am claiming is Robin Evans' immodesty – his desire to rethink some of the fundamental attributes of historical method and knowledge – is another kind of modesty – his refusal to project his personal judgement as representative of some teleological force of history, his refusal, in other words, of the position of operative critic. I will return to this latter position in a moment, but first let me speak of, as he said, revisions and contradictions.

Robin Evans' acts of revision and contradiction are, for the most part, not merely some minor correctives to an otherwise uniform and solid block generally labelled as the History of Art and Architecture, nor are they, for the most part, some alternative interpretations to add alongside other interpretations. He wanted, at the very least, to thoroughly complicate, and preferably to dismantle, some of the most fundamental and cherished notions held by historians and architects. His enemy was that sort of reductionism that is a subtraction from complexity, particularly the sort of reductionism that emerges from oppositional thinking. 'Some people have in their heads a pair of intellectual scissors which cut things in half', is how he put it.[3] He wanted, in other words, not just to complicate received opinion, but to show how received opinions have often reduced the complications and contradictions of objects, thoughts and situations. Some of his fundamental re-envisionings and thus revisions are exemplified here with just a few of the innumerable examples of his that could be cited.

On the so-called concept of centrality in the Renaissance:

From what has been said so far it would not seem reasonable to regard the Renaissance world picture as especially certain or especially coherent; nor would it seem any more

reasonable to regard the centralised churches as attempts to copy such a picture in all good faith. Is it not more likely that the delectable fancy we indulge ourselves in, looking back at these buildings as if what they appear to represent *had been there*, is itself an aftereffect of their original mendacity? ... This then was not an architecture that reflects a culture in its fullness, but an architecture that supplements culture's incompleteness with a compensating image... It does not exemplify the spirit in the times but a spirit standing next to the times ... ('Centrality')[4]

On the so-called concordance of whole-number proportion in architecture and music in the Renaissance:

The history of Western tuning is the history of the extinction of whole-number ratios... The striking thing is that, in architecture and painting as in polyphony, a countervailing rationality was established at the same time, and by the same people: Brunelleschi and Alberti introduced 'harmonic' architectural proportion as well as the linear perspective that distorted it, just as Dunstable and Dufay used proportional isorhythms as well as the thirds and sixths that destroyed numerical proportionality... There was no single species of proportion, no unified idea of it, no general relation of theory to practice, no seamless weave of numerical correspondence and similitude. ('Dufay, Brunelleschi and the Trouble with Numbers')[5]

On the so-called distinction between the formal and the social:

There was, after all, more than a passing parallelism between the ways in which the art of architectural composition treated the arrangement of iconographic and representational elements and the way in which reformed institutions treated the organisation of staff and inmates. *(The Fabrication of Virtue)*[6]

ROBIN EVANS
53, DIGBY CRESCENT
LONDON   N42HS

tel:(01)802-4304
8th June 1988

Dear Mark,
        It was nice hearing from you yesterday. I had forgotten all about
the revised book outline. It took me ages to do it but then I just let it
hang around after sending it to John V., to give him an idea of what I
wanted to work on. I would be very interested in your comments on it. At the
moment I feel that it at least gave me a clearer and more certain idea of
the connections between the parts, and how they sit in relation to one
another. In the end though, one is never sure whether this is a private
reverie or something conveyed in the document. The only way of finding out
is to ask other people.

        The articles you asked about are enclosed as photocopies (I have run
out of off-prints). Figures Doors & Passages I find too polemical in
retrospect, although I get the impression the punters like it more than my
other stuff. The book, also enclosed (you can't miss it), cost me £33. That
must be something like $60 at todays ludicrous exchange rate. I do not even
know whether that is less than the American retail cost. I think it may be,
but only just. I appologise on behalf of Cambridge University Press. Can you
believe that it retails over here at £47? I can't.

        I hope our paths might cross in the fall, but if not, I hope you have a
good time in Chicago. Good luck.

Yours

Bob Evans.

London
Je 88

Dear Mark,

Here's the Stereochem piece
and also Slides of the ills.
Some of these may suffice for reproduction.
but certainly not all! — there are anyway a
few missing.

Bob E.

On Mies's so-called structural rationality:

Since the mechanical structure of a building is nothing but a response to gravity, any architectural expression of mechanical structure would surely declare the transmission of load, not conceal it. Yet conceal it Mies does – always and in all ways. ('Mies van der Rohe's Paradoxical Symmetries')[7]

Robin Evans constantly registered the contradictions, indeterminacies and ambiguities both within the objects produced by architects and within the statements about these objects produced by architects, critics and historians. Once attuned to the constant occurrence of such indeterminacies – and few have ever been so carefully attuned as Robin Evans – the mere noting of such is a relatively easy task. What is crucial in his work is the precise tracing and unfolding of these contradictions, indeterminacies and ambiguities – these relations – precisely along the lines of what appear to be the most distinct, determinate and stable concepts in architecture. And thus he was at his best in his longer essays, where he could deploy the argument of these tracings through a series of repeated attacks, all the more fierce for the calm and measured delivery of their careful and cunning rhetorical skill.

His writing, in other words, is all the more immodest for its modesty.

Such is the case, for example, in his exemplary essay 'Drawn Stone' (on stereotomy, the use of projection in stone-cutting),[8] where he takes the seemingly fixed subjects under investigation (Classical and Gothic, ornament and structure, geometry and style, technique and effect, among others) and turns them inside out – as he literally does with the example of the vaults of the Henry VII chapel – showing how each of these pairs of subjects can no longer be thoroughly distinguished from the other, from its seeming opposite. He does so not by merely pronouncing a contradiction or a reversal, but slowly, step by rhetorically persuasive step, so that you hardly notice the disjunction, the extreme disjunction until suddenly you find with a shock that all your received notions on these subjects have been turned inside out and outside in, to the point that they lose any fixed and limited meanings they may have had. What is even more remarkable is that he performs this trick not once but at every turn in the course of this essay. It is a beautiful construction, as carefully fitted and as astonishing an enfolded act of structure and ornament as the stereotomic structures he was writing about.

Although in the past I had seen him perform such feats in formal public presentations, informal presentations seldom allowed him sufficient time within which to develop and connect all his necessary unfoldings and reconstructions. This is why he keeps apologising for the incomplete and summary nature of his explanations in this last Columbia University lecture. We should be grateful nonetheless for this transcription – knowing the thoroughness of a finished Evans essay, one can imagine how he might have developed the necessary turns and provided the transitions to fill in the outlines provided here on this particularly complex subject.

Having begun where he ends, let me continue where he begins – with the gesture of his beginning:

Some preliminary remarks about what this *isn't* meant to be – it's not meant to be an account of the way in which architecture should have, or must have, some sexual identity projected on to it. It is simply some observations about what has tended to happen, with the tense here being quite important, what *has* tended to have happened. ('Le Corbusier and the Sexual Identity of Architecture')[9]

Why does Evans refrain from developing a projective position, a 'should' or a 'must', on the question at hand? Perhaps one aspect of this restraint might be indicated in a comment he made in another letter to me, referring this time to his seminal essay on the relations between architecture and social forms of the domicile, still his most well-known text:

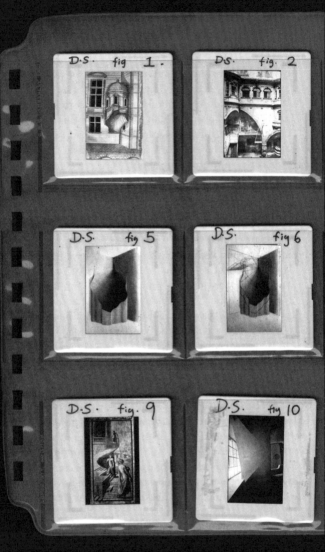

'Drawn Stone' slides, presented at the conference
Architectural Representation: History and Problems, Harvard University
Graduate School of Design, October 31–November 1, 1987

S.   fig 7   D·S·   fig 8.

S.   fig 11   D·S·   fig 12

Figures Doors & Passages I find too polemical in retrospect, although I get the impression the punters like it more than my other stuff.[10]

Punters. Ah, what a word. In its most common British usage, 'punter' means 'customer', your average consumer. But given Evans' linkage of this word to some notion of the polemical I would suggest that he means something more than just a lay person, a non-specialist, a non-historian. Let me suggest one of the other dictionary usages specified in my *Oxford*, not the one meaning 'prostitute's client', but the one meaning 'someone who bets'. It is not the sense of speculation that is at stake here, because Robin Evans often referred to his own work as speculation, understanding that all historical work is speculative construction, even as it attempts to hide behind the mask of objective reportage. But there is a difference between speculation that opens up to approximate the complexity of objects in the world, and speculation that closes down that complexity in order to develop a singular line, in order, that is, to develop a line to wager on, upon which to place one's bet. In other words, as is most often the case, one fabricates oppositional sides and is then pressured by one's own fabrication to choose between them. This does not mean that the architect, the critic or the historian cannot judge or even advocate a position – one cannot help but do so – but that one should not confuse advocacy for history. Just as he took historians to task for reducing the complexity of history to some manageable theme, now he takes himself and his audience to task for the same simplification, in other words, in Tafuri's words for example, the simplification of an operative criticism: 'the planning of a precise poetical tendency, anticipated in its structure and derived from historical analyses programmatically distorted and finalised … We could say, in fact, that operative criticism *plans* past history by projecting it towards the future.'[11] This is of course what Evans himself did in 'Figures, Doors and Passages', ending as he does with the nostalgic and operatively polemical evocation of a matrix of connected rooms (which he opposed to some notion of a 'frictionless' modernist space) as somehow being able to reestablish social connectivity in architecture.[12]

It is in response to his own early operative and oppositional position that he would, several years later, take such a fierce stand against the operative and oppositional position of what he felt was an otherwise well-informed book (Perez-Gomez's *Architecture and the Crisis of Modern Science*), a stand against, among other things, what he would call the 'debilitating' problem of 'nostalgic idealisation'.[13]

It is interesting now, in terms of potential operative usage – and nostalgic idealisation – that his book on geometry will be published at a time when there is a renewed interest in complex geometries in architecture. He would, I believe, have been very intrigued by some of the recent rigorous work on anexact geometries, but also concerned that this work – and now it would seem his own book – might spawn some less than rigorous appliqué (rather than application) of such ideas. He understood the inevitability, even usefulness, of metaphor in architecture, the metaphoric process that is always enacted as one translates ideas from one realm to another, but thus also the calamity of taking these ideas literally and symbolically, rather than suggestively *yet* rigorously. The former, in this contemporary case, would just repeat the simplifications of the avant-garde of the 1910s and 1920s, who having 'done away with the metaphysics of classicism … cobbled together a new metaphysics, out of the mysteries of modern mathematics and science'.[14] On this matter, his subtle argumentation on the use and abuse of mathematical models (such as topological transformations and fractals) in his review 'Not to be Used for Wrapping Purposes' remains unrefuted.[15]

Even though we will be robbed of the book on which he was about to begin work, the book that would have more directly interwoven the social and the formal (intimations of which one can get from his essay 'The Developed Surface'[16]), we are extraordinarily fortunate that *The Projective Cast* was essentially completed prior to his death. It will rank with Tafuri's *The Sphere and The Labyrinth*, both in

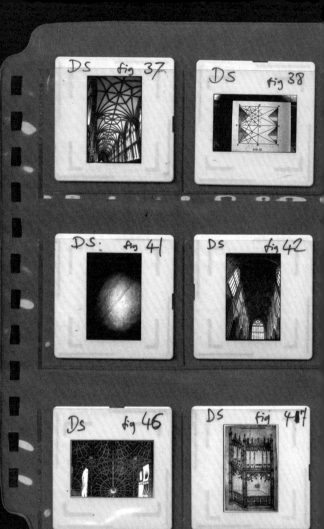

DS fig 37

DS fig 38

DS: fig 41

DS fig 42

DS fig 46

DS fig 47

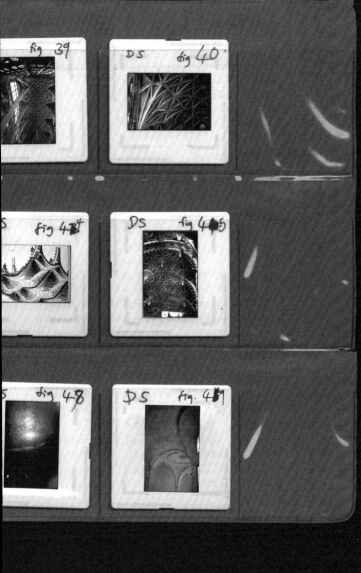

fig 39

DS fig 40

DS fig 44

DS fig 445

DS fig 48

DS fig. 49

terms of content and method, as one of the most important and, probably, tragically, least mined works of architectural history of the twentieth century. What do I mean by this? I mean that it will be enormously appreciated, even referenced, without, however, its profound historiographic methods having much impact on the obdurate discipline of architecture, as numerous architectural myths, the living dead, which both he and Tafuri ruthlessly attempted to eradicate continue to live on without end.

So thus now to the end, his end, the end. The last time he and I were together, at a conference at Rensselaer Polytechnic Institute, we comprised a panel the organisers had entitled 'Technology: *Poiesis* and Instrumentalism', where once again he tried to eradicate yet another easy oppositional notion:

So if we don't take sides then, all we've got is just a divide line and a bunch of stuff over there and a bunch of stuff over there. But we're not even sure that they're overlapping at this point. So the next thing then is to suggest this *poiesis*, which has a wonderful aura, might, if you look at it in a certain light and from the right angles, not be quite what it's cracked up to be. And instrumentalism, which has this terrible burden, might not smell so badly. So I'm going to suggest that *poiesis* stinks a bit and instrumentality is actually kind of okay, it can sort of smell sweet.[17]

As we parted after breakfast the day after the end of the conference, it seemed to me that he had never, in the time I had known him, seemed healthier or calmer or more at ease with his acuity. Never more modest, that is, about his immodesty.

Five days later he would be dead. At forty-eight. Several times while writing this I have had to restrain myself from telephoning him.

He was – as I have been trying to say without reducing the complexity of the man – one of the most penetratingly insightful of our time, and also one of the most genuinely gracious. Two rare qualities – the combination of which is nearly nonexistent. But anyone who ever met Robin Evans felt that way about him. So I will not imagine that I am the only one who now finds themself caught short by his absence, who finds themself at odd moments shaking their head and murmuring or mumbling his name, as if forgetting what he taught, as if on the edge of some nostalgic idealisation, as if our murmurs or mumbles or shouts or stories could bring back what is no longer here.

Originally published in Bernard Tschumi (ed.), *Columbia Documents of Architecture and Theory* 3 (1993), 175–82.

NOTES

1. Robin Evans, 'Le Corbusier and the Sexual Identity of Architecture', *Columbia Documents of Architecture and Theory*, vol. 3 (1993), 173.

2. Evans, personal correspondence.

3. Evans, 'Book Review: Lost Treasure', *9H* 7 (1985), 3.

4. Evans, *The Projective Cast: Architecture and Its Three Geometries* (Cambridge MA: MIT Press, 1994), 43.

5. Evans, *The Projective Cast: Architecture and Its Three Geometries* (Cambridge MA: MIT Press, 1994), 265–67.

6. Evans, *The Fabrication of Virtue: English Prison Architecture, 1750–1840* (Cambridge: Cambridge University Press, 1982), 412.

7. Evans, 'Mies van der Rohe's Paradoxical Symmetries', *AA Files* 19 (Spring 1990), 60.

8. Evans, *The Projective Cast: Architecture and Its Three Geometries* (Cambridge MA: MIT Press, 1994), 178–239.

9. Evans, 'Le Corbusier and the Sexual Identity of Architecture', 149.

10. Evans, personal correspondence.

11. Manfredo Tafuri, 'Operative Criticism', in *Theories and History of Architecture* (New York: Harper & Row, 1980), 141.

12. Evans, 'Figures, Doors and Passages', *Architectural Design* (Autumn 1978), 267–78.

13. Evans, 'Book Review: Lost Treasure', *9H* 7 (1985), 4.

14. Evans, unpublished précis.

15. Evans, 'Not to be Used for Wrapping Purposes', *AA Files* 10 (Autumn 1985), 68–74.

16. Evans, 'The Developed Surface: An Enquiry into the Brief Life of an Eighteenth-Century Drawing Technique', *9H* 9 (1989), 120–47.

17. Evans, transcript, 'Technology: Poiesis and Instrumentalism' panel, History Theory Criticism Design conference, Rensselaer Polytechnic Institute, 1993. I would like to thank David Bell and Reinhold Martin for providing me with this transcript.

KRZYSZTOF WODICZKO: WHY THE FIGURAL

Someone asked, someone will always ask, it is necessary for someone always to ask:

Why the body?

or

Why the anthropomorphism?

or

Why the figural?

Krzysztof Wodiczko's *Alien Staff* suggests many questions, but these questions above are all shortened versions of another, more primary, question. Because if the question is (and it is) how to proceed beyond a naive humanism, a humanism that represses any difficulties or complexities by presenting the body as something whole, complete, total, autonomous, safe and free in spirit – then it must be said that the figure *per se* is not the problem.

The problem is the evocation of the figure as a stand-in, as a surrogate, as a substitute, for dealing with, for addressing, the problem that the figure proposes – the problem, that is, of the social and psychological construction of the human subject.

The figure, in other words, is all too often evoked in order to repress the problem of the figure.

But of course any aesthetic abstraction, such as an abstract spatiality, also attempts to repress the problem of the social construction of the subject. Even though, or perhaps precisely because, the spatial is already thoroughly inscribed by and simultaneously inscribes physical, psychological and social figurations.

But perhaps these categories – the figural and the abstract – are already part of the problem. Hasn't Gerhard Richter, to give a distinct but comparable contemporary example, already demonstrated the uselessness of these as exclusive categories, focusing instead on the operations under which these categories (in his case, in painting) arise and are forever enfolded?

It might be said that Wodiczko has also focused on the operations under which these categories (in the public sphere) arise and are enfolded, focusing on how the social and psychological construction of the subject always circulates around the simultaneous yet complex abstraction of ideologies and their figuration. In other words, Wodiczko has focused on how the figuration of subjects reveals itself as a series of social abstractions and how the abstraction of buildings (or monuments or vehicles or instruments) reveals itself as a series of figural gestures.

So then let me propose a concept, or rather reapply a concept, that seems to me not only capable of redirecting the problem proposed by the figure, but also of revealing linkages throughout the diverse body of Wodiczko's work. The concept I am referring to is Bertolt Brecht's concept of the gestic. For Brecht, all gestures are social gestures, indicating the "attitudes which people adopt towards one another'.[1] Physical gestures, aesthetic gestures, design gestures, are never abstract matters of fact for themselves – they are always *directed* towards another, towards others. But if these gestures are already social, their repetition as conventions requires that they be interrogated as such to reveal this condition.

I have discussed the possibilities of a gestic architecture elsewhere,[2] so let me apply the concept here to figure the design work of Wodiczko.

Or is it his art work?

If one can even separate them into exclusive categories. Because, for one thing, he began his career as an industrial designer. So it might be said that he has never ceased to be a designer whose designs circulate around the subject of human industries, around certain forms, certain gestures, of human labourings.

From the beginning, the whole of Wodiczko's work demonstrates the critical potential of evoking the figural gests through a variety of tactical assaults in order to problematise both the figural and non-figural – relaying, oscillating, resonating in the space between the 'subjective' body and 'objective' architecture.

I say relaying, oscillating, resonating, because to say that the gestic occupies the space between the body and architecture would not be correct. A gestic approach does not occupy any one place, any ideal other place. A gestic approach does not reside: it finds within a figural gesture a social abstraction, and within an abstraction (of the spatial, for example) a figural gesture. A gestic approach problematises both the figural and the spatial, finding the social and psychological relations between bodies and architecture – without residing in either of the two impossible extremes of a 'pure interiority' (subjective figuration) or a 'pure exteriority' (abstract spatiality).

A gestic approach uses the fiction of subjectivity to question the position of the subject, just as it uses the fiction of instrumentality (in Wodiczko's case: of buildings, monuments, vehicles and instruments) to question the position of the object. And equally so the reverse: it uses the fiction of instrumentality to question the position of the subject, just as it uses the fiction of subjectivity to question the position of the object. Wodiczko:

My work attempts to enter and trespass this field of vision: the position of the individual as a subject being constructed, or produced, through the urban space in relation to others and in relation to monuments. I try to disrupt this continuous process of reproducing the individual in space.[3]

A gestic approach considers any situation as an entrance into a field – this field of vision and position, as Wodiczko says – as an opportunity, not as a *problem* that can be *solved* by one particular intervention (including its own). By revealing the construction and reproduction of conventional figuration through the figuration of new associations and disassociations, the gestic construction poses questions that open up the possibility of the re-configuration of the conventional, of the hegemonic.

I have already said that Wodiczko is a designer whose designs circulate around forms of human labourings, that is, around the gestures of certain forms of labouring. In fact, his early works would seem to be the most gestic of all his work, in that they seem to translate directly the physical materialisation of social gestures into form and movement: the pacing and pondering and other 'self-expressive' gestures of 'the artist' (*Personal Instrument*, 1969 and *Vehicle*, 1972), the vocal and physical gestures of 'coffee-shop critiques' (*Vehicle – Coffee Shop 1* and *Vehicle – Coffee Shop 2*, both 1973/1979), the Sisyphean physical labouring of 'the worker' (*Vehicle for the Worker*, 1973/1979), the 'free and multi-directional' movement of people in the square (*Vehicle – Platform*, 1973/1979), the gesticulatory qualities of 'the orator's voice' (*Vehicle – Podium*, 1973/1979). Although the rate of motion varies in response to these gestures, the potential movement of all of Wodiczko's early vehicles – regardless of whether they are propelled by the labourings of the artist, the intellectual, the orator, the masses or the worker – is 'in one direction only'. Thus the social and psychological aspects of gestures are evoked, but this critique of the possibility of any critique, this irony bordering on cynicism, threatens to erode the critical potential of the gest by reducing complexity to futility. But this was Poland in the early 1970s, Poland under the 'liberal autocracy' of party leader Edward Gierek, whose post-Stalinist reforms insufficiently veiled the fact that there was only negligible loosening of state control of art and design. And, of course, this is why Wodiczko calls these projects the *Allegorical Vehicles*.

But something else might be said here of allegory and its relation to the gestic, and about the difference between Wodiczko's early vehicles and his later ones, something not specifically about Poland in the 1970s, but about critical gestures under any 'liberal' forms of government. This something else is the difference between enactment and symbolism. Wodiczko's most recent objects – the *Homeless Vehicle* (1989), the *Poliscar* (1991) and the *Alien Staff* (1992–94) – do not symbolise their condition in some other, separate, place. They enact their (inevitable) symbolisms in the place of their enactment, in real time, as a direct event. The event *is* the event, the event is not taken out of context, taken out of the place of its enactment and deposited in some other abstract and thus safe place – which is a problem, a limit, of most installations, whatever else their value.

This problem is not a problem of Wodiczko's projections, as they do not set themselves up in some separate place, nor do they *arbitrarily* project some other place, some other imagery from some other place, against their site.[4] At their best, Wodiczko's projections attempt to 'draw out' from their site social and psychological gests, even though, or especially because, what they do is so clearly not literally a drawing out but an act of artificial superimposition. But if these works are acts of projection, they are not projections on some 'blank screen' of the site. As Rosalyn Deutsche has pointed out, Wodiczko's projections are 'projections onto projections', projections onto the 'projections of viewing subjects who, through the modes of identification solicited by traditional architecture, "ensure" an imaginary self-coherence by looking at naturalised images of the city'. In order to 'disengage viewers from habitual modes of perceiving and inhabiting the city: of receiving its messages', Deutsche notes, Wodiczko's work 'mobilizes in its audience an awareness that the architecture on which it projects images is not merely a collection of beautiful or functional objects but, rather, speech acts endlessly transmitting messages about the meaning of the city'.[5]

Thus, instead of importing some charged imagery arbitrarily to a given site that has, inevitably, its own complex

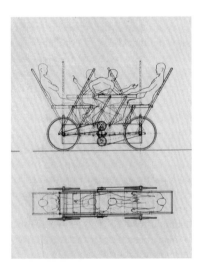

Top: *Vehicle (Pojazd)*, 1972, in motion, Warsaw, Poland
Above: *Vehicle - Coffee Shop*, 1977–79

Top: *Massachusetts Institute of Technology Projection*, 1981, Cambridge, United States
Above: Campanile di Santa Maria Formosa Projection, 1986, Venice, Italy

and charged imagery – which is another variation of this same problem of many installations (and many architectures) – Wodiczko emphasises gestures of the transmitting messages of the site (the building or monument or landscape) and returns them back to the site at the scale of the site. As these projections last from one hour to at most three weeks, Wodiczko can act swiftly and cunningly, addressing a range of topical issues from environmental destruction (*R.C. Harris Filtration Plant*, 1988) to nationalist reawakening (*Huth-Haus*, 1990). And as most of the sites he proposes are cultural institutions, he has developed diverse ways of emphasising the gests of cultural politics circulating through and around these institutions: the grasp of collecting hands in *Museum of Natural History* (1983), the containment of the archive file-cabinet in *Seattle Art Museum* (1984), cultural redevelopment as containment in *Astor Building* (1984), cultural tourism/terrorism – camera aiming – in the Venice Biennale (1986), the degree of governmental reflexivity of a national art institution – one hand holding one of the 'thousand points of light' and the other hand holding a gun in *Hirshhorn Museum* (1988), and the contrast between one nation's increase in cultural freedom and another nation's increase in censorship – the entombed hands inscripted with 'GLASNOST IN USA' in *Whitney Museum of American Art* (1989).

These projections use a range of imagery, from the specific and topical (Pershing missiles) to more general, everyday, bodily actions – turning the gestures of these images into gests.

For example, the projection *Massachusetts Institute of Technology* (1981) is just a pair of hands – shirt sleeves peering from behind jacket cuffs (yes, well), watches (many people wear watches), male (all right, probably), the hands of two 'administrators' of whatever sort (perhaps) – all centred on the inscribed INSTITVTE of the building's cornice. Then (perhaps) this projection might have some relation to the applied handshake of MIT's applied (military-industrial) research. As well as, *of course*, to the *entire* range of other alliances that one finds at an academic institution – because, on the one *hand*, the gest should 'emphasise the entire complex' of relations and, on the other *hand*, one exclusive reading can never be determined with certainty anyway.

But it's just a pair of hands.

Just a friendly gesture.

It's a pleasure: doing business with you.

Wodiczko's projection on the Bern Parliament building (*Bundeshaus*, 1985) is a single eye. But then the eye looks this way (towards the national bank) and that way (towards the canton bank) and now this way (towards the city bank) and now that way (down at a parking lot in front of the Parliament, under which lies the 'national vault containing the Swiss gold') and then this way (towards the 'clear, pure Calvinist sky').

But whichever way the eye is looking, the eye *is* looking, looking around.

But it's just an eye.

Wodiczko:

It was a question of what would be accepted, and then, when accepted, what would make a point. I figured no one would object to the image of the eye, and at the same time they wouldn't have to know that the eye would change the direction of its gaze...[6]

There are several moments in Wodiczko's discussions of his projections where it would seem as if he wholly subscribes to the myth of the *direct* anthropomorphic identification of classical architecture, but like the shift of the Bern eye, he slips away from this trap:

In earlier projections I dealt with the ideas of the body – an official body which is the body as facade – from images in which the media present people like buildings. I dealt with the way the media turns those photographed people into monuments. I also dealt with the way buildings are constructed and their facades are often photographed, by emphasising their symmetrical features to show a human

Top: *Bundeshaus Projection*, 1985, Bern, Switzerland
Above: *Bundeshaus Projection*, 1985, Bern, Switzerland

Top: *The Homeless Projection: A Proposal for Union Square*, 1986,
49th Parallel, Center for Contemporary Art, New York, United States
Above: *Poliscar*, 1991 New York, United States

face and the force of the corporate body. Neo-classicism resembles our bodies because it is a deliberate morphology. The question, then, was always how far I should go with the similarity between the image and the building – between these parallel bodies – and how much I should alter them.[7]

This is one of many examples in Wodiczko's work of what in Greek culture was known as *metis*, cunning intelligence, which proposed that one of the best ways to battle an adversary is 'to turn its own weapons against it'.[8] Notice that his repertoire of images circulates around clichéd ornamental institutional buildings and monuments: bodies, 'heroic' animals (eagles, horses), armament, assorted symbolic equipment and inscriptions. What Wodiczko does is to use the figural myth of neo-classicism against itself.

This is a disfiguring – a disfiguring to show the disfiguration of historical time already at work, a disfiguring in order to allow for a refiguring. This swerved repetition is particularly useful in the projections on monuments, where Wodiczko uses the political compulsion to repeat against itself. He cunningly uses the gestures of yesterday's history, yesterday's battles – usually considered as both inevitable and yet 'dated' with all the strange quaintness of the past (the costumes, the looks, the slogans) – against the gestures of today's history, today's battles, which, with the alienating distance of time, will seem as quaint, as contrived, as constructed as those of the past. And thus the present might be seen as not inevitable, and thus the history of the past might also seem less than inevitable, less a matter of fact, and thus the constant rewriting of history that always occurs after the fact might also allow for a rewriting of the present. While many of the images that Wodiczko uses on his monument projections might be said to be didactic, they might also be said to match cunningly the didactics of the past, bringing these issues up to date, to reflect on both the past and the present (and thus on the future).

Such is the case in the *Homeless Projection* (1986) in which, as Deutsche observes, Wodiczko 'manipulates the statues' own language to challenge the apparent stability of its own signification, transforming the classical gestures, poses and attitudes of the sculpted figures into those used by people begging on the streets. George Washington's left forearm, for example, presses down on a can of Windex and holds a rag, so that the imperial gesture of his right arm is transformed into a signal used by the unemployed to stop cars, clean windshields, and obtain a street donation.'[9] Or take the recent projection on Franco's Civil War victory monument (*Arco de la Victoria*, 1991) three days after the outbreak of the Gulf War: a gun in one hand and a gas nozzle in the other, over which hangs the open question of the gas station: *¿Cuantos?*, which can mean either How much? or How many?

But having shown the gestic at work in the gestures of these hit-and-run projections, it should be said that what is most interesting about Wodiczko's recent objects is that they are able to address social and psychological abstraction and figuration with neither the allegory of the earlier objects, nor the direct evocation of symbolic figures of the projections. This is particularly true of the *Homeless Vehicle*, another example of cunning disfiguration and refiguration, in this case, of the urban mobilisations of the homeless supermarket cart. This object, as I said earlier, does not symbolise its condition, it enacts it. It does not symbolise life in some other (separate) place. In use or as exhibit it already suggests a real intervention in urban life. The object itself now gestures – extends and contracts, transforming and projecting its varied figurations into local and urban space. The object *literally (and figuratively)* refigures the figuration of the supermarket cart in relation to the figuration of labourings, gestures, inhabitation – walking, sleeping, sitting, defecating, cooking, washing, storing, monetary labouring – but at the same time, it reveals the social gests of public and private gestures: the gestures that are proper if someone has some property, if that someone has an inside that that someone owns or rents. The *Homeless Vehicle* is an inside that is not inside, an inhabitation that is outside (physically, psychologically and socially) but also somehow an outside that is not totally outside.

It is property, after all.

The *Homeless Vehicle* thus problematises not only inside and outside, but also public and private, use and symbol, subject and object, machine and architecture, local place and urban network, self and community, body and space, figuration and abstraction.

It resides in neither side, but reveals the one in the other. It relays, oscillates, resonates.

The *Poliscar* continues this investigation of the operations under which these categories arise and are forever enfolded by giving another transforming form to the gestures of mobile inhabitation. But this time the emphasis is on the gestures of communication and community – recording, transmitting, planning, distributing information or aid – as it functions as 'an urban communications network for the homeless… [establishing] links between various encampments of the homeless, forming new social ties and leading to greater intercommunity and urban organisation…' [10] The form of the *Poliscar* seems less articulated than that of the *Homeless Vehicle*, but then again it is not mimicking the structural instrumentalism of a supermarket cart but the (ludicrous) attempted stealth of, say, a military or a surveillance vehicle. Wodiczko:

… it [the *Poliscar*] is simply a response to the image of the contemporary city, which the uniformed police and the real-estate armies have made a militarised zone. And the image of the city being overtaken by a force of communication vehicles everywhere, an impossible insurrection, accounts for the ridiculous aspect of its appearance. [11]

The *Poliscar* subsequently refigures this figuration of the stealth vehicle in relation to the figuration of the gestures of walking, driving and sleeping. This problematisation of subject and object is furthered by the juxtaposition of the gestures of the bodies seen on the screen and heard on the loudspeaker of the conical 'head' of the vehicle, projecting now in 'real time', with the gestures of the vehicle operators, also, one might say, projecting in 'real time'.

This disfiguring and refiguring of subjects and objects brings us to the *Alien Staff*, which continues the investigations of the *Poliscar* to question the ideological abstraction and social figuration of identity and community, especially as these issues relate to the situation of the immigrant. The immigrant must always allow for the possibility that circumstances will require yet another migration, and thus the previous mobilities of the *Homeless Vehicle* and the *Poliscar* are further developed in this project to the point of portability. But, at the same time, the object has to have a presence – the object of the object is to set, to create, 'a scene', a situation where immigrants can bring their so-called private stories to the so-called public sphere, which *Alien Staff* does by cunningly disfiguring and refiguring the 'attribute-cliché of a wanderer': 'The owner of the staff appears to be one with a history of wanderers, the tradition itself a cliché, but it is a cliché used here strategically … The strangely familiar shape of the staff allures the "non-stranger" to come closer to the operator/storyteller.'[12] And further, the object of the object is to be a 'consumer-quality' object (as one of the participants in the *Homeless Vehicle* project requested of Wodiczko), so as to legitimatise the presence of the immigrant operators, so that the public-sphere police do not come along and ask them to be less public.

With a video monitor, loudspeaker and storage space, this is certainly a consumer-quality walking stick. On the monitor appears, and from the speaker emerges, the gestures and voice of the same operator that holds this staff and speaks and gestures to, say, the smaller objects contained in its mid-section. Objects like: 'rejected visa applications, immigration and legal documents, apartment keys, old photographs and the various identity cards acquired by the owner'. But if these objects and stories and gestures would seem to, or are supposed to, add up to the whole of a single identity, they do not. The disparities in the multiple representations reveal the abstractions of the figural gestures, enacting a gestic doubling or trebling that provides an alienation effect between the character and actor

Top: *Homeless Vehicle*, 1988-89, New York, United States
Above: *Homeless Vehicle*, 1988-89, New York, United States

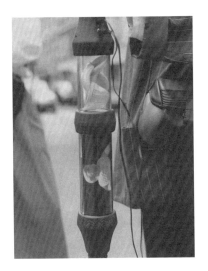

Top: *Alien Staff (Xenobacul)*, 1992 Operator: Patricia Pirreda, Paris, France
Above: *Alien Staff (Xenobacul)*, 1992 Operator: Patricia Pirreda, Paris, France

of the operator – in order to avoid the dismissive reduction of these stories to a single, humanistic, 'hardluck' story:

Usually when we look at the image of a speaker on our TV screens at home, we don't see the 'actual' person speaking behind the image. This confrontation, facilitated by the operator and his or her staff, is therefore unexpected; the story told by the staff's operator is interrupted and even contradicted by the pre-recorded image which tells other stories and vice versa. The image on the screen may show the operator recounting a tragic or comic moment concerning his or her alien status; however, the operator who holds the staff, thus relieved from the burden of telling this story, presents another face. Standing next to his or her own history, the operator asks the viewer, who now appears to be the stranger, to tell their own story. At this point a new space is created by the operator/object in relation to the spectator. The distinction between stranger and non-stranger is problematised here – maybe around this staff everyone becomes a different kind of stranger.[13]

Thus, if we were to be in Paris, or on page 157, we might come across Patricia Pirreda, one of the six *Alien Staff* operators so far, talking about her broken espresso cup, the pieces of which are visible in the container, her personal cup from the family set, while on the monitor we see her attempting to refigure these broken pieces, finding already in this disfigured object a network of resonate, open, inconclusive, enfolded, parallel meanings, around which she labours in order to have some control over the design of her own figuration, through her own labours, her own capabilities, not those of the state or her husband or child, even if, as she says, 'it is easy from those broken pieces to make a cup like that, but it is not easy from those broken pieces to make more than that', even if 'things … already have a form', and even if only, or especially, 'in order to make something else'.

There is always something else to be made, even if only from those things that already have a form, those clichéd social and psychological forms and gestures. As Wodiczko develops new versions of the *Alien Staff*, adding microphones and speakers, transforming the staff into some kind of techno-clothes, expanding it into an 'alien network', or reducing it (in his latest version) to a gaglike apparatus with video lips, these versions will emerge, as in all his previous work, through an integration of the history of the gesture of forms and form of gestures: the clichéd gestures of the past and present, and the already clichéd gestures of the cyber-Buck Rogers-future (headsets, power gloves, prosthetic appendages), the already past of sci-fi. Because, of course, all gestures are already clichéd, which is why they require the framing distance of the gest to be perceived and thus critiqued.

But Wodiczko's work functions not only as critique but also as proposition, not a universal proposition, but a local proposition, a proposition of questioning, a proposition for change. It functions as a series of open questions, not final solutions, as it thematises both the desire for and the impossibility of universal solutions, both the desire for and the impossibility of definitive instrumentality.

In other words, if these works relay, oscillate and resonate, they do so to bring forth questions, but also to allow no easy or rushed answers.

This is Wodiczko's intervening in the figuration of what is present. So that someone might ask a question. So that questions might be asked. So that it might be possible to consider a refiguring of the present, the present now past, and the present to come.

Originally published in *Assemblage* 23 (1994), 18–27.

TECTONIC ACTS OF DESIRE AND DOUBT

NOTES

Thanks to Steve Kolliopoulos for his assistance in the interview transcriptions that accompanied the original publication. All photographs copyright of Krzysztof Wodiczko (courtesy of Galerie Lelong, New York).

1. Bertolt Brecht, 'A Short Organum for the Theatre', in *Brecht on Theatre*, ed. John Willett (New York: Hill and Wang, 1964), 198. See also John Willett, *The Theatre of Bertolt Brecht* (London: Eyre Methuen, 1977), 173. For other commentary on Brecht's concept of the gest, see Walter Benjamin, *Understanding Brecht* (London: Verso, 1983), 1–25; Roland Barthes, 'Diderot, Brecht, Eisenstein' in *Image–Music–Text* (New York: Hill and Wang, 1977), 69–78; and Gilles Deleuze, *Cinema 2: The Time-Image* (Minneapolis: University of Minnesota Press, 1989), 189–203, 315.

2. Mark Rakatansky, 'The Gestic Body of Architecture', *Journal of Philosophy and the Visual Arts*, 1993, 70–79, and in this volume 'Identity and the Discourse of Politics in Contemporary Architecture'.

3. *Krzysztof Wodiczko: Instruments, Projeccions, Vehicles* (Barcelona: Fundació Antoni Tàpies, 1992), 64.

4. The sole exception being *New York City Tableaux: Tompkins Square* (1989). As for his other gallery projections in the same series: *The Homeless Projection* (1986) is a proposal more than an installation, while *The Real Estate Projection* (1987) focuses on its site by examining the intimate connection between cultural development and gentrification.

5. Rosalyn Deutsche, 'Architecture of the Evicted', *Strategies* 3 (1990), 167.

6. 'A Conversation with Krzysztof Wodiczko', *October* 38 (1986), 50–51.

7. *Krzysztof Wodiczko: Instruments, Projeccions, Vehicles*, 51.

8. Marcel Detienne and Jean-Pierre Vernant, *Cunning Intelligence in Greek Culture and Society* (Chicago: University of Chicago Press, 1991), 43. Ann Bergren first brought this concept to the attention of the architectural audience. Among her many writings, see, for example, 'Architecture Gender Philosophy' in *Strategies in Architectural Thinking*, ed. Whiteman, Kipnis and Burdett (Cambridge MA: MIT Press, 1992), 8–47, and her 'Educating Architecture as a "Total Woman": *Programmata* for an Architecture of *Metis*', in The Harvard *Architectural Review* 8 (New York: Rizzoli, 1992), 136–59.

9. Rosalyn Deutsche, 'Krzysztof Wodiczko's *Homeless Projection* and the Site of Urban "Revitalization"', *October* 38 (1986), 93.

10. *Krzysztof Wodiczko: Instruments, Projeccions, Vehicles*, 286.

11. Ibid., 63.

12. 'Dissonant Identities: A Conversation between Krzysztof Wodiczko and Julie Carson', *Thresholds* 7 (1993), 2.

13. Ibid.

MOTIVATIONS OF ANIMATION

Take Christopher Walken, for example. Two examples:

'He has no time for The Method. He just turns up and does it. [Walken:] "It boils down to: Can you act? Who cares what you *think*?"'[1]

And:

'He [Walken] pulls out his script and every word had a note on it about what he wanted to do.'[2]

What this is an example of is something other than contradiction.

There is no contradiction between saying 'Who cares what you think' and having thought written all over your script. Notice Walken didn't say: 'Who cares *if* you think?' He said: 'Who cares *what* you think?' Who cares what your creative preparation is if it doesn't make it into your performance? Who cares what your diagram is or what my diagram is if it doesn't make it into your act or my act, into the act of your design or of my design, in a way that is legible, perceptible, perceivable?

It makes no *difference* whether you prepare for your role through Method Acting or any other form of diagrammatic preparation (such as notes on a script) unless it results in a performance that gives the appearance of being (complexly) motivated, of being (complexly) animated, of being more than just a diagrammatic sum of individual lines of script. More: because you find the differences, the differentials, of motive and animacy and gesture within (and between) those diagrammatic lines in order to translate, to bring forth, those differences that might make a difference in your performance.

'A difference that makes a difference': that was Gregory Bateson's definition of 'information'.[3] I heard that expression often in the second year of my undergraduate

education, attending what was to be the last year of
Bateson's teaching. That expression and, along with many
other expressions, this one: *the map is not the territory*, echo-
ing and elaborating, as he often did, Alfred Korzybski's
famous dictum.

Meaning: the fact that I cannot peel the words *Fresh
Tagliatelle with Wild Mushrooms and Mint* off the surface of
this menu (at this restaurant in the East Village I am sitting
in right now, jotting down these lines while waiting for the
cheque to arrive) and eat those lines of ink for my dinner.
'The fact', in other words, in Bateson's words, 'that a mes-
sage, of whatever kind, does not consist of those objects
that it denotes' – for which Bateson cites the example: 'The
word "cat" cannot scratch us'.[4]

Ditto the diagram, as the dictionary defines: 'A
graphic design that explains rather than represents: a drawing that shows arrangement and relations (as of parts to
a whole, relative values, origins and development, chrono-
logical fluctuations, distribution).'

I started out this essay wanting to question certain
kinds of diagrammatics, but let's just admit it: isn't every
building a built diagram (from some plan, professionally
inscribed or not)?[5] Isn't every kind of music, theatre and film
a performed diagram (from some score or some script, tran-
scribed or not)? Isn't every essay, every novel, every poem
a written diagram (from some outline, jotted down or not)?

Everything is a transcription, everything is a translation, every artefact, every object begins as notional form as
it makes its way to its representation as material form. How
it might make its way there is what I want to begin to
address here.

Here was my beginning, my first sentence in the very
first draft of this essay: 'The question is – is always – how
to begin: begin your design: begin the design of your architecture or the design of your essay about architecture.'
You see, I started mixing things up, right from the very
beginning, mixing up the object and some representation
of the object, but you see the dictionary says the word
diagram comes from the Greek *diagramma*, from the Greek

diagraphein (*dia-* [through] + *graphein* [to write]), meaning *to mark out by lines*, so the marking and the writing of lines, the object and its representation, are already mixed up, at least in the dictionary, even before I arrive there on the page, or on screen, to make matters worse.

Which is what I did in that first draft of this essay: it's not *how* you begin – the how comes later – but *with what*? With what do you begin: what diagram, what outline, what idea, what motive, what do you have in your mind (or up your sleeve). Then – here's the *how* – how does that diagram, that outline, that idea, that motive give the appearance of working its way through your beginnings and through to your ends and so into the objects of your design?

Any historical or recent urge in architecture to equate, to collapse this difference between the what and the how, this difference between idea and representation, between the map and the territory, to assert the diagrammatic map *as* the territory of architecture, will reveal, as Bateson noted, the naive desire to 'get back to the absolute innocence of communication by means of pure mood-signs' – for which Bateson gives the example of 'the flag which men will die to save'.[6]

But: there are no pure signs of *any* sort, there is no absolute innocence in *any* communication, every diagram is a representational form of some idea and some motivation toward that idea: nothing is unmediated, the map is *not* the territory.

But: it would be foolish and pointless and futile to insist on the absolute and unequivocal separation of the map from the territory, for at least four reasons:

First, there are certainly relations, between the map and the territory, which, as Bateson noted, are relations of difference:

'What is it in the territory that gets onto the map?' We know the territory does not get onto the map. This is the central point about which we here are all agreed. Now, if the territory were uniform, nothing would get onto the map except the boundaries, which are points at which it ceases to be uniform against some larger matrix. What

gets onto the map, in fact, is *difference*, be it a difference in altitude, a difference in vegetation, a difference in population structure, difference in surface, or whatever. Differences are the things that get onto a map.[7]

Second, in aesthetic operations, it is *difference* that must be used to bring what is in the map back into the territory, because in aesthetic operations, to turn that dictionary definition around, a diagram is a representation in reverse. Aesthetic diagrams, in other words, are just as often made after-the-fact as prior-to-the-fact of the object. *Either* way, in the end, the object is always a representation, not of itself but of the diagrams, the outlines, the motives, the ideas – the ideas of certain 'arrangements and relations', as said dictionary definition said, which the object then represents.

Third, the failure of old identities (or the manifest diagrams of those identities) will not eradicate the recurring desire for new 'stable' and 'true' identities – and thus, in architecture, for new 'stable' and 'true' diagrams.

I have been trying to say that no one is exempt from this condition of the translation between the diagram and the object, *whatever* your position on the use of diagrams, but that in this play that is your work it all depends on the quality of your translation, the quality of your performance.

To wit: Christopher Walken.

'The inner life of the characters is irrelevant … *except in so far as* it is expressed in their outward attitudes and actions.'[8]

That's a quote from drama theorist Martin Esslin, not from Christopher Walken, but what he is saying is the same as what Walken said. And further, this description of a Brechtian theory and practice of performance could stand for the performance of architecture as well, for architectural elements are always acting as characters within the architectural drama. This makes the resourcefulness, responsiveness and expressiveness of the characters within both your map and your territory all the more important.

The map that is the name of the dish *Fresh Tagliatelle with Wild Mushrooms and Mint* (those inky lines, those graphic designs, those words on a page of a menu or on a page of a disciplinary journal or book), or that 'inner' map that is the recipe for this dish, is of no interest to me (whether I am eating it at this restaurant or cooking it myself at home) *except in so far as* the ingredients and the operations performed on those ingredients accrue to a *greater* effect in the 'outward' territory that is the dish, so as not to remain merely a diagram of a dish, so as not to remain merely a diagrammatic sum of those individual ingredient parts, which unfortunately remains the sum of my experience with *this* particular tagliatelle.

Even though the *New York Times* recommended it just the other day!

Thus: *the proof of the pudding is in the eating* – an expression that the actors of the Berliner Ensemble heard often from Bertolt Brecht, with respect to the act of developing a play from its initial conception through the diagrammatics of its script to its performance – attending as they were what was to be the last year of Brecht's directing.

And finally, the fourth and perhaps most important reason why it would be foolish and pointless and futile to insist on the absolute and unequivocal separation of the map from the territory is this: if, as Bateson noted, in that psychical condition designated as primary process 'map and territory are equated' (because the primary process operates under the pleasure principle to speed gratification by collapsing difference), and if, in that condition designated as secondary process map and territory 'can be discriminated' (because the secondary process operates under the reality principle to manage gratification by asserting difference), then in the performance that is the *act* of play (animal play, child's play, grown-up play) map and territory are 'both equated *and* discriminated'.[9]

In Jean-Luc Godard's film *King Lear*, for example, to the partially ironic imperative 'Tell me Professor!', the partially ironic response is 'Show … Show … Show, not Tell!' It is precisely both the showing *and* the telling that give Godard's work its 'virtue and power' (to cite one of the film's inter-titles), not by collapsing showing and telling together, but by treating showing and telling as two equal (representations of) realities through which relations are to be developed. There are few finer-grained and more deeply rendered moments of realism in cinema than the scenes of Burgess Meredith as father Lear and Molly Ringwald as daughter Cordelia, moments of fine-grained and deeply rendered *showing*, mimetic representation, which then are tactically put in relation with every manner of both coarse-grained showing (absurd scenes, ridiculous puns) *and* fine-grained and course-grained *telling* (inter-titles, complex manipulations of soundtrack and image). Here is an object that is constructed through the refusal to believe *either* that map and territory can be equated *or* that map and territory can remain discriminated, that refuses to believe in these *false* distinctions between realism and abstraction, between criticism and lyricism, between *mise-en-scène* and montage, and yes, between tragedy and comedy:

This is where the trouble begins. Is the cinema catalogued as a whole or as a part? If you make a Western, no psychology; if you make a love-story, no chases or flights; if you make a light comedy, no adventures; and if you have adventures, no character analysis.

Woe onto me, since I have just made *La Femme Mariée***, a film where subjects are seen as objects, where pursuits by taxi alternate with ethnological interviews, where the spectacle of life finally mingles with its analysis: a film, in short, where cinema plays happily, delighted to be only what it is.**[10]

Samuel Beckett, Marguerite Duras, Max Frisch, Jamaica Kincaid, Gordon Lish, Grace Paley, Dennis Potter, Gerhard Richter, Krzysztof Wodiczko: just a few examples of those who also produce works that play happily between the map and the territory.

I guess that helps explain why most people are not all that interested in architecture – let's just admit it – compared to novels or movies or just about *any* other art form.

Because you hardly need me to draw your attention

to the fact that most people do not pay much attention to architecture.

Because most architecture is not all that complexly rendered, you might say, in relation to what counts as complex (or even noticeable) rendering for most people.

Too diagrammatic, you might say.

Which brings me to what the editors emailed me to get me to write about, what they had heard I might be interested to write about, which is animation and the animated diagram.

Cartoons, for example. An interest of mine. And pleasure. Like wild mushrooms.

So why is it then, that *still*, in a design review, whenever I want to suggest that a building might need to be worked more, developed more, in relation to its concept, why is it that I still say: 'It's a diagram of a building' or 'It's a cartoon of a building'?

I am tired of discriminating myself from myself.

So let me now try to write it out as it seems to me *right now*: it's not that these buildings are cartoons that is the problem, it's that they're not engaging cartoons, not (complexly) animated enough (in form *and* in content).

It's not that all buildings begin as bubble diagrams that is the problem, it's that so many end there – whatever their styles and however embellished their details. It's the beginning-and-the-end problem, it's the means-and-the-end problem, it's the translation problem. It's a question of whether the diagram is a means of exploring an idea or an end *in and of* itself. Fortunately there are a number of individuals struggling in architecture, art, film, graphics, writing, attempting to work on and with these problems today.

What in the process of design would resist such a simplistic translation, what differences and differentials are in the ingredients of architecture (of site, of programme, of tectonics) and in the operations performed on those ingredients, such that more complex interweavings of object *and* diagram, of territory *and* map, of discriminating *and* equating, of the spectacle of life *and* its analysis, might be possible?

This is where Chuck Jones, renowned animation director, can come in, can make an entrance of the stagings on these pages, along with his books *Chuck Amuck* (1989) and *Chuck Reducks* (1996), from which I will attempt to draw out a number of points, seven for now, more on some other occasion, for architectural consideration:

1   *'Animation means to invoke life, not to imitate it.'* [11]

Chuck Jones summarises his position with the preceding statement in *Chuck Reducks*, but in his earlier *Chuck Amuck* he goes to the dictionary first before concluding with the *same* point, and *his* dictionary says: 'animate: [*Webster's*] From Latin, *animatus* – to invoke life, to make alive, to give life to, bring to life, to stimulate to action or creative effort'.[12]

Like Jones, I would say that the only one of these definitions relevant to the *process* of architectural design is 'to invoke life', not to imitate it. It's not possible to make architecture alive. It's not possible to give life to. Or bring to life. Or even to stimulate to action. It's only possible to *invoke* the possibility of action or effort, the possibility of the performance of action or effort. A simulation, in other words, that *might*, in turn, cause a stimulation of the user.

A building cannot move as a body moves, a building is not a body, needless to say, but, needless to say, given how dull, how *un*animated, most buildings are, whatever considerations it takes to get a building animated – or at the other extreme, to obdurately, albeit *futilely*, *attempt* to resist any and all animation – could be worth the consideration.

And, anyway, isn't the art of animation animating what isn't?

Likewise, the art of art?

After all, a painting is just pigment on canvas, an essay just ink on a page.

Here's a story Chuck Jones, in the 1991 documentary *Chuck Amuck: The Movie*, tells: a little boy's father introduces him to the little boy with the following introduction: 'This is the man who draws Bugs Bunny.' The little boy, as Chuck Jones tells it, was furious: 'He looked up, threw his lower lip out and said "He does not *draw* Bugs Bunny! He draws pictures *of* Bugs Bunny!"' Chuck Jones, in the film, comments approvingly: 'And that to me is the whole *difference*. That's the whole point.'

2   *'Animation is not the art of drawings that move,
         but the art of movements that are drawn.'* [13]

In the book *Chuck Amuck,* Jones follows his dictionary definition of animation with the preceding quote from Norman McLaren, another renowned animation director. Animation is not movement, but a series of representations of movement: this is as true for the older forms of celluloid animation as for the newer, computerised, *vector-based* forms of animation.

Not movement but the invocation of movement, not gesture but the invocation of gesture, not motivation but the invocation of motivation. *Looney Tunes, Merrie Melodies*: it's all just lines, after all, lines drawn on a 'cel', as animationists say, on celluloid, five or six thousand cels for a six-minute animated cartoon. There are no characters, there is no performance, only the invocation of characters, the invocation of a performance.

Lines drawn on a cel, at least that was the old technology. Not entirely unlike this institutional office I am writing this in now at *this* moment, one of a set of cells all in a row, lines drawn using whatever technology was new or old at *that* moment, a plan 'marked out by lines', *diagramma, diagraphein*, a bubble-diagram of a building with the bubble-lines turned into wall-lines, a built diagram showing 'arrangements and relations'. Except Chuck Jones's cels and Norman McLaren's cels do not just repeat, they iterate, they iterate to provide animation and movement in the characters as the characters respond to difference from cel to cel, whereas these office cells are drawn all the same, so the story (of this space, this social space) is not animated.

No iteration, no animation – in the territory, that is, regardless of how much (or even whether any) iteration is visible in those diagrams that make up the architectural map.

But the animation of life happens *in* the office space, with the *people*, not with the architecture, *right*?

So I've heard – from many surprisingly distinct quarters of this discipline. Well, it makes a good excuse anyway. How convenient it would be if someone else were responsible for the animation of the spaces we are supposed to be designing, and not us.

3   *'Character* always *comes first, before the physical representation.'* [14]

'What we did at Warner Bros is often called "character animation", but if one considers Webster, that is redundant.' [15]

In other words: 'We must have a clear idea of what our character is doing before we start to draw him.' [16] That sentence follows the Norman McLaren quote when Jones evokes it again in *Chuck Reducks*. It is Chuck Jones's explication of what those movements that are being drawn are being drawn *as* and *for*, in order to clarify what and how these characters are being drawn *towards* and *away from* in their responsiveness: so not just abstract movements, but movements of characters, movements as characterisations: 'For instance, when Daffy Duck plays Robin Hood, we must be thoroughly familiar not only with Daffy himself but with how he would approach the role of Robin Hood. If Bugs Bunny played Robin Hood, it would be with a different manner, attitude, and body movement.' [17]

In order to animate you have to have some 'character' in mind first, you have to have some 'arrangements and relations' within and between characters in your mind first. This is what Chuck Jones calls: *attitude*. That's the map, that's the diagram.

You can see right here in this parade of some of Chuck Jones's characters, Elmer Fudd and Bugs Bunny and Daffy Duck and Pepé Le Pew and Porky Pig, that these 'arrangements and relations' are conveyed as internal differentials, let us call them vectors, that Chuck Jones has diagrammed for us here in his parade. And you can see in this severely reduced diagram – that's redundant: isn't every diagram severely reduced? – that all of these characters, as a minimum requirement, have vectors that are going in two different directions. In other words, with two (or more) vectors, characters already have within them internal conflicts, internal differentiations, internal differentials, and that is the nature of their conflictual and differentiated and differential character, which is always in response to external conflicts, external differentiations, external differentials.

The common definition of a vector force is that it involves magnitude *and* direction, as opposed to a scalar force, which involves only magnitude. But in fact, there is a third vectoral *dimension*, so to speak, to add to magnitude and direction, and that is the dimension of *sense*: 'The word "direction" used here is sometimes replaced by "direction and sense" to denote the fact that a vector is an orientated line segment which points in a particular sense.'[18] In that mappy space of pure mathematics, two dimensions are all that is necessary, but when a vector is used to analyse properties of this territorial and third-dimensional space that is our impure materialised world, it 'requires', as this dictionary says in the first of the three definitions it enumerates under 'vector': '… for its complete specification, a magnitude, direction and sense'.

A vector is thus not just a physical force: it is said to be 'directed', to be 'oriented', to have some 'sense'. This sense, this orientation, is its motive force. A vector is motivated, like a gesture is motivated (as all knowing actors know), as a relational complex of motivation, a dialogical motivation, not as a reflection or illustration of a single motive. A deeply rendered performance is precisely that which cannot be rendered as an enactment of a single, uniform, homogeneous, monovalent, pure motive – given that human beings are incapable of feeling only one emotional vector at any given time. The simultaneity and complexity of conflictual emotions is precisely what a deeply rendered performance enacts at every micro-level of gesture and speech, revealing not a fixed character, but a character

Chuck Jones, *Chuck Amuck: The Life and Times of an Animated Cartoonist*
(New York: Farrar, Straus and Giroux, 1989)

FOGHORN   HENERY   TWEETY   SYLVESTER

in the process of acquiring form and sense. An actor or a director wanting to know the one true and definitive motivation of a character misses the point, as does the stereotypical Method Acting query 'what's my motivation?', as this is usually just long-hand for 'what's my motive?' – as if a single experience, a single motive, a single force, could define and explain the complexity of behavioural motivation and performance.

Motivation is always plural, as Gerhard Richter has said: 'I have no motive, only motivation',[19] which is another way of saying, as Godard has: 'We need to show that there is no model; there's only modelling'.[20] Ditto: there is no map, there's only mapping. Ditto: there is no territory, there's only territorialising.

Or as Deleuze and Guattari might have said it: there is no territory, there's only deterritorialising and, in turn, reterritorialising – de-coding the territory as certain mappings (*operating on certain vectors*), and then over-coding and re-inscribing these mappings back into the territory.[21]

That a vector is not just force, but has some 'sense' that may be operated on should not be too surprising, considering that 'vector', as this dictionary says, comes from the Latin *vectus*, meaning 'carrier', meaning 'to convey' ('to impart of, communicate either directly by clear statement or indirectly by suggestion, implication, gesture, attitude, behaviour or appearance').

Which leads us to the second of these three dictionary definitions for vector: 'an agent capable of transmitting a pathogen from one organism to another'. You could say that a vector thus acts both as a force and as a conduit, but it would be more accurate to say that if a vector acts as a force of sense, it is because it is a conduit of sense. The vectorial force of architecture is the agency which makes it capable of transmitting (and infecting) social and cultural sense from organism to organism – exemplifying the capillary action of Michel Foucault's 'micro-technologies of power': the 'circulation of effects of power through progressively finer channels, gaining access to individuals themselves, to their bodies, their gestures and all their daily actions'.[22]

One trick for architecture to learn to play might be this: how to acknowledge and make legible, *in the object*, the inevitable cultural and ideological transmission of architecture while showing its potential to reconfigure that transmission – simultaneously showing that every act of transmission, like every act of character, is always a form of configuration, and that every act of configuration (or reconfiguration) is a form of transmission. This is the sort of simultaneity of transmission and reconfiguration that Angelika Hurwicz, one of those Berliner Ensemble actors who was in attendance during those last years of Brecht's directing, spoke of when she spoke of Brecht's characterisations: 'He demonstrates persons as products of the conditions in which they live, and capable of change through the circumstances which they experience.'[23]

This simultaneity is what (a) character is, whether that form of character is revealed as a person or as an architectural element.

4   *'If you start with character, you probably will end up with good drawings. If you start out with drawings, you will almost certainly end up with limited characters, caught in the matrix of your limited drawings… For identity, you do not draw differently, you think differently.'*[24]

Here are just a few of the characters that will be coming soon or sooner to a building near you: Door, Wall, Window, Ceiling, Floor, Cabinet, Signage.

Or pick another category of character, if you prefer: Lobby, Meeting Room, Working Room, Eating Room, Sleeping Room – Rooms and Rooms and Rooms and Rooms.

There are many characters in any given project, and each character contains many characters or, rather, many (diverse and conflictual) characterisations. In other words, there is no (fixed) character, there's only characterising. Only character – only identity – in process, and to animate their identity, it is not just a matter of drawing them differently, as Jones says, but of thinking them differently.

5   *'Our characters are based on individual personalities,*
       their anatomy abstracted only in the most general way
       from their prototypes – rabbits, ducks, cats, canaries,
       etc… What they looked like grew in each case from our
       discovery of who they were. Then and only then could
       their movements and voices uniquely demonstrate each
       of these personalities.'[25]

Jones's point is particularly relevant to architecture here.
Say, for example, you were to consider using any of the
architectural characters mentioned in the previous section,
then one way you might consider using them would be,
first, to consider their personalities through their anatomy
– their social, psychological and physical anatomy – abstracted, say, *only in the most general way* from their conventional or normative 'types' – because anyway that is more
or less what we all do sooner or later in the design process.
And then, second, what you design these characters to look
like – for that particular project – *could* grow and develop
in each case from your discovery of who they were and
could become. The important point is that the architectural
character is not just predetermined and then repeated, but
rather that the character is discovered through the responsive iteration of its multiple characteristics throughout
the project.

I say abstracted only in the most general way, because,
even though Chuck Jones says he animates 'realistically' …
'compared to the … "abstractions" of some of the so-called
avant-garde animators', he goes on to demonstrate how
dissimilar Daffy is from a normal duck, how Bugs's movements and gestures bear surprisingly little resemblance to
a conventional rabbit, how the only thing Porky shares with
a pig is its tail.

And yet: Daffy is (and remains) a duck, Bugs is (and
remains) a bunny, Porky is (and remains) a pig. That
remaining is necessary for the exploration of character.

'With Bugs, Daffy, etc., we invented our own anatomical structures', Jones says in *Chuck Amuck* – but this is of
course not true: what Jones did was to *adopt* and *adapt*

comparative zoological anatomy, but he finishes his sentence with a statement that *is* quite true – 'and were faithful to them'.[26]

Faithfulness: 'We are dealing in shapes, shapes with individual characteristics, variations on a common anatomical structure … individual personalities, so that in the same circumstance they react in different ways… If you want believability in your characters, you must have visual consistency. In animation, each character must move according to its own anatomical limitations: Daffy Duck must move with Daffy Duck's anatomy, Donald Duck with Donald Duck's structure.'[27]

Believability: 'One principle he learned is that believability is more important than realism.'[28] That might be some film director or film critic speaking of Christopher Walken, but actually it is the literary scholar Hugh Kenner speaking of Chuck Jones. Jones himself says: 'We must all start with the believable. This is the essence of our craft. All drama, all comedy, all artistry stems from the believable, which gives us as solid a rock as anyone could ask from which to seek humor: variations on the believable – that is the essence of all humor.'[29]

Believability, Visual Consistency, Faithfulness to Anatomy: these principles do not constitute a reduction of variation but, on the contrary, allow for that proliferation of variation – variations on *and* in the believable – that *is* the character.

If a proliferation of variation is what a character is, that is because, as Mikhail Bakhtin has said: 'A man never coincides with himself. One cannot apply to him the formula of identity A=A.'[30] Which accounts for the variation within character, as Max Frisch has said: 'The individual is a sum of various possibilities, not an unlimited sum, but one which goes beyond his [specific] biography. Only the variations reveal the common centre.'[31]

There is no Daffy, no Donald, no Lear, no Cordelia, no Christopher Walken, no you, no me. There is no definitive common centre, only some set of common intersections, no true and stable self, no true identity or map or

It has been said that our characters are realistic . . . Well . . .

RABBIT -

AND BUGS

THIS IS NO MORE A NATURAL
POSITION FOR BUGS THAN IT
WOULD BE FOR A HUMAN BEING
— BUT, I'M TRYING TO BE FAIR

DUCK AND DAFFY DUCK

— THERE IS A CERTAIN SIMILARITY
IN FOOT STRUCTURE - AND NEITHER
OF THEM WEARS GLOVES

CAT AND SYLVESTER

THE EARS DO LOOK SOMETHING ALIKE
EVEN THOUGH THERE IS A PAINFUL
DISCREPANCY IN THE NOSES

PIG

PORKY PIG.
— THE TAIL IS A DIRECT STEAL.

Chuck Jones, *Chuck Amuck: The Life and Times of an Animated Cartoonist*
(New York: Farrar, Straus and Giroux, 1989)

COYOTE

WILE E. COYOTE

VITAL DIFFERENCE: WILE E'S EYES ARE $1000 SHUT.

ROADRUNNER
(GEOCOCCYX CALIFORNIANUS) (ACCELERATII SUPERSONICUS)

TASMANIAN DEVIL   TASMANIAN DEVIL

...THEY ARE BOTH FROM TASMANIA

WELL, THEY BOTH HAVE
WINGS AND EYES AND......

diagram to be revealed, there are only the variations – the way you see that character on the screen or in a book, or, say, you or me in life, respond in various ways to various situations – that *retroactively* suggests some character, some you, some me, some map, some diagram.

If you look at what is called the model sheet or the character sheet for any Looney Tunes character, say Daffy, you will see that there is no single Daffy, no Daffy *qua* Daffy, no Daffy *Ding-an-sich*, there is only a series of Daffys, a series of Daffy responses, gestural and verbal.

Only: Now-look-here-Buster-Let's-have-an-under-standing Daffy *and* It's-mine!-All-mine!-I'm-rich!-I'm-wealthy!-I'm-comfortably-well-off! Daffy *and* Slight-pause-whilst-I-adjust-my-accoutrements Daffy *and* Now-then-we'll-just-see-who's-boss-in-this-bailiwick Daffy *and* It-isn't-as-though-I-haven't-lived-up-to-my-con-tract-Goodneth-knows-I've-done-that Daffy *and* That-sir-is-an-inmitigated-frabication!-It's-wabbit-season! Daffy *and* I-say-it's-*duck-season*-and-I-say-*Fire*! Daffy *and* I'll-start-it-this-time! Daffy *and* Okay-this-time-*You*-start-it! Daffy *and* You're-dethpicable! Daffy.

And out of those multiplicitous characterisations, you create the character: Daffy.

So given that there is no character, only characterising, then how could you abstract the 'anatomy' of one of those architectural characters I mentioned in the previous section?

This is where the editors of this special issue can make another entrance on these stagings, because when the editors emailed me, they emailed me the following statement: 'The way the diagram operates that distinguish-es it from an icon, inspiration or *objet trouvé*, is related to the difference between representational and instrumental techniques. An image becomes a diagram only when you instrument it toward organisational effects.'

Now when the editors sent me that email they were trying to discriminate the diagram from the image, and you already know I have been trying to discriminate *and* equate the diagram and the image, but this is where the editors can help with the question of how you might abstract an image like an architectural character: by deterritorialising and reterritorialising the image or the *objet trouvé* or character, by instrumentalising it toward organisational effects (as they would say it), by operating on its organisational effects (as I would say it).

Thus: the diagram is not imported *to* the image (or the object), the diagram is exported *from* the image (or the object). It is found already at work metonymically in or around the image or the *objet trouvé* or the character, and drawn forth. But then, it should be said: the image (the character) does *not* become a diagram, what the image (the character) *does* is to reveal its own diagrammatics. Diagrammatics that will only be recognisable by virtue of how they are drawn forth in the act of responding to internal and external forces, growing and developing, as Jones suggests, *'in each case from our discovery of who they were. Then and only then could their movements and voices uniquely demonstrate each of these personalities'.*

6   *'We are left to ponder, oh, the reluctance of Being to
       succumb to Mutability.'* (Kenner)[32]

But why worry about believability, visual consistency, faithfulness to anatomy, anyway? Or characters, even? Animation is *great* because *anything* can transform into anything *else*, a character can become *anything* at all, *right*?

Or so it's said, at least in some cyber circles. Oh, that dreamy talk again. On the contrary: what the art of animation and the art of art reveal is the possibility – but also the difficulty – of transformation, which only occurs not in spite of but because of that difficulty, in the struggle *of* and *for* identity – a struggle not in order to transform into something *else*, but in order to find the differential characterisations, the differential transformations, from within (the) character.

Transformation is easy. It is not difficult, say, for a handrail to change into a bench or a coat rail, just, you know, for example, or, say, a counter to turn into a dish-

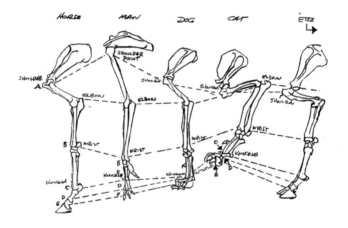

Chuck Jones, *Chuck Amuck: The Life and Times of an Animated Cartoonist*
(New York: Farrar, Straus and Giroux, 1989)

Chuck Jones, *Chuck Reducks: Drawing from the Fun Side of Life*
(New York: Warner, 1996)

rack, or, say, a shelf to turn into a table, nothing could be easier really, it's only a question of what you get for this labour, what you get out of it, what relations can be drawn out of such transformations.

As in montage: a juxtaposition does not a relationship make – so, too, in animation: a transformation does not a relationship make.

If you want to maintain the productive tension of the transformation, in a way that would articulate difference *and* relation, then that transformation should resist being too smooth, too easy, because then it will not be legible as to what transformed into what. And why. And how.

But, given that, what *is* particularly instructive in animation is the 'amazing, elastic play' that the film director Sergei Eisenstein notes:

With surprise – necks elongate.
With panicked running – legs stretch.
With fright – not only the character trembles, but a wavering line runs along the contour of its drawn image…
For if, in terror, the neck of a horse or cow stretches, then the representation itself of the skin will stretch, but not … the contour of the drawing of the skin, as an independent element! …
And only after the contour of the neck elongates beyond the possible limits of the neck – does it become a comical embodiment …[33]

This amazing and elastic play is due to a *limit* of physical identity already having been established and then *temporarily* elongated, extended, *in relation to, in comparison to*, that limit. This limit, of course, is not just the limit of that physical identity but the limit of that set of cultural identities that circulates around that physical identity. What is enacted, in other words, is the *temporary* re-formation of the object and its representation. 'The comicality here', Eisenstein notes, 'stems from the fact that any representation exists in two ways: as a set of lines' – *the map* – 'and as the image that arises from them'[34] – *the territory*.

Eisenstein used the example of a clock to further illustrate this principle: if the relation between 'the graphic drawing of numerals and hands on a clock face, and an image of the time of day that comes from their specific combination' is 'normally … indissoluble', then 'in a comical construction there is … dissection, but of a special type: the perception of them as independent of' – *as discriminated from* – 'each other, *and simultaneously* as belonging together'[35] – *as being equated to* each other.

This productive tension is maintained by simultaneously establishing *and* exceeding a particular identity. In order to work, in order for the transformation of identity to be perceivable as a transformation, this transformation has to be developed in relation to, within range of, that identity, that *identifiable* identity. That was one of the many lessons Jones learned at Warner Bros from the master animation director Tex Avery:

Tex showed us that we could go beyond rationality. At a time when we were learning to animate and realizing that respect for anatomy is vital for believability, Tex showed us that a character can come out of that anatomy very briefly for a violent, distorted reaction. However, the distortion can't continue for long, or … credibility is gone.[36]

This is one of Chuck Jones's principal points: 'Our characters achieve believability *because* of their limitations'.[37]

Your architectural characters, your architecture: by their limits shall you know them. The limits, say, of their mutability, which will give you the very possibility of enacting what might be noticeable and in fact notable.

Here's Hugh Kenner's example, from his discussion of the differentials of Wile E. Coyote's fall from whatever edge of whatever cliff Coyote was falling off of in his forever failing pursuit of the Road Runner:

Wile E's torso drops away, leaving a stressed face atop the stretched-out neck. Two seconds later the contracted

**neck snaps the face down out of sight, leaving two long
ears. When those in turn vanish we are left to ponder –
oh, the reluctance of Being to succumb to Mutability.**[38]

What a wonderful line: 'When those in turn vanish
we are left to ponder – oh, the reluctance of Being to succumb to Mutability.' But, actually, it's not just the reluctance
we are left to ponder, it's the reluctance *and* the possibility,
the necessity, the difficulty, the inevitability, of Being to
succumb to Mutability.

This play between reluctance and inevitability,
between establishing and exceeding identity, leads us to
Jacques Lacan and to anamorphosis, the principles of which
Lacan first discussed in his seminar of 1959–1960: 'It is any
kind of construction that is made in such a way that by
means of an optical transposition a certain form that wasn't
visible at first sight transforms itself into a readable image.
The pleasure is found in seeing its emergence from an indecipherable form.'[39] And returned to again in his seminar of
1964, where he seemed to emphasise just the reverse, focusing then on: '…the pleasure of obtaining not the restoration
of the world, but the distortion … of the image … and I
will dwell, as on some delicious game, on this method that
makes anything appear at will in a particular stretching.'[40]

Both of these pleasures – the pleasure of finding the
readable image in the indecipherable form *and* the pleasure
of its distortion – are already implied, as the literary scholar
Stephen Greenblatt has noted, in the etymology of anamorphosis, which 'suggests a back-and-forth movement,
a constant forming and re-forming'.[41]

A constant de-forming and re-forming: a constant
deterritorialising and reterritorialising.

This possibility of a constant de-forming and re-
forming in architecture, this possibility of an anamorphic
architecture, is perhaps better exemplified not by a single
painterly image, but by an example from music, say, John
Coltrane's 'sampling and scratching' in his various versions
of 'My Favorite Things', which not only show how you can
find radical abstraction from within the figural, but even

more radically: just how *close* the abstract is to the figural, say a note or a pitch or an octave or a beat away, in other words, how instantaneously the indecipherable form of abstraction is ready to snap for us into melodic lyricism or the readable image of figuration.

Hip hop may be an even better musical example here. Say you sample and scratched a line something along the lines of: 'ch … ch … ch … chec … chec … checit … check it … ch . .. ch … check it ooouuuuuttt.' This is not some uniformly graduated transformation or deformation, this is an anamorphic play with a very figural phrase, one that maintains the set of diverse but specific connotations of the phrase, while at the same time revealing the entirely abstract sonic tectonics of its construction. If it were all abstract – if it were: 'uh … uh … uh … uhuh … uhuh … uhuhhh … uhuhh uh … uh . .. uh … uhuhh uh uuuhhh-hhhhh' – there would be *no* transformation, not even an orgasmic one, which would require quite a different array of sounds (which anyway are not an abstract set of sounds, but already and conventionally have assumed the figuration of the 'orgasm-sound').

If those particular abstract sounds hold none of the tension of that anamorphised 'check it OUT', well that is due to the fact that when sampled, or stretched, what is lacking in the abstract uhuhh uh sounds is the way *sense* might be held in suspension. This holding in suspension of both form *and* sense *is* the anamorphic act, and it is the means by which Lacan links anamorphosis to those techniques of suspension that are found in (courtly) love – and in tragedy and in comedy – wherein the relation between action and desire is held within various states of suspension.

Further, what anamorphosis and animation point to in this play is the pointlessness anyway of making such absolute distinctions between, say, the abstract and the figural – precisely by keeping the categories of abstraction and figuration *in suspension*, in process, precisely by *neither* allowing for the instant gratification of these categories as fixed or stable, *nor* the displacement of the one category by the other:

This also allows us to approach a little closer to the unanswered question on the ends of art: is the end of art imitation or non-imitation? Does art imitate what it represents? If you begin by posing the question in those terms, you are already caught in the trap, and there is no way out of remaining in the impasse in which we find ourselves between figurative and so-called abstract art...

That's a trap one must not enter. Of course, works of art imitate the objects they represent, but their end is certainly not to represent them. In offering the imitation of an object, they make something different out of that object. Thus they only pretend to imitate. The object is established in a certain relationship to the Thing and is intended to encircle and to render both present and absent.[42]

In the end, anamorphosis can either be an end *in and of* itself – say, a kind of cute party trick – or a means: 'At issue, in an analogical or anamorphic form, is the effort to point once again to the fact that what we seek in the illusion is something in which the illusion as such in some way transcends itself, destroys itself, by demonstrating that it is only there as a signifier.'[43] In other words, by showing that the image, the picture, as Lacan said, is 'what any picture is, a trap for the gaze', but showing it to us in a way that shows us: 'that, as subjects, we are literally called into the picture, are represented here as caught'.[44]

We are already entangled, here, between the map and the territory, in the picture, in the object – between being equated to and being discriminated from our own forms of representation. And left to ponder the reluctance and the inevitability of Being to succumb to this form of Mutability.

But then the question is: how can architecture be animated so as to cause us to recognise our own entanglements, as it responds to us, and we to it, in our various differentials of characterisation? This is how we might recognise ourselves – as already called into our own pictures – in the enactment of our entanglements.[45]

7 *'All of our characters are recognizable, not only by their
personal characteristics, but by how they express these
characteristics in response to conflict or love or any
adversarial situation.'*[46]

What is wrong with this statement in *Chuck Amuck*, Chuck
Jones goes on to correct seven years later with the following
statement in *Chuck Reducks*: 'It's not what or where a character is, nor the circumstances under which he finds himself
that determines who he is. It is only how in a unique way
he responds to that environment and those circumstances
which identify him as an individual'.[47]

 In other words, there is no personality – no map –
of a character in the film or in the book or in the architectural space. The only thing you can perceive is the character's responsiveness to various conditions. In a building,
in a book, in a film the only thing you can see of the conceptual map is that which is inscribed in that part of the
territory that you do see, as Christopher Walken indicated,
because you never see the territory whole, you just see bits
and pieces. Only those bits and pieces of responsiveness,
those bits and pieces of entanglement, give you the character – or more precisely: it is only those bits and pieces
from which you will attempt, *retroactively*, to construct
some character.

 Here is Theodor Adorno's beautiful quote about vectors: 'Beauty is either the resultant of force vectors or it is
nothing at all.'[48] But I would say, perhaps less beautifully,
that forces are most strongly represented not directly in
and of themselves as frozen entities nor as a pre-(in the
computer)-established result but as resultant effects *in relation* and in *responsiveness* – 'It is only how in a unique way
he responds to that environment and those circumstances
which identify him as an individual' – through transformations in the configuration of the character or the building,
transformations visible to anyone looking at the character
or at the building. 'The subject is neither a result', Alain
Badiou has said, 'nor an origin. It is the *local* status of the
procedure, a configuration that exceeds the situation.'[49]

Like watching a kick-off return for a touch-down in a football game: all the tension and drama of the kick returner's gestures would be eviscerated if the forces were reduced to the resultant that is merely the run. That is, if all the relational forces at work in the responsive gestures of the run – the other team trying to tackle the runner, his own team blocking the other team or getting in his way, the near out-of-bounds at the sideline, the final sprint to the goal line – were entirely erased from view, so that the only thing one would see would be the *resultant* wacky dance in some abstract space by some helmeted nutcase with a big number on his shirt.

This is why it is important to avoid the mere direct expression(ism) of forces as resultants, lest we as designers become, say, glorified traffic engineers instrumentally calcifying *maps* of circulation flows – *as if* those maps of flows were the socially and psychologically complex territory that is the circulation of individuals through institutionalised spaces. Rather, architecture might gesture relationally to these forces, inferring forces as well as expressing forces, which is a way, to shift the association yet again, back to music, of being simultaneously on *and* off the beat, developing a syncopation of beats, a syncopation of (responses to) forces.

Both materialising the map and not materialising (but alluding to) the map, happily playing between the map and the territory.

In animation and in human performance the lesson is that these vectors of character are expressed not as some general movements, not as some general shapes, but as shapings through physical and vocal characterisations,[50] as gestures in relation and in response. Indeed not just expressed but rather enacted as gestic movements of complex motivation (to use Brecht's term for the social connectedness of all gesture[51]), motivated between desire and drive – action being that which is suspended not just between various desires, but between that which the character desires and that which the character does not desire, yet nevertheless is compulsively driven to do (this is the Lacanian notion of drive): 'Daffy rushes in and fears to tread at the same time'.[52] Just like an architect.

This brings me finally to the third of the three dictionary definitions for vector: 'a behavioural field of force toward or away from the performance of various acts; broadly: DRIVE.' So it should not come as too much of a surprise if in his discussion of the Lacanian notion of drive, Jacques-Alain Miller speaks – in terms of cells and diagrammatic graphs – not only of conflict and love and other adversarial situations, but speaks of these situations by speaking of vectors:

It is for this reason that, in this seminar [*Encore*], Lacan places right away, at the side of *jouissance*, its Other, namely love – which, on the contrary is itself representable, by a vector that goes from one point to the other. And, we won't even hesitate to bring the vector of return, which we find in a fundamental cell on Lacan's graph. His entire graph is constructed on these departures and returns.[53]

Conflict and love and other adversarial situations: this is the social connection, the social link – 'In the final analysis', say Lacan, 'there is nothing but that, the social link'[54] – the 'affiliative relations' (to utilise a phrasing of Greg Lynn) through which to develop 'connections that occur through vicissitude'.[55] These 'behavioural fields of force toward or away from the performance of various acts' in architecture are related to the conceptual and real vicissitudes of site, programme, structure, type, tectonics, material, ideologies. It is these adversarial vicissitudes (including those of love), these vectorial movements from one point to the other, these departures and returns, which motivate and animate our character. And could in turn motivate the character of (and the tectonic characters in) our architecture.

There's more, but: there's always more. Where these last two sections on anamorphous and vectorial responsiveness have taken me to is to the point of these departures and returns as the differential vectors, the differential motives, of our character, of our architectural characters.

What is left to discuss is how motives might be developed
into motivic improvisations, how points might be made
contrapuntal. For this I will need to have Chuck Jones
and Hugh Kenner and Tex Avery return, along with, say,
John Coltrane and Public Enemy and Glenn Gould, and
many others.

> Another time then: another interest, another pleasure.
> Another me then. And then, well, another you.

Originally published in *ANY* 23 (special issue:
Diagram Work: Data Mechanics for a Topological Age,
edited by Ben van Berkel and Caroline Bos, 1998),
50–57.

NOTES

1. Adam Higginbotham, 'Walken on the Wild Side', *Premiere* IV:5, UK edition (June 1996), 67.

2. Director Peter O'Fallon, quoted in Holly Millea, 'Tall, Dark, and Ransom', *Premiere* II:7 (March 1998), 75.

3. Gregory Bateson, *Steps to an Ecology of Mind* (New York: Ballantine, 1972), 453.

4. Ibid., 180.

5. For the operations and play of non-professional diagrams and plans in vernacular architecture, see, for example, Henry Glassie, *Folk Housing in Middle Virginia*(Knoxville: University of Tennessee, 1975).

6. Bateson, *Steps to an Ecology of Mind*, 183.

7. Ibid., 451.

8. Martin Esslin, *Brecht* (London: Methuen, 1984), 123.

9. Bateson, *Steps to an Ecology of Mind*, 185.

10. Jean-Luc Godard, *Godard on Godard* (New York: Da Capo, 1986), 208.

11. Chuck Jones, *Chuck Reducks: Drawing from the Fun Side of Life* (New York: Warner, 1996), 268.

12. Chuck Jones, *Chuck Amuck: The Life and Times of an Animated Cartoonist* (New York: Farrar, Straus and Giroux, 1989), 180.

13. Ibid.

14. Ibid., 261.

15. Ibid., 180.

16. Jones, *Chuck Reducks*, 120.

17. Ibid.

18. Richmond B. McQuistan, *Scalar and Vector Fields: A Physical Intrepretation* (New York: Wiley, 1965), 2. It is Jason Vigneri-Beane who reminded me of the importance of addressing the difference between the scalar and the vector.

19. Gerhard Richter, *Paintings* (Bolzano: Museum of Modern Art, 1996), 12.

20. Jean-Luc Godard, 'Introduction à une véritable histoire du cinéma',

in *Camera Obscura* 8-9-10 (1982), 95.

21. Gilles Deleuze and Felix Guattari, *What is Philosophy?* (New York: Columbia University Press, 1994), 67–68.

22. Michel Foucault, *Power/Knowledge: Selected Interviews and Other Writings 1972–1977* (New York: Pantheon, 1980), 151–52.

23. Angelika Hurwicz, 'Brecht's Work with Actors', in *Brecht as They Knew Him*, ed. Hubert Witt (New York: International, 1974), 133.

24. Jones, *Chuck Reducks*, 268.

25. Jones, *Chuck Amuck*, 261–62.

26. Ibid., 261.

27. Jones, *Chuck Reducks*, 131, 267.

28. Hugh Kenner, *Chuck Jones: A Flurry of Drawings* (Berkeley: University of California, 1994), 62.

29. Jones, *Chuck Amuck*, 261.

30. Mikhail Bakhtin, *Problems of Dostoevsky's Poetics* (Minneapolis: University of Minnesota Press, 1984), 59.

31. Quoted in Michael Butler, *The Novels of Max Frisch* (London: Oswald Wolff, 1976), 149.

32. Kenner, *Chuck Jones*, 67.

33. Sergei Eisenstein, *Eisenstein on Disney* (London: Methuen, 1988), 57.

34. Ibid.

35. Ibid., 57–58.

36. Jones, *Chuck Reducks*, 98.

37. Jones, *Chuck Amuck*, 263.

38. Kenner, *Chuck Jones*, 67.

39. Jacques Lacan, *Seminar VII: The Ethics of Psychoanalysis* (New York: Norton, 1992), 135.

40. Jacques Lacan, *Seminar XI: The Four Fundamental Concepts of Psychoanalysis* (New York: Norton, 1977), 87.

41. Stephen Greenblatt, *Renaissance Self-Fashioning: From More to Shakespeare* (Chicago: University of Chicago Press, 1980), 23.

42. Lacan, *Seminar VII*, 141.

43. Ibid., 136.

44. Lacan, *Seminar XI*, 89, 92.

45. The idea of an aesthetic object enacting entanglements in order to make its 'readers' enact their own entanglements is developed by Stanley Fish in *Surprised by Sin: The Reader in Paradise Lost* (Berkeley: University of California Press, 1971).

46. Jones, *Chuck Amuck*, 263.

47. Jones, *Chuck Reducks*, 268.

48. Theodor W. Adorno, 'Functionalism Today', *Oppositions* 17 (1979), 41.

49. Alain Badiou, 'On a Finally Objectless Subject', in *Who Comes After the Subject*, ed. Eduardo Cadava et al (New York: Routledge, 1991), 27.

50. All the voices for almost all of the classic Looney Tunes characters (including Elmer and Bugs and Daffy and Pepé and Porky) were enacted by Mel Blanc, whose job description was 'Vocal Characterisations'.

51. For a discussion of Brecht's concept of the gestic, see 'Identity and the Discourse of Politics in Contemporary Architecture' in this volume.

52. Jones, *Chuck Amuck*, 239.

53. Jacques-Alain Miller, 'The Drive is Speech', *UMBR(a)* 1 (1997), 20.

54. Jacques Lacan, *Seminar XX: On Feminine Sexuality, The Limits of Love and Knowledge: Encore* (New York: Norton, 1998), 54.

55. Greg Lynn, 'Multiplicitous and Inorganic Bodies' *Assemblage* 19 (1992), 39: 'Affiliative relations, by contrast, typically exploit possible connections that occur through vicissitude'.

GREG LYNN

Date: Mon, 25 Jan 1999 14:25:28 -0600
To: 'Sarah Whiting'
From: 'Mark Rakatansky'
Subject: Greg Lynn

Sarah, you are even crueller than I had imagined you to be: enticing me to return to these pages I had removed myself from, with a subject you knew I would be enticed by.

But, Sarah, a proper essay, even a proper review, I cannot write in four pages, and anyway not in two weeks' time, but yes, I will agree to send you some four-page kind of something that will act as a review of Greg's new book, until some other occasion allows me to do this subject or this book justice. Only it's books, isn't it, because when you emailed me I thought you meant *Folds, Bodies, and Blobs: Collected Essays* (Brussels: La Lettre volée, 1998), which I had already, whereas I guess you meant *Animate Form*, which I received from you today, just hot off the Princeton Architectural presses, but really what's the point of reviewing one without the other, which is another one of my points anyway. Yet when you said '… the book is important; why it is, is the single point you have to get across in four pages', I have to say that I no longer believe in getting across some single point – single points they come, they go – I'm only interested in the getting there, which you already know is what I've been saying all along about the process of narrative and character and identity. And anyway isn't Greg's work about multiplicity, about – let's use his words – 'a complex relationship which is not reducible to either the contradiction of the many or the wholistic unity of one' (*Folds, Bodies, and Blobs*, 162)?

That's part of the problem isn't it, single points written in four or forty or four hundred pages, single points designed in four or forty or four thousand square feet. But ditto as to forty conflicting points written in forty pages, forty conflicting points designed in forty thousand square feet.

I know: this has to be post-scriptive, well that's not exactly right either, let's just say … affiliative to the Garofalo-Lynn-McInturf project, which is situated somewhere outside of this review – and I know: you're just about full up on this issue, so there's no way around the page limit – but since I can't possibly explicate all the vital points in these two books of Greg's, then I might as well put at least one of these points into practice, like, say, this one: 'It is important for any parameter-based design that there be both the unfolding of an internal system and the infolding of contextual information fields' (*Animate Form*, 42). I am *trying* to unfold the particular *internal* system and infold the particular *context* of *this* particular 'review' at *this* particular moment here, but you can write until you're red in the fingers or blue in the face, and still, it's like Stanley Fish says, half the people will understand that everything is already a rhetorical construction and the other half will just go on saying 'no, you're the one with the rhetoric, not me, so why can't you just get to the point and summarise the book already?'

Warm-up points, summarial points, pointed points: a point's only as good as the extent to which it performs in relation to that mix that is the performance. Anyway, aren't all those diagrams in *Animate Form*, in the book and on the CD-ROM, about not getting rid of the warm-up – the throat-clearing – to get to the point, but developing the warm-up into iterative and inflective and responsive values? Not in order to get to some 'reduced essence of the project', nor merely to provide 'the historical trace of the project's developmental process', but to utilise those diagrams as 'machines for proliferation; they are generative; they incorporate specific information; and they unfold in their complexity' (*Folds, Bodies, and Blobs*, 232).

'Prolific', 'generative', 'incorporative', 'unfolding in complexity': these certainly are some of the phrases you could use to describe the production exemplified in these two books. *Folds, Bodies, and Blobs* contains a selection of eleven essays published between December 1992 and May 1996, while *Animate Form* documents four building projects and two installations, all designed between January 1994 and October 1995. The quantity of this production is of less interest, in and of itself, than the fact that this proliferation has been generative both of innovative concepts and innovative forms. Which would also not be so important except to the extent that – through its incorporation of a variety of conceptual and contextual influences – this production has unfolded over this short span of years in its complexity, to the point that it is easy to say, with these two books in hand, that Greg is developing one of the most articulate, sustained and rigorously elaborated discourses in architecture. That is why I can't reduce all of these points to some single point, because there isn't a single page in any of the essays in these books where there isn't one kind of incisive and iterative point or another.

This unfolding is one of the great pleasures of these two books: the exceedingly rare pleasure of witnessing an architect set out a line of research and actually follow it through in a rigorous yet innovative way. Or to use the term Greg borrowed from Derrida's reading of Husserl: in an *anexact yet rigorous* way. Anexactitude is only interesting, it seems to me, if it means not just different from normative exactitude (as, say, CAD-exact curvy shapes vs CAD-exact orthogonal shapes), but as that which is resistant to prediction, capable of surprise. And rigorousness is only interesting if it means not a closing down to essentials, but an opening up through a thorough and sustained follow-through. There is no contradiction in the combination of these terms: for how could one even recognise a surprise move unless a certain rhythm has been rigorously and rhetorically enacted through which and from which this move, this surprise, might venture, in the tension between rigour and surprise? All surprise of course means no surprise.

As a means of bringing 'both a degree of discipline and unanticipated behavior' (*Animate Form*, 20) to the design process, Greg has pioneered, in architectural design, the use of a particular form of *computer-based* animation techniques of motion and force. This use of computers, or more specifically certain kinds of animation software, has, of course, become both his medium and his trademark, especially to all those yearning for a victim or a hero to pin the word 'cyber' on to, or at the very least to designate the Cyber Architect for the Millennium. Well, it makes good copy either way, and in truth it is one of the genuine aspects of what is intriguing about Greg's work: that he is attempting to develop architectural uses for the computer beyond mere instrumentalism, dreamy cyber-escapism, or formal expressionism: 'The challenge for contemporary architectural theory and design is to try to understand the appearance of these tools in a more sophisticated way than as simply a new set of shapes' (*Animate Form*, 17). But if others take up the shapes over the principles, well it won't be the first or the last time *that* happened, and it certainly won't be Greg's fault: over and over again in his writing he sends out the cautions. Of course, it's easy for anyone, no one excepted, to forget the cautions. In fact, the designated person that architects write cautions for is always probably mostly themselves, as a reminder to themselves, so that what might get expressed will not just be formalised expressions, but concepts manifest as formal expressions.

Right from the beginning, from the first of those essays selected for *Folds, Bodies, and Blobs* – 'Multiplicitous and Inorganic Bodies', published in the pages of this journal some seven years ago – Greg set out not to develop a computer architecture as such but with a greater task in mind, as he says: a 'monumental task'. And in fact it is the rigorous working on and through of this task that is so extensively exhibited in these two books: 'To disentangle the pact between organic bodies and exact geometric language that underlies architecture's static spatial types is a monumental task. Any attempt to loosen this alliance must simultaneously *deterritorialize* the autonomy of whole organisms and replace the exactitude of rigid geometry with more pliant systems of description' (*Folds, Bodies, and Blobs*, 41).

Setting that doubled task in motion, Greg began by developing specific designs and a theory of design that simultaneously loosened certain static models and developed certain more pliant systems of symmetry and proportion, gravity and tectonics, typology and geometry, in order that 'rather than as a frame through which time and space pass, architecture can be modeled as a participant immersed within dynamical flows' (*Animate Form*, 11). This loosening and developing is evident in the designs of the projects in the books: the inflected aggregation of variously scaled context-derived figures in the Cardiff Bay Opera House project, the simultaneous reach and lift of the glass-clad tubular frames in the Port Authority Gateway project, the intertwining tubular volumes of the Yokohama Port Terminal project – and thus we could now come to the collaborative church in Queens, but that is outside this review – I mean, it's not included in the books that I'm supposed to be reviewing here.

Now if architecture can be 'modeled as a participant immersed within dynamical flows', then what character animation software may productively animate in architecture is not so much the character of physical forces as the character of architectural elements and forms as they relate and respond to these and other forces. Forces, as Deleuze said, are already social. There are no physical forces as such, in and of themselves, in architecture. There are no such things, no stable entities, no personified abstractions as Light or Gravity or View – as if they were characters in some Medieval Morality play – there are only our complex and conflicted and ever-changing social relations to differentials of light and gravity and views. The characterisations of forces, in other words, are already encultured as they make their way rhetorically – whether it's through the rhetoric of symbolism, expressionism, functionalism, or abstraction – into architecture. Thus when Greg says: 'This multi-type, or *performance envelope*, does not privilege a fixed type but instead models a series of relationships or expressions between a range of potentials' (*Animate Form*, 13–14), then the question arises as to how this kind, or any

Greg Lynn, Cardiff Bay Opera House, Cardiff, Wales, 1994

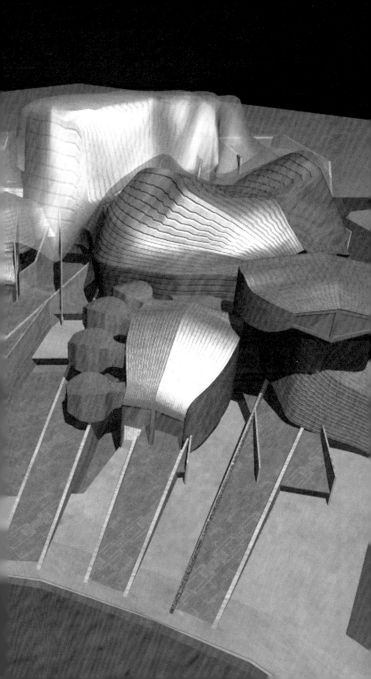

kind, of architecture will show itself to be in the midst
of this performance, in the act of its act, which perhaps
then gets us into not a *performance* model as much as a
performative model.

Thus context may not be best 'understood as a gradient field of unorganised information rather than as a
repository of fixed values, rules, and codes' (*Folds, Bodies,
and Blobs*, 66), but as *both* identifiably but contingently fixed
and therefore capable of gradient or other differential kinds
of reorganisation – *not* through a staying in the middle of
'two poles' just to avoid aligning with 'either the exact and
scientific or the literal and expressionistic' (*Folds, Bodies,
and Blobs*, 226), but through a traversing throughout those
poles in 'fluid and continuous differentiation' (*Folds, Bodies,
and Blobs*, 31). This is why it might be more productive *not*
to cross over entirely 'from models of cinema to models
of animation' (*Animate Form*, 42), but continually to cross
between – as the exaggeration and nuance of animation is
particularly instructive towards enacting in architecture
the exaggeration and nuance of our cinematic architectural
drama. (Thus the entire model of cinema cannot be reduced
to, or dismissed as, some single concept such as serial static
frames, whatever its particular history has been in recent
architectural discourse.) Even more productive would be
not to (definitively) periodise, especially micro-periodise,
aesthetic models – which reaches a point of absurdity when
we find ourselves saying: cinematic model = early 1990s,
animation model = late 1990s. This is why Chuck Jones can
say (and we can use this kind of fictive transhistorical statement to help us perceive anew or not, as we will): 'Animation could therefore apply to all … drama from *Lysistrata*
through *King Lear, Waiting for Godot*, to Chaplin, Keaton,
and us.'

But, for whatever circumstantial or market-driven
reasons, these books are split between the drama of design
and the drama of theory, between a project sort of book
(even if it has an excellent theoretical introduction by Greg
and serious captioned commentary running throughout)
and a theory sort of book (even if there are occasional

references to a few of his projects), the former kind of polished and the latter kind of unpolished, which inadvertently and unfortunately perpetuates the conventions of what design and what theory are supposed to look like. I can readily understand, in some instances, a rationale for some forms of this kind of split, but in this instance, in Greg's instance, I would say it is particularly important to have both of these books to appreciate, fully, either one.

One matter that adds to this split is that Greg does not, in either of these books, thematise the form and the content of the writing and presentation to the degree of some recent exceptional exceptions of monographic form by some other rigorous and anexact practices (practices of rigorous surprises), such as Diller + Scofidio's *Flesh* or Koolhaas's *SMLXL*. I mean he doesn't design the presentations or the writing in the same iteratively active and responsive ways as he does his architectural designs. Greg's books are more 'direct' in this aspect, which some will prefer and others will not, even if 'directitude' is just another kind of rhetorical … call it *style* if you like, *trick* if you prefer. But like the aforementioned practices, Greg's practice is already deeply influential in the most productive sense, not in terms of how many stylistic copies may result, but in how it is providing conceptual and formal grist for the mills of many different – and different kinds of – practices.

For many practices the production pace that generated these two books would result in either reductive repetition or widely unrelated projects – reduction to a single point or proliferation without focus. But if some forms of repetition may be found in the essays selected in *Folds, Bodies, and Blobs* or in the projects of *Animate Form*, that repetition pushes its concepts forward to test and evolve them in new areas, and thus is a form of iteration, allowing for development and refinement as it evolves. An iteration – to again use Greg's descriptions of his design practice to describe an aspect of his writing practice – that is not 'reductive to ideal essences', but is 'evolutionary, flexible, and proliferating' (*Folds, Bodies, and Blobs*, 63). An iteration that is 'continually, dynamically, and fluidly transforming itself in response to

Greg Lynn, Yokohama Pier, Yokohama, Japan, 1994

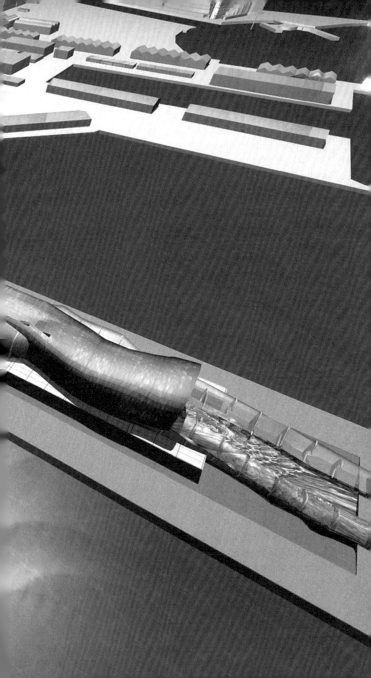

its intensive involvement with external forces in its context' (*Folds, Bodies, and Blobs*, 45), whether that context – that subject – be Gwathmey, Rowe, van Berkel, Deleuze, Bateson, Symmetry, Proportion, Gravity, Tectonics, Typology, or Geometry. Regardless of whether these subjects might be seen as already allied (van Berkel) or already in opposition (Rowe) to Greg's project, because as he says: 'Affiliative relations, by contrast, typically exploit possible connections that occur through vicissitude' (*Folds, Bodies, and Blobs*, 47–48).

Transformation, responsiveness, differentials, animation, performance: now knowing what you know of me, Sarah, it won't come as much of a surprise to you that I've selected these particular issues as the terms through which to discuss Greg's books. Obviously, anyone else would have selected a different set of affiliative or oppositional issues to discuss (so much for the veracity of book reviews). It's like this other email I received the very day I received your email request for this review – it said: 'We like your work very much, which is not too surprising: we can find a lot of ourselves in what you do!' Well, that's the bittersweet truth of it, I guess: anyone, designer or historian or critic or theorist, who writes about anybody or anything else, is looking to – lo and behold – find their pet issues residing before them in whatever they select to reside before them. (But pets have a degree both of domestication and of wildness, which is why Greg likens the computer more to a pet than a tool.) I'll put this another way: every designer, every historian also and every theorist too, uses whatever subject he or she selects – or is suggested to her or him by some review editor like yourself – to set the stage upon which he or she will attempt to climb upon and perform, with whatever acknowledged or unacknowledged rhetorical style he or she happens to utilise. (I've already suggested that this is no less the case for Greg's incisive essays on his subjects Gwathmey or Rowe or van Berkel.) And yet – no, no 'yet' because there are still no contradictions in these terms – *so then*, there is another pleasure besides that of self-reflection, which is *the unexpected*, which is the pleasure of finding how dramatically different someone else's work can be from yours even as you seem to be working on similar issues or forms – or vice versa: similar when the issues or the forms seem so different. An anamorphic reflection then – of the subject who's writing, of the subject who's written. Not a distorted reflection so much as a reflection of the differential distortions and transformations within. This is the pleasure of finding the performance taking surprising turns, which thankfully keeps those issues and those forms – and those subjects – open and evolving.

The only thing in these books I don't really believe is some of those occasional (mostly early) polemical overstatements that strike a unitary pose – phrases like (I'll go ahead and add the emphasis): 'A reformulated concept of the body … *mandates* 'anexact yet rigorous' topological descriptions …' or '*The* most difficult task *for the moment* is …' (*Folds, Bodies, and Blobs*, 136, 158). Or 'The *now apparent failure* of deconstruction to develop an adequate theory in architecture … is most likely due to its proclivity for arresting internal difference in forms of contradiction and conflict' (*Folds, Bodies, and Blobs*, 137). But of course, no theory or practice of architecture will ever be adequate. Thankfully. Oh I know, that's just the rhetorical style of polemics, after all, all of this is all just polemics – even this sentence is – but the problem with *that* kind of polemical statement is that it's easy to be caught in one's own trap, I mean it's just as easy to arrest internal difference in forms of *continuity and flow* as it is in forms of *contradiction and conflict*.

I would like this polemical point to be a smaller point than it is, just some kind of tagged-on point to create the impression that I'm giving you a fair and critical review. But this zeitgeist business, and the profits that are assumed to be had thereof, this assigning forms or models or references to a given retro or avant micro-period, this periodisation sickness of our discipline to be *of the moment or ahead of the moment* is something we should continually try to cure ourselves of. Maybe we could work on and through this repetitive compulsion not to repeat the same way Freud

suggested we work on and through our compulsion to
repeat (as both are just ways of resisting critical analysis):
through some thematised, iterative, forms of repetition.
As Freud said: 'We render it harmless, and even make use
of it, by according it the right to assert itself within certain
limits.' Just look at Gerhard Richter or read Thomas Pyn-
chon or watch Dennis Potter's *Singing Detective*, or (if you're
going to NYC anytime soon) check out what the Wooster
Group does with Gertrude Stein's *Doctor Faustus Lights the
Lights* and Joseph Mawra's *Olga's House of Shame* in their
performance *House/Lights*: *any*thing and *every*thing may be
used from *any* period, *any* modality, *any* image-repertoire in
order to iteratively develop 'a complex relationship which is
not reducible to either the contradiction of the many or the
wholistic unity of one.'

Otherwise, if you end up writing those kinds of zeitgeistian statements, you may just end up writing your own
epitaph. Now Sarah, now don't get me started on that, on
all those reasons why we still disagree about the funerary
foreclosure of the pages of this journal. Well, it's inevitable
I guess: I guess we are all of us writing our own epitaphs
all the time, just by the fact and the act of our writing and
our designing. Only it seems to me that there's a difference
between, on the one hand, stating your place *as* history – to
track yourself as history, to make history tractable to you –
and on the other hand, acknowledging in your work your
awareness of history (including your history as a writer or
as a designer or as a journal) as a *dialogical placing*, as an 'infolding of [historical] information fields', as a process that
is 'continually, dynamically, and fluidly transforming itself
in response to its intensive involvement with [historical]
forces in its context'. The conceptual gaps and temporal lags
between theory and design will always assure that theory
and design will never be totally tractable each to the other,
however influential each dialogically might be to the other,
the degree and coordinates of which will always remain
ultimately unknowable at its own time, at the moment of its
moment. And in point of fact, except for the odd polemical
over-statement, an attempt at a rigorous dialogical

placing is precisely what Greg is working at throughout these books. But if these works are, as Greg says they are, *experiments* – modellings instead of some unitary Model – then I say let's let others strive to judge which movement or which shape or which building or which disciplinary journal is *of* the moment or *ahead* of its moment or *past* its moment or whatever other kinds of momentary and impossible judgements – those seemingly cheap but really rather costly zeitgeistian thrills – may be passed and then be passed by and then be past.

I do not know where the Korean Presbyterian Church in Queens, New York belongs vis-à-vis the zeitgeist, or even the cyber*geist*. What I know is this: I am eagerly looking forward some few months from now to when I will be able to step, in Queens, into this finished work of Doug and Greg and Michael's, which is still and always I guess will be residing somewhere outside this review, on some other side of the pages in this issue of the journal. Well, I'm hardly the only one looking forward to this moment – the buzz already resounds – which will be an important moment, to many, for however long that moment may be. Why don't we meet up there, you and I, take the tour, see what we might see.

That's all for now. Except to say: with that opening email stuff and this closing salutation of love to you and Ron, there's my four, maybe now six, but whatever the number, always too many and never enough pages, for you.

Mark

Originally published in *Assemblage* 38 (1999), 22–27.

Douglas Garofalo, Greg Lynn and Michael McInturf,
Korean Presbyterian Church of New York, Queens, New York, 1999

SPEAKING IN SYLLABLES

Before trying to speculate about future positions or practices – whether critical or post-critical (stereotyped as 'criticism and resistance' vs 'a language of physical appetites as well as formal operations') – we might talk about *possibly* practising, about how all our practising is going to make its way into all of our objects.

Every issue of every journal, every piece of writing, every building, is always only its performance at the moment, in other words, is nothing but another rehearsal, another practice run.

That's what we all do: we make performances, but these performances, as is the way with all performances, are of their moment, frozen as objects: our buildings are objects, our texts are objects, they're all only objects. So we ought to say it as a verb: I *ob*ject. So that it can convey both meanings: I *ob*ject and I ob*ject*: I make ob*jects* but, or rather, because I *ob*ject within the ob*ject* to this or that, and this is how my object is formed, as an objection to one thing or another, if only to the under-articulation and under-characterisation of certain appetites. In other words: appetite *and* criticism: appetite as criticism, criticism as appetite. Just like the double condition of the subject, as Foucault said: 'subject to someone else by control and dependence; and tied to his own identity by a conscience or self-knowledge', which is also always a performance, a practising, a rehearsal of subjecthood. I *sub*ject and I sub*ject*. That's what we do: we subject ourselves and others and we object ourselves and others, at any given moment, to certain cultural operations and appetites and formulations. We rehearse ourselves. So if William Butler Yeats says: 'We make out of the quarrel with others, rhetoric, but of the quarrel with ourselves, poetry', then it should also be said that all rhetoric is also always a quarrel with ourselves, and all poetry also always a quarrel with others, or let us say in either case a quarrel with the other in our*selves*, a syncopation of the self to itself, a syncopation of the subjective and the objective. Not post-, but intra- and inter-critical.

Speaking of syllables, speaking in syllables: When Drea de Matteo, who plays Adriana on the television show *The Sopranos*, says 'The joke on the set is that I got the part because of the way I said *Ow*. It was like *Ooooowaah* – I turned it into a couple of syllables', well yes, there's humour in this, but it's not a joke, just the fundamental principle of inflection and vocalisation. That's why Christopher Walken spends all that time practising, as he says: standing in front of his Connecticut kitchen window, standing at the sink, looking out at the back woods, repeating line after line, over and over, looking for rhythm, looking for cadence, looking for character, looking for The Voice:

The way I do that is I read the script with an Italian accent, I read it like a certain kind of actor … like Marlon Brando … like Pee-wee Herman … I'll very often try to get Woody Allen's rhythms. One of my favorites – this is going to sound strange – but I think Bugs Bunny is one of the most interesting movie characters of all time. His rhythms, his intelligence, his attitude is very amazing. So I'll do the part like Bugs. I'll do it as a woman… I'll do it as many ways as I can think of.

And all that practising makes its way into his syncopated performances and vocalisations, his em*pha*sis on the right and then the wrong syl*lab*le, his stressing, in prosodic terms, and unstressing those syllables. His voice is always made up of many voices, many stresses and unstresses, many appetites, many criticisms. As at the very end of *Dogs of War,* where he plays the mercenary Jamie Shannon. His mission completed, the ruling dictator deposed, he is sitting with his back to the just arriving wannabe dictator who hired him. 'Youu'rrrrree *late*!', he says, and with his equally syncopated hand and eye and facial gestures

expresses rage, weariness, cunning, belief beyond belief
– all within nine (I timed it) seconds. Just before he gets up,
goes to the presidential desk, opens a draw, pulls out a gun
out, and shoots the dictator. Or as when I saw him performing on Broadway a few months ago, and he, as James Joyce's
Gabriel Conroy, pronounced the word 'ham' as if it had
three syllables, finding syllables where there were none
to be found. That's a trick, of course, that's already in early
and middle and late Joyce: 'Gabriel smiled at the three
syllables she had given his surname and glanced at her.'
Well, isn't that always the trick, the secret? It's what gets
you to look, what gets you to glance: finding syllables, say,
syllables of architectural elements and spaces and writing,
where there are none (seemingly) to be found.

Just analyse the scenes as rendered by Meryl Streep,
Anthony Hopkins, Helen Mirren, Kate Valk, you pick your
favourite, the syncopated rhythms and counter-rhythms
between and within the bodily and vocal gestures, and
compare those to the paucity of most architectural scenes.
Now there's an appetite architecture and architectural
writing could cultivate – in whatever taste seems tasty
to whomever is setting up the tasting. Take Judi Dench's
minimalist performance as Queen Elizabeth in 'Shakespeare in Love', for example: all of the nuanced differentials
between her slow laconic gestures and her rapid laconic
vocalisations, developed in her portrayal an agile and
penetrating wit – indeed in Shakespeare wit is wisdom,
an animated and acute form of revelatory intelligence
(like Hamlet's) – in contrast to the ponderous simplification
of all but the most intensive architectural minimalism.

Or take John Coltrane: while everyone else in the
band would be relaxing between sets at whatever club they
were playing at, Coltrane would be off in some way-back
part of the backstage, practising … *scales*! And it is that
motivic play, that motivic practice, between and within
various scales (chromatic, diatonic, octatonic, pentatonic)
that you can hear throughout Coltrane's (early and middle
and late) work. Or take hip-hop: you could sample and
scratch some syllables, anamorphically moving between

and among sonic abstractions and realisms: ch ch ch chec check checit checkit check it ouuuuuuuuuutttt, or you could add some syllizables: chizeck it out, or take some away: check it. Or some or all of each at once, which is even better, as the most rendered vocalisations in drama and in music (from classical to hip-hop) operate through a syncopation, a differential of syllabification. In the 'you be', 'we be', 'I be' case it's all the better, as DJ Tim B says, so as to get past, present and future tenses working together. Which is more interesting than always trying to occupy, in architecture, say, the past tense or, just as bad, the forever future tense. More interesting to get all the tenses working tensely together.

Originally published in *Assemblage* 41 (2000), 64.

JOHN COLTRANE'S
SAMPLE AND SCRATCH

Lots of people imagine wrongly that 'My Favorite Things' is one of my compositions; I would have loved to have written it but it's by Rodgers and Hammerstein… 'Favorite Things' is my favorite piece of all those I have recorded… This waltz is fantastic: when you play it slowly, it has an element of gospel that's not at all displeasing; when you play it quickly, it possesses other undeniable qualities. It's very interesting to discover a terrain that renews itself according to the impulse that you give it.

John Coltrane interviewed by François Postif in *Jazz Hot*, January 1962

MARLOW: In fact, now that I look at you properly,
                 I can see what you are.

NURSE MILLS: Oh. Can you indeed.

MARLOW: You are the girl in all those songs.
                 Dee dum.

NURSE MILLS: What songs?

MARLOW: The songs. The songs. The bloody,
                 bloody songs.

NURSE MILLS: I wish I knew what you were talking
                 about –

MARLOW: The songs you hear coming up the stair.

NURSE MILLS: Sorry?

MARLOW: When you're a child. When you're
                supposed to be asleep. Those songs.

Dennis Potter, *The Singing Detective*, 1986

I have for so long utilised Coltrane's versions of the Rodgers
and Hammerstein song 'My Favorite Things' as a kind of
guide, one of many, for the operations of my own architecture and art and writing – so long considered his various
versions, or rather his various versionings, not as a model,
but as a *process* of modelling. For, as Godard says: 'We need
to show that there's no model; there's only modelling'. So
when Fareed Armaly asked me to produce something for
his haus.o series at the Künstlerhaus in Stuttgart, but suggested that, due to budgetary reasons, I make not my usual
spatialised multi-media constructions, but a sound-work
based on 'My Favorite Things', this particular piece seemed
so fundamental to me, so already tied up with my work,
that I persisted with numerous nos until his persistence
brought me around to yes.

   Well, it's a tune to be tied up with, to be entangled
with, or so it seems at least from Coltrane's own account,
which may explain why he himself was so tied up with it,
playing it year after year, hundreds of times between the
original recording in 1960 to his last live recording three
months before his death in 1967. Over the years I've searched
– obsessively – for all 28 bootleg and officially released
versions in jazz stores and record auctions from Brussels to
Tokyo. Each version is different of course, from the original
13 minutes to the longest one of 59 minutes in Tokyo in 1966,
and of course I have favourite moments in all of them.

   Coltrane obviously favoured that song, loved that song,
as he himself says in the interview I quote above, but he (or
you) could just as well have hated it – as Dennis Potter says:

> ... it's sometimes the ones I hate the most that give me the most traffic because I become aware of saying to myself, 'Why the hell is it in my head then?' ... The purpose is ... to re-see, re-hear what may be an extraordinarily banal tune and nonsensical lyric. In other words, to give the song the meaning of the emotional and physical surround out of which you are made to re-hear it.

Those bloody, bloody songs, as Marlow says in Potter's *The Singing Detective.* Either way, it's what you're tied up with, it's about entanglements, about whether you choose to re-see and re-enact your entanglements.

What I have been imagining is this: John Coltrane as the first hip-hopper, as the first to sample and scratch lyrical sonics, as hip-hop will do later on with actual lyrics. Coltrane's versions are not just simply and slightly swinging versions, not just formulaic jazzed-up versions. The song says I *simply* remember – 'When the dog bites / When the bee stings / When I'm feeling sad / I simply remember my favorite things / And then I don't feel so bad' – but memory is anything but simple, as Coltrane and hip-hop so vividly demonstrate. Just like hip-hop, it's a mix of sampled histories, cross-histories, counter-histories. Coltrane is remembering, but not simply. His is a complex counter-history of his entanglements. Coltrane as MC.

Among the (favourite) things that he is in the act of re-membering is the melody that is the character that is Mary/Maria: 'the girl in the song', to use Dennis Potter's phrase, who is not Julie Andrews from the film, that's 1965, long after Coltrane's first recording in 1960, but Mary Martin from the Broadway production, that's 1959, the original date. And the scene is not as in the movie, not the forced and frenetic version of Hollywood Maria (Andrews) before all the anxious children at the von Trapp estate, but a duet in the abbey between Broadway Maria (Martin) and the Mother Abbess (played by Patricia Neway). Not a solo governess lesson for anxious children, but an entangled duet between anxious adults, postulant Maria and the Mother Abbess all tied up in various desires and doubts.

Finding that the girl is in the song, finding the desire and doubt, the joy and fear, that already is in the song, well, that can happen, it's how you listen to it. Here, for example, is another Maria: it has been proposed that Bach's *Ciaccona* – the heretofore assumed instrumental section that concludes the Second Partita (in D-Minor) of his six solos for unaccompanied violin – is a 'tombeau', a musical epitaph, for his wife Maria Barbara after her unexpected death in 1720. This discovery by the musicologist Helga Thoene has been recently enacted by Christoph Poppen and the Hilliard Ensemble in their album *Morimur*. Thoene has revealed the choral phrases of death and resurrection – the *feeling sad* ('Grant us patience in times of sorrow'), the fear ('In my beloved God I trust in fear and need'), the doubt ('Where shall I refuge find') and its corresponding desire ('Command now all my pathways'), and finally the *feeling not so bad* ('For this shall we joyful be') – that are encoded into the abstract instrumental music. The entanglements *between* lyric and metre speak to the speaking of entanglements *within* the lyrics: 'Christ lay in death's bondage' and 'From this came, then, death so quick / And seized power over us / Held us in his realm as captives'. Thoene proposes that Bach encoded this lyrical (choral) material in the Partitas, just as he encoded his name and a variety of numerical plays in many of his works, and went so far as to find a way even to encode Maria's name in 'cryptographic form at the opening of the *Ciaccona*'.

And if it seems odd to evoke death in relation to the supposed cheeriness of 'My Favorite Things', then it should be noted that the lyrics for the *Sound of Music* were the last written by Oscar Hammerstein II, the final versions being written with the knowledge of his own stomach cancer that killed him less than a year after the Broadway opening and almost two months to the day, October 21, 1960, that John Coltrane walked into the Atlantic Recording Studio, 234 W 56, to record his original reversioning, just ten short Manhattan blocks due north from the Lunt-Fontanne Theatre, 205 W 46, where *The Sound of Music* had opened 11 months earlier and was still playing on the day Coltrane recorded

Lunt-
Fontanne
Theatre

PLAYBILL

a weekly magazine for theatregoers

THE SOUND OF MUSIC

his version and would continue to play for another year. Who knows: Mary might even have been singing the (very) moment John was playing into the microphone, just blocks from each other. Not within earshot, but certainly within eyeshot, right down Broadway. Close yet far, far yet close?

Finding the lyrics entangled in Coltrane's music is not limited to his interpretations of popular songs: Lewis Porter has rigorously demonstrated how *Psalm*, the concluding section of Coltrane's own 'abstract' composition *A Love Supreme* is nearly word for word, syllable for syllable, a recitation of Coltrane's 'poem', that sentimental prayer that was included in the liner notes of the album, filled with phrases of feeling bad and fearfulness ('Help us resolve our fears and weaknesses'), doubt ('No road is an easy one') and its corresponding desire ('But they all lead back to God'), and joy ('His way is so lovely'). Coltrane's lyrics are, of course, no more or less mawkishly sentimental in conventional and hackneyed religious phrasing than Bach's chorals or Hammerstein's *Sound of Music* lyrics. And while Coltrane, unlike Bach, is not generally known to encode lyrical materials in his abstract sounds, Coltrane made this technique and play quite clear in another interview in the French journal *Jazz Hot* three years after the interview quoted above. Coltrane was then asked about this *Love Supreme* poem and about whether the text aids 'in understanding the music.' He replied: 'This is the longest that I ever wrote but certain pieces of the album *Crescent* are also poems, like "Wise One", "Lonnie's Lament", "The Drum Thing".' I sometimes proceed in this manner because it's a good approach to musical composition. I am also interested in languages, in architecture.'

This manner, the mannerism that is a fundamental principle of every language and every architecture, is among the many ways of finding the lyrical figuration within abstract instrumentation (and instrumentalism), as well as of finding the abstract structuring within the figural (the lyrical). It's a mode (a modality) of questioning: what is form, what is figure and how they are tied up with each other – whether in music or language or architecture – whether you're writing (or designing) your most abstract composition or trying to figure out what your reversioning of 'My Favorite Things' for the Künstlerhaus Stuttgart will be.

Now the question is this:

How do you solve a problem like Maria?

That is the question Rodgers and Hammerstein and Martin and Coltrane and I had to ask ourselves. Even Bach had to.

In the first section, entitled 'Duet Anticipated', of *My Favorite Favorite Things*, my own reversioning, I took what in the original is the vocal alternating of the complete song – Mary sings through all verses first, then the Mother Abbess sings through all the verses, then they alternate the first two bars in the final section, then they duet at the very end – and turned it (through many tactical micro-snips here and there) into the continuous duet between Maria and the Mother Abbess that was already anticipated in the original. Mary Martin in the original is singing slightly faster than Patricia Neway, so removing the gaps between certain vocalised notes allowed the two voices not so much to *totally* match up (that recording studio tendency had to be avoided), but to enact the vocalists' desire to be matching up in time, which in fact reveals their subtle and not so subtle differences and discrepancies and anticipations, revealing also the complex entanglements between the vocalisations and the orchestrations, the entanglements between lyrical (and melodic) desire and doubt. The double orchestration now duets against itself, simultaneously speeding up and slowing down, slowing up and speeding down, dragging against itself while rushing ahead of itself.

In the second section of *My Favorite Favorite Things*, 'MC' (as in Mary Coltranised *or* MC (Master of Ceremonies) Coltrane *or* Martin and Coltrane), I have Mary sing along with John, considering that it was John singing along with Mary to begin with. The pitch and time of her melody has now been adjusted to (almost but not always) match his melody through countless micro-operations involving lyrical annunciation, phrasing and tone – in order to enact its own desires and entanglements to match up in time, to be entangled in time. I say countless because the decisions and iterations have been beyond count, but the computer can and does count, say, the notes of hers that have been operated on, which as of today count up to one thousand, four hundred and five.

The third section 'Dual / Duel / Duet' is an alternate version, an alternate take, of 'MC'. Well, all the sections are alternate takes really: transforming and decoding matter by taking alternatives already available within the object – showing what has been altered by showing that it is alternating with what already was there, but now in an active and animated way. 'Duet Anticipated' and 'MC' are developed as continuous duets, continuous entanglements – alternate versions made simultaneous – in order to show both the continuity and discontinuity between Martin and Neway, between Martin and Coltrane, given that there are moments in 'MC' that are beyond the legible range of Mary, too low, too high, just as there are moments in 'Duet Anticipated' that are too slow, too fast. 'Dual / Duel / Duet' was developed in response to the strict alternating of Maria and the Mother Abbess in the last section of the Broadway original. So now the moments when Mary is dueting with John in 'MC' are no longer layered over the Coltrane track. Now when Mary sings John does not play, when John plays Mary does not sing (those are the moments he is out of her range, after all). What results is a more extreme form of disjunction, but it is also – given that Mary has been Coltranised – uncannily continuous. The structure and the operations are in a way more revealed here, but also more concealed, because the reasons for the operations are no longer made evident. In 'Dual / Duel / Duet' you hear the transformations of Mary more clearly, you hear just how strange her new vocalisations are – in 'MC' you hear the reasons, the motivations, for the transformations (of both Mary and John) more clearly.

What all this constitutes is a retroactive illumination of just how much the girl is in the song, just how continuously (rather than intermittently) faithful Coltrane was to the lyrical material of the original, and just how extraordinarily inventive he was with its reinvention. The process used here to make this lyrical material and its distortional encryption audible and evident is not so different, it turns out, from that employed to decode Bach's *Ciaccona*, as described by Thoene:

The choral melodies employed as a *cantus firmus* can be made audible by prolonging the notes of the violin part with the aid of additional instruments or voices. In order to blend into the musical fabric, the rhythm and metre of the hymns have been freely manipulated. This becomes particularly evident when the chorale quotation has the same pitch sequence as a fugue subject but has been subordinated to its rhythm.

This dialogue in Bach, between the lyrical and the sonic, made evident by the Poppen/Hilliard reversioning, thus now reveals the instrumental version of *Ciaccona* as a self-dialogue – in the way the best dramatic monologues (comic or tragic) are really dialogues with others, or rather, the other(s) in your self. Jazz critic Ekkehard Jost has already called attention to the self-dialogue in Coltrane's music from 1960 through to the late work, which he calls a 'simulated polyphony, in which a single instrument appears to take on the role of two' (or more, as in Bach). This self-dialogue only increases in Coltrane's last years:

In almost all of Coltrane's pieces, there is at one time or another a passage in which he strings together a quick succession of related phrases, two, sometimes three octaves apart. These 'dialogues' … hark back to one of the most traditional elements of jazz, however new and strange it may appear in Coltrane's music. They are highly compressed logogram call-and-response patterns, such as occur in the earliest forms of religious Afro-American music, or – to go back further yet – in African music. Not least for this reason, they would seem to be symptomatic of free jazz as a whole.

This should explain the lyrical resonance of Coltrane's gospel comment regarding *My Favorite Things* in the earlier *Jazz Hot* interview: 'This waltz is fantastic: when you play it slowly, it has an element of gospel.' And it might also explain Jost's use of the word logogram, meaning a sign or character representing a word, which as he says are in call-and-response dialoguing patterns, given that gospel music in performance is a lyrical form of dialogue. It is Coltrane who says in the later *Jazz Hot* interview that this lyrical generator 'is a good approach to musical composition', like, he says, 'in languages, in architecture'.

This self-dialogue between sense and structure, lyric and sonic, or to use Jost's terms 'emotion and construction', is a form of comparative *double description*. As Gregory Bateson said, it doesn't take one to know one, it takes *two* to know one. A syncopation: close yet far, far yet close?

Like when Coltrane switched from his principal tenor saxophone to the soprano saxophone he plays on *My Favorite Things*. In the linear notes to the album he notes the distance this gave him: 'It let me take another look at improvisation. It's like having another hand.'

On and off register from each other, on and off the beat.

Double entanglements: brown paper packages are the things that are tied up with string in the song: from white artist to black artist back now to white artist again: *brown* paper packages, *cream*-coloured ponies, girls in *white* dresses, *silver white* winters. Rodgers' next musical, following Hammerstein's death, the one he wrote both the music and the lyrics for, was called *No Strings Attached*, which was about inter-racial romance, Rodgers having already tried his liberal hand at issues of racism in *South Pacific* and *The Sound of Music*.

As for the entanglement of my collecting that caused Fareed to suggest my entanglement in this project for the Künstlerhaus: although I get much philological pleasure comparing all the various 28 recorded versions of *My Favorite Things* I won't try to convey that favourite kind of thing here, that would be piling abstraction upon abstraction. I just picked my favourite favourite: the Newport Jazz

Festival, 1963, from the middle period, as whatever other
benefits there are to be had with the increased abstraction
of the later versions, they become too atomised by the end,
and the lyrical tension gets muddy, homogeneous, out of focus. Newport was the first live version I heard, long before
I began my quest to collect them all. There is a Stuttgart
version from the same year, and happy I would have been
to have reworked that bit of historical entanglement to the
Künstlerhaus, but *that* bootleg recording is of a lesser quality,
the version is less driven, and it's really not my favourite.

I was only five-years-old and only 35 miles away from
the Newport performance, that night of July 17, 1963. Was
I outside playing still in the late light of July? Was it hot,
was it humid that night in Providence, in Newport, in
Rhode Island? Was I already asleep? Maybe I was already
asleep, or perhaps just drifting off to sleep. Was there music
playing then, not coming up the stairs as in Potter's *Singing
Detective*, as ours was a modernist house and my bedroom
was on the main level, but under the door as in Benjamin's
Berlin Chronicle ('the strip of light under the bedroom door
on evenings when we were 'entertaining'')? Whatever music
may or may not have been playing that night, it wasn't the
music of Coltrane that was playing in our house, we didn't
even have the hi-fi yet, just an older record player for the
then already old 78s: Leadbelly, Woody Guthrie, Talking
Union, Six Songs for Democracy, Marlene Dietrich, Gilbert
and Sullivan, Gershwin, Jazz at the Philharmonic, Mozart,
Beethoven, Bach – the pop and the Broadway musicals and
the rock n' roll would all happen later.

Originally published as 'My Favorite Favorite Things:
Meine liebsten liebsten Dinge' (German translation:
Constanze Ruhm) in Fareed Armaly (ed.),
>REDIRECT (Stuttgart: Künstlerhaus, 2002), 39–45.

AS SETTING, AS SCENE

What distinguishes a locale from a place, let alone a space, at least according to all the dictionaries, is that a place becomes a locale only when it references a particular event or events connected with that place.

Apparently the people who write the dictionaries have not read the anti-space pro-placemaking theories in architecture, even the most recent ones, say just from Aldo van Eyck on, because according to them a 'place' is as empty as a 'space' – another empty vessel, empty of meaning, another empty bag o' building. Which is what van Eyck was positioning himself against in the postwar Team 10 attack on CIAM and its modernist concept of Space, Time and Architecture: 'Space has no room, time not a moment for man. He is excluded … Whatever space and time mean, place and occasion mean more.'

Locale, on the other hand, is a 'scene or setting, as of a novel', or of a film, 'the scene of any event or action'. And thus every architectural and urban scene and scenography that we can imagine is a 'place where some action occurs'. This of course is the problem, this is why architecture hardly seems to be needed, in that any place, whether designed by an architect or not, no matter how lo-cal (or high-cal or no-cal), will be a space where some action occurs.

The lesson of locavore cooking and the slow food movement (as well as nouvelle cuisine) is that the intensification of flavour occurs through developing the relations in and of the ingredients rather than by the addition of rich high-cal sauces, blandishments to cover bland masses of meat. Just like so many tricked out building envelopes with bland background masses. If lo-cal can mean less auxiliary richness, then similarly locale can mean more flavour from the thing itself, however simple or elaborate the cuisine.

Thus if the generality of space-making needs to be avoided, then it is equally important to avoid the xenophobia and latent conservatism that always seem to attend 'placemaking' and 'locavorism'. The current slow food movement, like some other instances of preservation movements in the past, while conserving traditional culture, is resistant to evolution, resistant to innovation. And as is often cited, in certain cases the 'carbon footprint' of a locally grown tomato may even be greater (and the flavour much less) than a can of San Marzano tomatoes shipped halfway round the world. Local does not guarantee anything.

Every architect should realise that they are simultaneously inside and outside – local *to* and distant *from* – their own culture. Architects are always anthropologists – in their particular area of professional attention. But isn't that the very definition of practice, of being a professional, any professional? You need to be outside your culture in order to practise an intensification of your professional area of expertise – in order to bring it (back) inside the general culture.

So it's impossible to practise as an architect totally from inside a local culture and context. Thankfully. By definition you are no longer part of the vernacular, you are on the outside looking back in, which indeed is your expertise, so from that outside distance you may perceive some aspects of *in*habitation, some attributes of inner intimacy that are always impossible to perceive from the normal inside.

If being totally within the local context is an impossibility for an architect, so is being totally outside the context. Thankfully. If Rem Koolhaas in *SMLXL* infamously said 'Fuck Context' (or to be more precise said that's the subtext of Bigness), what is called for (however you take the literal meaning of the first word in that phrase) is engagement and relationship, making love, making war, but definitely not oblivious or autonomous what*ever*ness. So no one should be surprised when the shaping of Seattle Public Library is explained or justified through its directional relation to Mount Rainier and Elliott Bay. Or that the diagonal void through the Netherlands Embassy in Berlin is described as being formed in relation to the existing landmark television tower (the former East German *Fernsehturm*). Or that the first double-page spread of the Casa da Musica in *Content* (you can see it on their website too) is looking towards its bare white sloping surface from the adjoining bare sloping white rendered surfaces of the low housing units, the laundry hung out to dry cantilevering toward the theatre. Or that in each of these projects OMA has sought to burrow an exterior public space into and through the interior of the building.

In the psychological register, what Jacques Lacan called extimacy is, as Jacques-Alain Miller notes, not the opposite of intimacy, but the exterior that 'topologically' is immersed in the very most intimate interior. Architecture always attempts to hold within itself the social and psycho-logical scene of its cultural context. It is its own anthropol-ogy, the study of its own local and global rituals, if only we had the distance to see it. So beyond space, beyond place, what all these dictionaries suggest is that architecture may not merely be any old local container for an event, but can enact its events in its manifestation of enacting itself as setting, as scene.

As locale: novel, film, architecture, urbanism.

Originally published in Stella Betts and David Leven (eds.), *LoCal City* (New York: Parsons the New School for Design, 2012), 32.

DESIRE
AND DOUBT

IDENTITY AND THE DISCOURSE
OF POLITICS IN
CONTEMPORARY ARCHITECTURE

In speaking of the discourse of politics *in* contemporary architecture I have turned around the title of the conference, *The Politics of Contemporary Architectural Discourse*, in order to speak to the question of this 'in' – the question of what discourses, what politics, may be said to be in contemporary architecture.

I am going to say that this 'in' is a problem of identification. And its failure.

And the failure of this failure.

Following Ernesto Laclau, I would say the political may be defined as the very constitutive, the very instituting, dimensions of social practices – which attempt to give a fixed, stable and unified identity to these practices (whether psychological, social, nationalistic, familial or sexual) in order to conceal the very contingencies of these practices. Laclau:

The social world presents itself to us, primarily, as a sedimented ensemble of social practices accepted at face value, without questioning the founding acts of their institution. If the social world, however, is not entirely defined in terms of repetitive, sedimented practices, it is because the social always overflows the institutionalised frameworks of 'society', and because social antagonisms show the inherent contingency of those frameworks. Thus a dimension of construction and creation is inherent in all social practice.[1]

There is, in other words, no identity that is definitively fixed, stable and unified. The constructive act of identification always fails – there are always supplements, instabilities, fragmentation, slippages, there are always 'unwelcome effects' – 'distortions and excesses that point at its precarious and contingent constitution'.[2] The search for such an ideal identity, that obscure object of desire, that desire, in Freud's words, 'to convince oneself that it is still there', never results in the ideal object.[3] As Jacques Lacan observed: 'The object is encountered and is structured along the path of repetition – to find the object again, to repeat the object. Except, it never is the same object which the subject encounters. In other words, he never ceases generating substitutive objects.'[4]

The history of architecture is a history of substitutive objects. Of surrogate objects and stand-in objects. And of their failure, the failure of these substitutive objects to hold, the failure of these objects to shore up the failure of identification. The complex and conflicting desire in the Renaissance to find the objects and principles of antiquity, to repeat those objects and principles only to generate substitutive representations of antiquity, is one particularly poignant moment in our history.

There have been and continue to be both architectural tendencies that embrace the attempt to develop stable, fixed and unified identities (certain neo-classicisms, certain neo-vernaculars) and architectural tendencies that embrace the failure of any such identification to hold (certain neo-avant-gardisms).

But there is a further turn: this failure of identification also always fails to hold – this failure is not the permanent undoing of identity, but rather the constitutive condition for identity – as further attempts to shore up identity are effectuated in order to fill the lack generated by this failure: 'Failure will trigger new acts of identification … which attempt (vainly) to master those destructuring effects… This is why there is a permanent and alternating movement whereby the lack is rejected and invoked, articulated and annulled, included and excluded.'[5]

This might also explain another failure. The failure to sufficiently confine the concept of political architecture to buildings that unashamedly display their ideology – say, to use yet again that overused example: Nazi architecture. Because as we should know by now the so-called stripped-down classicism of Hitler's Germany is not *sufficiently* un-like the so-called stripped-down classicism of Stalin's Russia or the so-called stripped-down classicism of Roosevelt's New Deal America.

This failure of pure and definitive ideological expression does not prove that there is no ideological component to architecture. On the contrary, the failure of ideological identification forever triggers further attempts at explicit or implicit ideological identifications in architecture.

It is a common notion of our 'postmodern' times that different programmes can inhabit the same space because, it is said, programmes are completely independent from architectural spatiality. But it is the similarity, not the disparity, between institutional identities, and between the identities of institutions and architectures, that allows for this interchangeability of inhabitation and management. It has been said, by Viktor Shklovsky, and repeated, by many, that the colour of art has never reflected that of the flag atop the citadel. Given the temporal lags and conceptual gaps at work between built form and ideologies, one could say, provisionally: yes, the 'colours' of art and the 'colours' of government have varying rates of change, so as never to allow a total or definitively reflective identification of one to the other.[6] But – here's the provision – the social form of this thing we call government and this thing we call architecture remains surprisingly the same. That is because government, the act of government – and one might say the act of architecture – remains the same; that is, '"the conduct of conduct" … a form of activity aiming to shape, guide, or affect the conduct of some persons or persons',[7] regardless of whether any particular government or act or conduct or architecture might be judged to be of negative or of positive value.

Thus the most significant forms of ideological identification in architecture are not the Big Symbols – the Classical

Orders, the Flags, the Animals of Political Myth (the Eagles, the Lions), the Medallions, the Exhortative Inscriptions, the Instructional Frescos and Murals and Sculptures – but the accrual of the *small symbols*, the small interpellative symbols: the ways in institutional space that architecture organises, hierarchises and systematises activities, behaviours, orderings, visibilities, movements.

Thus the flag over the citadel may change, but there will always remain that architectural element: the Flagpole. Specified, no doubt, from *Sweet's Catalog* – or the historical equivalent – or delegated by some senior architect to some junior architect to be design-developed in some more or less jaunty style, handed over with that phrase that more or less translates to:

'Here, have some fun with this.'

If it's not the flagpole, then it's its ideological equivalent – say, this Speakers' Table I am sitting behind, or the rows of Audience Chairs you are sitting in, facing this table.

This is why there may be little difference between, say, a doorway surrounded by neoclassical mouldings and a doorway stripped of all mouldings. Neither doorway necessarily addresses in an aggressive manner the constitutive construction, the political instituting, of the social and psychological identifications of threshold interaction (and its failure) that circulate around the architectural condition of every doorway. Herein lies architecture's compulsion to repeat, which rather than being acknowledged as a symptom – as a mechanism for organising the desires around which we circulate – instead functions as a defence mechanism against actively questioning the constitutive dimension of its forms.[8]

But may it not be possible to construct an architecture that embraces neither identification nor its failure, that *renders visible* the construct of both the inevitability of the attempts at identity and the failure of these attempts – that renders visible the construct of its own identity and the identity of the inhabiting subject?[9]

Mannerism, as an aesthetic model, might seem to be precisely the sort of model to address architectural identity

and its failure. Except that to this day, architectural mannerism has focused, with few exceptions, on the private
architectural language of columns, cornices and mouldings, rather than on the public language of the mannerisms
of everyday life. There is, of course, no point in privileging
one or the other, as each should be used against the other
to reveal more about each other.

Jean-Luc Godard has addressed the ridiculousness
of privileging either so-called private ('high-art') languages
or so-called public ('everyday') languages:

**Such distinctions have never been made in music. No one
says, 'Rock is documentary and J.S. Bach is fiction.' It just
isn't said. In cinema I don't know how it happened … but
we think we know what documentary and fiction mean.
Actually, I do believe that there is a difference between
the two modes and I see to some extent what it is, but it's
not so easy. When is a worker's gesture fiction, or that of a
mother toward her child, or of one lover toward another?
At what point? One calls it documentary if, at the moment
he was filmed, the person was really saying that: that is,
if he wasn't asked to say it. The director did not ask him
to say it. But when a child says 'Mom' to his mom, it may
have been his mom who got him to say it, so that his mom
becomes the director at that point.**[10]

'A film for me, then', he continues, 'is a documentary,
or fragmented view of reality, with a certain amount of dramatisation.'[11] This might stand as a significant definition for
architecture as well: a documentary, or fragmented view of
reality, with a certain amount of dramatisation. What might
be considered to be the documentary aspect of architecture, and what is its fictionalisation or dramatisation? Let's
take … function, for example: function as something that's
supposed to be direct, straightforward, matter-of-fact,
without fiction, without drama – function, let's say, in both
senses: the functions of everyday life and the functions of
the architectures that are supposed to respond to, to solve,
the functions of everyday life. What, to use the Lacanian

formulation, is in function more than function? What 'cannot be swallowed, as it were, which remains stuck in the gullet of the signifier'? What are the 'unwelcome effects', one might even say unwelcome architectural effects, what are the 'distortions and excesses that point at its precarious and contingent constitution'?[12]

If, as Lacan posited, desire is the difference that results when you subtract need from demand, the demand that will not be satisfied by the functional satisfaction of the need – in Slavoj Žižek's example of the cry of the infant, the need (for milk) from the demand (for the attentions of love)[13] – then what are the demands of function that exceed the needs of function, what, in other words, are the desires of function? The desires of programme? The desires of everyday life? The desires that circulate around a door, say, or around the way a window penetrates a wall, or around the way a wall confronts a ceiling, or around the way one mass confronts another mass, or around the way a building confronts a city. The desires, say, that pertain to the inevitable topological enfolding of self and other, absence and presence, inside and outside, private and public at work at every level of social and psychological inhabitation – and that thus might be engaged architecturally in terms of revealing their political constitution.

This formulation, by the way, might explain the politics of yet another architectural failure: the failure of social housing. The satisfaction of need (minimum housing) seldom produces satisfaction, because the demand is not for the instrumental act of housing but for social care and architectural attention, beyond any reductive functionalism. As Lacan says, 'the subject remains all the more deprived to the extent that the need articulated in the demand is satisfied',[14] which should explain why those provided with what passes for the brute documentary of most social housing continue to feel socially and architecturally deprived.

A particular locus for this enfolded condition of documentary and fiction, of refined art and quotidian life, for Godard, is the everyday gesture, as he indicates in his comments on Robert Flaherty's 'documentary' *Nanook of the North* and his own 'drama' *A Married Woman*:

What is interesting in *Nanook*, for example, is the moment during which Nanook raises his harpoon and then waits ... and the waiting begins. In fact the look – Nanook is indeed looking at his wait – is closely tied to waiting... We all know very well in love relations, as in work relations, there is a point at which one makes a gesture toward the other... It was precisely this look onto the gesture, and the gesture of waiting itself, and then the catching of something, instead of a fish, let's say we catch a hand, and this hand – depending on what it does for you – will gratify your hunger as well.[15]

Godard's interest is not in the specific humanistic gesture of this act, but in the act of this act, in the generality of this act, in how one occupies oneself in these acts – how one occupies oneself, and is occupied, by and through the occupation of social and psychological roles in space and in time. By extension, one might suggest that these forms of occupation are always in relation to the spatial and temporal occupation of buildings and spaces, the occupation, that is, of institutional, and thus political, space.

What gestures does architecture make in response to the gestures of bodies? The gesture that conventional architecture tends to make toward bodies is to reduce the body to a series of documented and documentary standardised measures, proper behaviours, ergonomic formulations. In other words, architecture's gesture is to match, and thus spatially constitute, these already socially determined reductions of the body.

In other words, the gestures of architecture already precede the body, are already in place before any bodies interact with them, and thus architecture constitutes and manages these bodies (that eventually do interact with it) through socially determined architectural configurations of walls, doors, tables, chairs, podiums, desks, file cabinets, closets and so on – whose purpose is to put into place socially determined 'proper' ways (proper identities) of working, waiting, eating, and so on. Conventional architecture attempts to mask this social determination of behaviours by giving its gestures the appearance of economy, naturalness, matter-of-factness.

But, as Bertolt Brecht noted, gestures are not matters-of-fact, rather they are always *adopted and directed* toward another, toward others. Brecht entitled this social condition of the gesture its *gest*:

The realm of attitudes adopted by the characters towards one another is what we call the realm of gest. Physical attitude, tone of voice and facial expression are all determined by a social gest: the characters are cursing, flattering, instructing one another, and so on. The attitudes which people adopt towards one another include even those attitudes which would appear to be quite private, such as the utterances of physical pain in illness, or of religious faith.[16]

This is what Brecht said about gestures, but what does the *Oxford Dictionary* say? *Oxford* says: 'significant movement of limb or body; use of such movement as expression of feeling or as rhetorical device'.[17]

It says: '(fig) step or move calculated to evoke response from another or to convey (esp. friendly) intention.'

It says: 'L *gerere* gest – wield.'

As in: the way you and I may wield our hands during the lunch break in that social and psychological gesture known as the Hand Shake. Or: the way I am wielding my hand right now in that sort of Committed Public Speaker gesture that is supposed to emphasise my points. Or: the way you are wielding your hand right now in that Thoughtful Audience gesture: poised on your leg, folded across your chest, or positioned on your face.

Following Brecht (and *Oxford*), one might say that the gestures of architecture, like the gestures of the body, are already rhetorical gestures toward others – already steps or moves 'calculated to evoke response from another' – are already social gestures.

In other words, the social is not restricted to, and cannot be reduced to, selected programmes focused on selected groups of narrowly designated 'users' – the homeless, the poor, the aged, the disabled. It is rather too easy for architecture to appear under the 'sign' of the social by selecting and 'constructing' one of the aforementioned programmes in some diagrammatic manner (under the excuse of budgetary constraints) without ever addressing what is social within the programme or within the particular design. On the other hand, it is rather easy for 'high design' to avoid addressing issues of the social, never mind attempting any of these programmes.

In other words: all architecture is social architecture. All architecture is political architecture.

But if the gestures of architecture are already social, already political, their repetition as conventions requires that they be interrogated as such to reveal this condition. Brecht: 'This means that the artist has to adopt a definite attitude … he cannot let it [the gesture] just speak only for itself, simply expressing it as the fact dictates'.[18] As it does, for example, in this speaker's table. As it does, for example, in your chairs. As it does, for example, in these walls.

The drawing forth of what is social in the gesture, of the 'attitudes adopted by the characters towards one another', requires, according to Brecht, the finding and developing of the gest in the gesture. A gest is, in John Willett's words, 'at once gesture and gist, attitude and point: one aspect of the relation between two people, studied singly, cut to essentials and physically or verbally expressed'.[19] The term 'essentials' here refers to the framing of (what in dynamical systems theory would be designated as) singularities, not to some reduction of the complexity of the social and psychological field.[20] Brecht: 'These expressions of a gest are highly complicated and contradictory, so that they cannot be rendered by a single word and the actor must take care that in giving his image the necessary emphasis he does not lose anything, but emphasises the entire complex.'[21] And as architectural elements act as actors – actors, that is, that also direct – the focus in Willett's definition on the relation between two people might be extended to refer to the relation between two entities (such as subject and subject or subject and object or object and object).

There are, by the way, many directing actors in this drama of inhabitation we are enacting right here and now. We think we can sit anywhere or any way in this room, but just like the child in Godard's example, if you are sitting in one of these chairs in this big room, facing me, next to other people sitting in another of these same chairs, all facing me, and I am sitting up here behind this speakers' table, facing you and all these other people, it's because the architecture got us to sit and face this way, so the architecture has become the director at this point.

This directing is the interpellating, the hailing – hey, you there – effect of ideology posited by Louis Althusser:

Ideology 'acts' or 'functions' in such a way that it 'recruits' subjects among the individuals (it recruits them all), or 'transforms' the individuals into subjects (it transforms them all) by that very precise operation which I have called *interpellation* or hailing… The individual *is interpellated as a (free) subject in order that he shall submit freely to the commandments of the Subject, ie, in order that he shall (freely) accept his subjection*, ie, in order that he shall make the gestures and actions of his subjection 'all by himself'.[22]

It is this ideological hailing that we always feel is addressing us, this hailing, as Étienne Balibar suggests, not from 'a Big Brother, but a Big Other – as Lacan would say – always already shifting in an ambivalent manner between the visible and the invisible, between individuality and universality'.[23] And it is this ideological hailing to which we always respond 'all by ourselves' – whether our response is an attempt to refuse it ('sorry, you have the wrong person'), to ignore it ('I'm not listening'), or to accept it (as is the case with us today, all of us as we entered this room to attend this symposium, saying, 'yes, thank you' when these chairs said, 'hey, you there, sit – within these social relations – here'). In other words, each and every one of these responses already affirms, as *responses*, the very gesture of this hailing.

Just as with the case of the failure of a definitive ideological expression in architecture, these ideological interpellations – within or without architecture – never provide, and never can provide, a definitive identity for the subject. They will always fail, precisely because what this hailing addresses, above all else, is the ambivalence, the ambiguity, the doubt, the excess, the trauma, the radical uncertainty of identification. But this failure, far from inhibiting the process of ideological identification, merely triggers further attempts, both by the subject and by the architecture, to fill the gap caused by this failure.

This process is the same for the act of management. It is not that architecture itself manages us in some definitive way. It is we who desire to find ourselves already considered, already recognised, already managed – in some stable and unambiguous way. And it is precisely architecture's failure to do so without some slippage that causes us continually to structure architecture in such a way so as to be our director, our manager. Even the architects of the most 'radical' buildings find themselves under the sway of the entire range of (conscious and unconscious) interpellative codings at work in architecture: from site planning to space planning, from programmatic convention to 'way-finding' circulation, from the visual to the constructional systemisation of building components – the whole business of it all to get us to feel defined in our citizenship as architectural and ideological participants, architectural and ideological users, as inevitably it all will (attempt to), whatever the form of social organisation, whatever the historical moment.

In other words, to 'hey, you there' we will always (even, or especially, unconsciously) respond – hesitantly or defensively:

'Who me?'

Who, in other words, is this *me*? Who am I, such that I am within this hailing of the social field, within this hailing of the Other, within this desire of the Other? Who am I, in other words, such that my desire is to be recognised and identified in the desire of the Other?

Even the Lacanian reversal performed by Žižek – 'it is never the individual which is interpellated as subject, *into* subject; it is on the contrary the subject itself who is interpellated as x (some specific subject-position, symbolic identity or mandate)'[24] – leads us back to this room, back to the interpellative gestures of this room. If we have entered this auditorium to attend this symposium, obviously we desire to be identified within the (range of) social relations that pertain to this institutional type of individual and collective identification:

We do not recognise ourselves in the ideological call because we were chosen; on the contrary, we perceive ourselves as chosen, as the addressee of a call, because we recognise ourselves in it – *the contingent act of recognition engenders retroactively its own necessity.*[25]

This is why, in this otherwise undifferentiated field of auditorium chairs that you are sitting in – all of which face this table – you not only feel that you can choose to sit anywhere, feel that you can manage your immediate environment, but you even feel that you can choose *your* individual chair, the one that *fits* your *individual and collective* identity – the *one* in the front or the *one* in the back or the *one* by the window or the *one* next to … *what? who*?

And you feel this to such an extent that when you return to this room after the lunch break you may find yourself saying:

'Excuse me, but *you* are sitting in *my* chair.'

We work (this ideological interpellation) *all by ourselves*.

To such an extent that we do not know who or what is directing.

This is the very definition of ideology. And, as Laclau suggests, of the political.

And nowhere in this room is the politics of this remarkable event of social address and counter-address being addressed by this architecture, except as the so-called facts – the unexamined historical and social conventions – dictate.

This is the problem. This is the problem with the architecture of this room, and with the architecture of most rooms, of most buildings, no matter how 'avant-garde'. The problem is this: there is a complex (and always conflicted range) of social and psychological relations, narratives, desires, gestures and identifications that pertain to this 'auditorium' event – as to any and every architectural event – and yet only a narrowly restricted few of these relations are being consciously identified by the architecture of this room and by the architecture of most rooms.

Consequently, this is one condition of architecture and the architectural event wherein certain critical, engaging and constructive operations in architecture might be enacted. Every event, as it is constructed through an architecture, is already its own representation. So then, one might reveal it as such, construct it as such, enact it as such: in the gesture of its gesture, in the construct of its gesture, in the contingency and oscillation of its (interpellative) identity and failure. So that, *in use*, the subject's own gesture may be considered in relation to its representation – may be seen as already a construct – in relation to the reciprocal yet contrasting construct and construction of the architecture. Brecht: 'The actor must show an event, and he must show himself. He naturally shows the event by showing himself, and he shows himself by showing the event. Although the two tasks coincide, they must not coincide to such a point that the contrast (difference) between them disappears.'[26] And as every event is experienced as part of a larger complex, every event may be revealed to be involved with other events – with the various constructions and re-presentations of these events, with their affiliative tensions. In other words, with various constructions (identifications and failures of identification) of the subject.

Like the *tactical* operations suggested by Michel de Certeau, a gestic approach finds as its site the conventional form of the gesture, which it must interrogate, unfold, unpack, disengage from its interpellative, its hegemonic, identity – before reconfiguring, reinterpellating, refolding, reconstructing.[27] In other words, a gestic approach finds specific social and psychological narratives already within the physical form of conventional gesture, in order first to reveal them and then to operate on them.

The gest, in other words, is never general. The gest is a specific gesture situated within the general field of the social. Thus to articulate this specificity is not to find it in contrast with the abstract, but to find that the specific is already a (localised) form of social abstraction, of psychological abstraction, that nevertheless is repeatedly actualised by the subject as a 'genuine' (non-abstract) activity. Contrawise: that a gesture is perceived by the subject as 'genuine' does not make it any less of a social and psychological abstraction, any less of a construction.

But let us consider, for a moment, an opposing *strategy*: a rejection of such an enfolding of the specific and the abstract. A rejection of the specific, the local, the everyday, in favour of the abstract, would require more than just a benign ignoring, as this is business-as-usual for most architecture. It would require a refusal, a radical refusal, a refusal that would be in the end, of course, impossible, but that nevertheless might have more or less interesting consequences depending on the acknowledgement both of its attempt and of its failure. But it would require a refusal at more than just the macro-scale (this is a common strategy), which then gets filled up at the micro-scale with all the standard furniture, appliances, handrails, signage, all that which mocks the efforts at 'difference' and 'otherness' being made in the so-called *proper* place of architecture, at the periphery, in other words, of everyday life along the walls and the ceiling.

The everyday always returns, in a return of the repressed, to capture the subject's attention in the place where that – your, everyone's – attention always is: the everyday.

Thus the architecture that ignores the everyday allows itself, sets itself up – to be ignored in the everyday, or you could say, to be ignored everyday. But to ignore the wider, more abstract conditions in favour of the specific is to develop just another reductive form of instrumental 'problem-solving', and thus also to be ignored everyday. In other words, to reject the specific or the abstract in favour of the other is to miss the opportunity to play each off the other, to problematise each by the other.

But this is not about a casual mixing. The abstract may be considered to be most productively located and inter-rogated within that place where it is least expected: the spe-cific, the everyday, the concrete – as Ezra Pound suggested:

Don't use such an expression as 'dim lands of *peace*'. It dulls the image. It mixes an abstraction with the concrete. It comes from the writer's not realising that the natural object is always the *adequate* symbol.[28]

In other words, everyday objects, so-called natural objects: chairs, podiums, coatrooms, handrails, kitchens, closets, doors, walls are already *adequate* symbols for the exploration and interrogation of social and formal identities and meanings, as they are already the objects around which these identities and meanings circulate. But such an interro-gation would require a 'representation that … allows us to recognise its subject, but at the same time makes it seem un-familiar', in order to 'free socially conditioned phenomena from that stamp of familiarity which protects them against our grasp today'.[29] Thus, as in writing, what is required is a reframing, a reconfiguration, to bring out these meanings, precisely because these objects are perceived as 'natural'.

In this reconfiguration, on the one hand, form and detail and architectural effects are of primary importance, but not for their own sake, as Brecht's collaborator Kurt Weill noted in his comments on gestic theatre: 'It is inter-ested in material things *only up to the point* at which they furnish the frame of or the pretext for human relations.'[30] On the other hand, from the opposite direction: the conceptual basis of the work as it relates to human relations is only relevant to the extent that it can be, in Willett's words, 'conveyed in concrete terms', can be developed in form and detail and architectural effects. Or in Martin Esslin's words: 'The inner life [of the characters] is irrelevant

… *except insofar* as it is expressed in their outward attitudes and actions',[31] that is, in designed or built form.

In other words, no Big Symbols standing in for everyday events, just everyday events (even if, or rather, precisely because, these events are already within the symbolic field), but *events*, that is, reconstructed in the (Foucauldian) sense characterised by John Rajchman: as moments 'of erosion, collapse, questioning, or problematisation of the very assumptions of the setting within which a drama may take place – occasioning the chance or possibility of another, different setting … like those events in a drama which take the drama itself as an event'.[32] Brecht: 'The idea is that the spectator should be put in a position where he can make comparisons about everything that influences the way human beings behave.'[33]

In positing this possibility of a gestic architecture, let me propose two orders of architectural gest.

The first order of architectural gest might operate on a global level (while still being actualised at the local level) by revealing that architectural elements are actors in this social and psychological drama of interpellation and inhabitation, that in their acts and gestures of 'functional' accommodation these elements are, in fact, directing actors. This operation reveals and reconfigures gestic networks throughout the given institutional space – whether new or under renovation – thus providing opportunities for localised (second-order) gests. It is important to configure these localised events along a confluence of networks so that they become more than random, idiosyncratic gestures, so that they accrue in ways that refer to more general conditions. Just as it is important to reveal that desires are more than random and idiosyncratic, to reveal that they accrue in ways that refer to more general conditions. In both cases, one of the general conditions that might be referred to is the very process of interpellation, identification and identity. This play between local and global identity is also in accordance with the principle of complex emergent behaviours in dynamical theory, as posited by Chris Langton: 'From the interaction of the individual components … emerges some kind of global property… And the global property, this emergent behaviour, feeds back to influence the behaviour of the individuals … that produced it.'[34]

The second order of architectural gest might thus operate specifically on local singularities, local events. In fact, it needs these singularities to develop its own internal differences (of any significance) so as not to become just another totalising system. It needs, in other words, these singularities to problematise its own construction, its own interpellations, its own identities. It does this by actualising its accommodations in a directed (to wit: exaggerated) manner, by demonstrating its knowledge. 'Knowledge of what?' (asks one of the characters in Brecht's 'A Dialogue about Acting') 'Of human relations, of human behaviour, of human capacities' (replies the other). 'All right; that's what they need to know. But how are they to demonstrate it?' And the reply is: 'Consciously, suggestively, descriptively.'[35]

Consciously, suggestively, descriptively: the intensification and exaggeration of this knowledge in a simultaneously descriptive (documentary) and suggestive (fiction) manner is necessary because, as I suggested earlier, conventional architecture already accommodates, in Brecht's phrase, 'the habits and usage of the body',[36] but in a reductive, diagrammatic and 'trancelike' fashion, without acknowledging that these accommodations are socially constructed, provisional, ideological.

To reconfigure this accommodation is not a matter of constructing 'a better mouse-trap', but of revealing the social gests already within conventional accommodation, of interrogating the interpellative instrumentalism of these gestures, practices, narratives, events, even if the result must itself be instrumental in some manner – cannot, as architecture, not be instrumental – but might in its own instrumentality examine, thematise, problematise this instrumentality. The question, then, for this second order of gest is not, *have* you addressed ('accommodated') the event?, but *how* have you addressed the event?, how have you addressed it, such that in its architecturalisation some *form* of gest is revealed and, in addition, is reconfigured, is troped?

I will end by referring once more to Godard: 'We need to show that there's no model; there's only modelling.'[37] No social model, no aesthetic model, just the act of social modelling and the act of aesthetic modelling, which, if they do not amount to the same thing, at least one must say that they are forever inseparable, forever enfolded.

But perhaps now I should turn the title of the conference back around and make at least one explicit statement about the politics of contemporary architectural discourse before I end. So let me say this: some people are upset with theory. Or rather: some people are upset with certain current theoretical discourses. Why? Because certain current theoretical discourses refuse to posit definitive models. Some people, I guess, don't want theories – they want models, they want precedents, they want types, they want coefficients: ergonomic, thermal, structural, social, aesthetic coefficients.

And these certain current theoretical discourses just aren't delivering the coefficients.

So I must emphasise again that when I say that *some* form of gest might be revealed through the approach outlined in this talk, this is because no attempt could or should represent some definitive development of the gests of any event. There are any number of gestures in any event that might be reconfigured as any number of gests.

Like here, for example. At the end of this talk.

Because if you are listening to this right now, if your body is being directed toward me by some architecture and my body is being directed toward you by some architecture, then you know that I wrote this for you.

As a gesture to you.

You: my colleague, respondent, editor, client, collaborator, director, audience.

You: my user.

Originally presented at *The Politics of Contemporary Architectural Discourse*, Tulane University School of Architecture, October 1994, and published in *Assemblage* 27 (1995), 9–18.

TECTONIC ACTS OF DESIRE AND DOUBT

NOTES

1. Ernesto Laclau, 'Introduction' in *The Making of Political Identities*, ed. Ernesto Laclau (New York: Verso, 1994), 3.

2. Ernesto Laclau and Lilian Zac, 'Minding the Gap: The Subject of Politics' in *The Making of Political Identities*, 32.

3. Sigmund Freud, 'Negation' in Freud, *Collected Papers*, vol V, ed. James Strachey (London: Hogarth Press, 1952), 184.

4. Jacques Lacan, *The Seminar of Jacques Lacan: Book II, The Ego in Freud's Theory and in the Technique of Psychoanalysis*, ed. Jacques-Alain Miller (New York: Norton, 1988), 100.

5. Laclau and Zac, 'Minding the Gap', 33.

6. By temporal lag between ideologies and built form I am referring, for example, to the time between the height of the 'open classroom' pedagogical movement and the appearances of the first built examples, and to the degree to which these built examples may even have assisted in the movement's decline.

   As George Duby notes (in 'Ideologies in social history', in *Constructing the Past: Essays in Historical Methodology*, ed. Le Goff and Nora, 158–59) ideologies indicate changes in 'the lived reality of social organisation … slowly and reluctantly, because they are by nature conservative. They are the locus of a process of adaptation, but this is sometimes very slow and always remains partial. Moreover, in a subtle dialectical process, the weight of ideological representations is sometimes such as to hold back the development of material and political structures…'

7. Colin Gordon, 'Governmental Rationality: an introduction' in *The Foucault Effect: Studies in Governmentality*, ed. Graham Burchell, Colin Gordon and Peter Miller (Chicago: University of Chicago, 1991), 2.

8. I discuss the relationship between this compulsion to repeat and the uncanny in 'Spatial Narratives', in this volume.

9. Laclau, 'Introduction', 4.

10. Jean-Luc Godard, 'Introduction à une véritable histoire du cinéma', *Camera Obscura* 8–9–10 (Fall 1982), 76–77.

11. Ibid., 77. These issues inevitably lead back to the long-standing debate in cinema and photography between the *vérité* of documentary and the *vérité* of fiction. Bertolt Brecht's words only increase in relevance in this regard: '… the situation is complicated by the fact that less than ever does the mere reflection of reality reveal anything about reality. A photograph of the Krupp works or the AEG tells us next to nothing about these institutions. Actual reality has slipped into the functional. The reification of human relation – the factory, say – means that they are no longer explicit. So something must in fact be *built up*, something artificial, posed.' (Quoted in Walter Benjamin, 'A Small History of Photography', *One Way Street and Other Writings* (New York: Verso, 1979), 255. Emphasis in original.)

12. Jacques Lacan, *The Four Fundamental Concepts of Psycho-Analysis* (New York: Norton, 1977), 270.

13. Jacques Lacan, *Écrits: A Selection* (New York: Norton, 1977), 287: 'Thus desire is neither the appetite for satisfaction, nor the demand for love, but the difference that results from the subtraction of the first from the second, the phenomenon of their splitting (*Spaltung*).' Slavoj Žižek's example is from his *Tarrying*

with the Negative: Kant, Hegel, and the Critique of Ideology* (Durham: Duke University Press, 1983), 120.

14. Lacan, *Écrits: A Selection*, 263.

15. Godard, 'Introduction à une véritable histoire du cinéma', 81.

16. Bertolt Brecht, 'A Short Organum for the Theatre', in *Brecht on Theatre*, ed. John Willett (New York: Hill and Wang, 1964), 198.

17. *The Concise Oxford Dictionary*, ed. J.B. Sykes (New York: Oxford University Press, 1982), 414.

18. Bertolt Brecht, 'On Gestic Music', in *Brecht on Theatre*, 105.

19. John Willett, *The Theatre of Bertolt Brecht* (London: Eyre Methuen, 1977), 173. For other commentary on Brecht's concept of the gest, see Walter Benjamin, *Understanding Brecht* (London: Verso, 1983); Roland Barthes, 'Diderot, Brecht, Eisenstein', in Barthes, *Image–Music–Text* (New York: Hill and Wang, 1977), 69–78; and Gilles Deleuze, *Cinema 2: The Time–Image* (Minneapolis: University of Minnesota Press, 1989), 189–203, 315.

20. Sanford Kwinter, 'Landscapes of Changes: Boccioni's *Stati d'animo* as a General Theory of Models', *Assemblage* 19 (December 1992), 58: 'In a general sense singularities designate points in any continuous process ... where a merely quantitative or linear development suddenly results in the appearance of a "quality" ... A singularity in a complex flow of materials is what makes a rainbow appear in a mist, magnetism arise in a slab of iron, or either ice crystals or conventional currents emerge in a pan of water.'

21. Brecht, 'A Short Organum for the Theatre', 198.

22. Louis Althusser, 'Ideology and Ideological State Apparatuses (Notes towards an Investigation)', in Althusser, *Lenin and Philosophy and other Essays* (New York: Monthly Review Press, 1971), 174, 182. On the ambiguites and excesses of interpellation, see Slavoj Žižek's *The Sublime Object of Ideology* (London: Verso, 1989), 43–44.

23. Étienne Balibar, 'Subjection and Subjectivation', in *Supposing the Subject*, ed. Joan Copjec (New York: Verso, 1994), 9.

24. Žižek, *Tarrying with the Negative*, 73–74.

25. Slavoj Žižek, 'In His Bold Gaze My Ruin Is Writ Large', in *Everything You Always Wanted to Know About Lacan (But Were Afraid to Ask Hitchcock)*, ed. Žižek (New York: Verso, 1992), 224.

26. Quoted in Walter Benjamin, *Understanding Brecht*, 11. Althusser's interest in Brecht focuses on this problematisation by Brecht of the direct and stable identifications (of the audience to the hero) in traditional theatre, precisely through his exposing of the process of identification. See Althusser, 'The "Piccolo Teatro": Bertolazzi and Brecht: Notes on a Materialist Theatre', in Althusser, *For Marx* (London: New Left Books, 1977), 131–51.

27. Michel de Certeau, *The Practice of Everyday Life* (Berkeley: University of California Press, 1984).

28. Ezra Pound, 'A Retrospect', in *Literary Essays of Ezra Pound*, ed. T.S. Eliot (New York: New Directions, 1968), 5.

29. Brecht, 'A Short Organum for the Theatre', 192.

30. Kurt Weill, '*Gestus* in Music', *The Tulane Drama Review* 6:1 (Autumn 1961), 28–29. The emphasis is mine.

31. Martin Esslin, *Brecht* (London: Methuen, 1984), 123.

32. John Rajchman, *Philosophical Events* (New York: Columbia University Press, 1991), viii–ix.

33. Bertolt Brecht, 'On the Use of Music in an Epic Theatre', in *Brecht on Theatre*, 86.

34. Quoted in Roger Lewin, *Complexity: Life at the Edge of Chaos* (New York: Macmillan, 1992), 12–13.

35. Brecht, 'A Dialogue about Acting', in *Brecht on Theatre*, 26.

36. Brecht, 'The Literarization of the Theatre', in *Brecht on Theatre*, 45.

37. Godard, '*Introduction à une véritable histoire du cinéma*', 95.

THE BITTERNESS AND
THE SWEETNESS OF ARCHITECTURE

Is architecture really so boring that it constantly, perpetually, requires some supplemental some*thing*, some *and*? Architecture *and* film. Architecture *and* music. Architecture *and* food. Architecture *and*, it seems, anything *else*?

Yes – yes it is. Architecture is mostly so non-engaging that none of your non-architect friends can name more than one or maybe at the very most three architects, whereas they can name multitudes of artists, musicians, writers and directors.

But lest all this seem a little too bitter to begin with, let's begin with something a little sweeter perhaps, like, for example … a hot fudge sundae. Vanilla ice cream amassed, hot fudge poured, whipped cream piled, nuts sprinkled. Creamy, gooey, foamy, crunchy.

Here's how the story goes. A petulant little prince or princess wanted to befuddle the wise men of the court by asking for *paradox*: something simultaneously dark and light, hot and cold. So they came up with the Sundae. But why must we always make everything a battle of contrasts – *or* rather than *and*? Is dessert an integral part of dinner *or* something extra, something supplemental? Architecture *or* decor? Foregone conclusion *or* I really shouldn't splurge? Building *or* art?

Within this homely category of dessert there is already the tension between proper delimitation and excess, there is already unhomely desire and fear. Already within the familiar tectonics of the American Hot Fudge Sundae, there are the initially unfamiliar differential relations of nouvelle cuisine. Degrees of difference – the larger gestures of sharp contrast (dark and light, hot and cold) revealing more nuanced relations between these contrasts.

As texture: the various viscosities of the molten, the foamy, the creamy, the solid, the crunchy.

As appearance and proportion: the contained, the overflowing, the scattered, the poured, the amassed, the garnished.

As flavour: the simultaneous bitterness and sweetness of nuts, of vanilla, of chocolate (it's the darkest, the most bitter of bitter*sweet* chocolates, that will make a sauce of deep and differential flavour). A bittersweetness regularly achieved in film, literature, art and music, but rarely in architecture.

If various other media understand the principle of the bittersweet, it is because other media understand that desire is irresolvable and thus never to be resolved, but to be enacted, *within* the object, both the bitterness and the sweetness within the very same object. Which is why the deepest tragedies are rife with bittersweet ironies and comic moments, why deep comedy is rife with bittersweet poignancies and tragic moments.

Actually, I never eat ice cream – in America anyway. In Italy I eat it every day. Ah, Roma: ah, Giolitti. I keep by my computer a small stack of those crummy little green and white Giolitti napkins, which, every so often, while we are all in the office working on the next project, I lift up in the direction of Rome and kiss, a prayer to San Giolitti, patron Saint, so that our work may be as good to eat and as good to think. Even their simplest flavours have more differentials of taste than those mixed up mix-ups we Americans concoct here. Like their purest: *Gelato di Panna* – Cream Ice Cream. *Con panna*? *Sì*. And then with that flat metal paddle they use as a scoop – because their gelato is soft enough that they don't need the curved claw we use here – the whipped cream is spread on top. Cream iced and cream whipped. Ah.

But in America I never eat ice cream unless it's *with* something. Something *else*: a pie, a tart, hot fudge. So tonight, for example, Max, now ten, and I went out – out the door and down the avenue to the only local parlour (that franchise with the fake Scandinavian name), he for a scoop of Cookie Dough Dynamo in the crushed-chocolate-cookie-crumb-covered cone, and I for a small hot fudge sundae: vanilla ice cream, hot fudge, whipped cream, crushed nuts, the cherry.

Call it research.

You can get so sick of research after a while.

It's just too much: why is it that when they make a sundae they think it has to be more and yet more, loading it up with more ice cream, more fudge, more whipped cream, all of it spilling over the glass and down the glass and onto the plate and under the plate and on the table *and* my hands, so that half of a small one is about all I can stomach.

But it's also never enough, because it's already difficult enough to get the perfect proportion of that near perfect and delicious mix, which you only maybe possibly get in one bite or maybe three. Because what you get in the first spoonful is a mouthful of whipped cream. So for the second spoonful you overcompensate by really digging in on one side which causes the other side to overflow, and still all you get is a mouthful of … fudge. By the third spoonful you may just begin to get just the right proportion of fudge, ice cream, whipped cream and nuts, and all those differential interactions start interacting. Variously and varyingly. Bite by bite, spoonful by spoonful. You start to dig deep down now, but by then the fudge is cooling too quickly and the ice cream is melting too fast and the whipped cream is becoming more creamed than whipped, and you end up dredging up that sludge pool down at the bottom, where the degrees of difference are so reduced that they no longer maintain distinction, no longer maintain tension, and it's all just mush. It's like all those buildings that have just one fleeting moment before they all turn to mush.

You scream, I scream.

But the name sundae already speaks of certain excesses, certain delimitations, certain desires, certain fears, certain puritanical lacks, certain puritanical needs – certain (getting around certain) paradoxes. A sundae is called Sundae because Sunday was the day it was created for, in the 1890s, as a cunning variation on the immensely popular chocolate 'soda-fountain' frappe – which was being preached against by some ministers as being inappropriate for the Sabbath. (Evanston, Illinois being the first town to legislate against the 'Sunday Soda Menace', according to Paul Dickson's *The Great American Ice Cream Book*.) All of which led to the creation of the soda-less chocolate and ice cream concoction: 'This prompted confectioners to create Sundays so they could do business on the Sabbath.'

This is an old, even older, dilemma. In 1636, the Spanish priest Antonio de León Pinelo, in his book *Question Moral Si el Chocolate quebranta el ayuno Eclesiastico*, struggled with the moral question of whether or not chocolate (as a drink) could be used to break a holy fast: is chocolate nourishment or excess, structure or supplement? He found a way, of course, to morally justify his getting his (and Europe's) just deserts and desserts – by cleverly not calling it dessert. On the title page of his *Question*, an Indian maiden stands in an architectural niche, offering a miniaturised cacao tree in her outstretched arm: the deliverance of chocolate from the New World to the Old. She turns her face from the viewer, one could say demurely, but should one? – considering that it was the New World that was being ravaged by the Old precisely to facilitate the delivery of such goods, such goodies. And it is bittersweet, is it not (like her look), that meanwhile the miniaturised cacao tree she offers at the end of her outspread arm seems to be taking root to the tablet upon which the title of the book is displayed. The tablet almost covers her yet she also appears to be propping it up, the new colonial goods and goodies propping up the old, as all the while the cocoa roots on the title page are reaching around the back of the tablet and towards the 'Q' of 'Question', just as, lo and behold, a raging mania for chocolate took root and spread throughout Europe by the end of the seventeenth century, an addiction enough to worry clergy – the first introduction to Europe (just prior to coffee and tea) of that propping up chemical of choice, caffeine – consumed mainly and constantly as drink, but also as cake, as candy, and of course as creamed then iced: *glace, helado, eiscreme, semifreddo, gelato.*

We all scream. For ice cream.

That moment: it's what drives you, it's the carrot you donkey after, it's what Lacan called 'the drive', that gap between (you) the subject and its (your) desire. Only it would be more interesting, more delicious, if it wasn't like all those buildings that have just one fleeting intensive space, say a lobby or a part of the facade. Just one intensive moment where the parts are just beginning to be in a differential tension to themselves *and* each other, even if most of the time there are too many or too few ingredients that have yet to release their flavours in relation to the other spatial, tectonic, material, social, psychological and ideological flavours of that particular moment. As for the rest, it's mostly mush, just some undifferentiated consistency, however potentially yummy a small bit of that consistency might be. Some newer than new material, the latest of latest glazing or cladding technology now spread unvaryingly across its surface like paste, just another new texture-map to replace the old texture-map.

As compared to a dish that stirs you, wherein each bite delivers the tug, the pull, the grab, the drive of degrees of difference throughout the whole dish. That stirs you to experience that pull, and re-experience that pull, in the vivid present, over and over and over. Then the poignancy of the dish, the bittersweet poignancy, is in the rareness of its intensity. How it intensifies its moment between past and future, between past recipe and future innovation, going to *from*, going to something *from* something else, as in some memorable sunset. How it keeps changing differentially and intensely between relations of contrast (sometimes subtly, sometimes violently) with each moment until it ends. Ends not from some puritanical need for excess in order to be disgusted enough to stop, nor from some puritanical need for parsimonious purity in order never to risk beginning, in order never to risk difference, in order never to desire dessert.

That vivid mouthful is not so easy to find, but when you find it, at a street vendor here or an elaborate restaurant

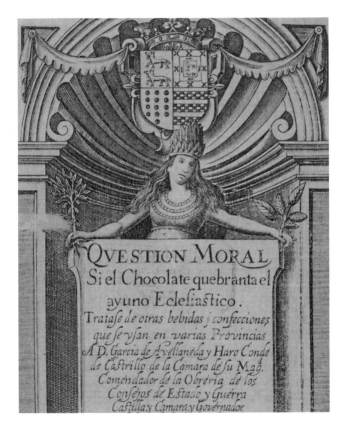

QVESTION MORAL
Si el Chocolate quebranta el
ayuno Eclesiastico.
Tratase de otras bebidas y confecciones
que se ysan en varias Provincias
A D. Garcia de Avellaneda y Haro Conde
de Castrillo de la Camara de su Mag.
Comendador de la Obreria de los
Consejos de Estado y Guerra
Castilla y Camara y Governador

there, you feel its tug, its pull of intense and poignant pres-
entness. It makes you pause: you feel your taste buds and
your brain thinking, experiencing, through the relations
of taste – as compared to all that food that's just okay, even
tasty in some way or other, but that doesn't make you stop
and consider. All that food, and all that architecture, that
you consume 'without thinking'.

Why isn't this *vividness* our experience in most buildings? Is it because most buildings are not cooked deeply?
I don't say not long enough – because sometimes they are
cooked for so long they are like the beef stew in the school
cafeteria. In buildings cooked deeply, the relations between
the ingredients (the tectonic ingredients, the programmatic
ingredients, the geometric ingredients, the ideological
ingredients, the geometric ingredients, the site ingredients,
the material ingredients) have the chance to draw out the
relations of flavours *in* and *of* each ingredient and each to
the others, to draw out the relations of the bitter and the
sweet, so you can *taste the separate tastes together*.

As with garlic and most meat, vegetable, fish or fowl,
balancing what is sweet and what is near-bitter savouriness
in that 'stinking *rose*' and ditto whatever it is in relation to.
Ditto apples and cinnamon. Ditto campari and grapefruit
juice and bitters. Ditto almost any dish, deeply developed.
Any dish you can think of. It doesn't matter what cuisine or
how many ingredients, how minimal or maximal, how raw
or cooked – it's how deeply you work the relations of the
dish. Drawing forth unfamiliar flavours from both new and
all too familiar architectural ingredients and recipes.

So is the hot fudge sundae really the model for
architecture? Hardly, well not the full experience anyway,
although within its concept and experience are moments,
fleeting as they are. But it's not easy to find a really tasty
one, and as for the hot fudge I had tonight, I would have to
say that, as for the question of hot, well … not exactly, not
even really *warm*, in temperature or taste, I'm sorry to say.

Bitter the lukewarm, yet perpetual, architectural
servitude to all too familiar institutions, spaces, materials,
tectonics, geometries, ideologies.

Sweet the possibility of elaborating, troping, reinventing all too familiar institutions, spaces, materials, tectonics, geometries, ideologies.

But never the one without the other.

However you begin – trying to work these existing codings or to free yourself from them – you'll always end in the midst of both transformation and fixity. Whether it's bittersweet for you, or – if you like your glucose first – 'sweetbitter', as Anne Carson translates *glukupikron*, Sappho's description of *Eros*:

Eros the melter of limbs (now again) stirs me – sweetbitter

That's love for you. Matter transformed: solids melting, stirrings in the vivid *now*, again.

As we walk down the avenue, with our desires, with our drives, with family or alone, it's not so easy to find a building that's good to eat, that's stirring. Not like in the magazines where each and every building is indeed, there is no point denying this, yummy yummy yummy, whatever the style of its cuisine (local or international, traditional or nouvelle) – tasty in material or in form or in tectonics, fleeting as these may be – even if it's not so easy to find one that's tasty in concept. Then there are those architectural projects indeed yummy in concept, but with barely enough substance even to taste a taste.

As for me, what I hunger for, walking down the avenue or sitting at this computer in the studio, is a few buildings, here and there, that are as good to eat as they are good to think. A few buildings as stirring – as bitter and sweet – as the writings, films and music that cover all the shelves and surfaces closest to this machine and to me.

Originally published in *Log* 1 (2003), 27–32.

WHY ARCHITECTURE IS
NEITHER HERE NOR THERE

When I say architecture is neither here nor there, what I mean is this: architecture is neither purely specific nor purely abstract, neither purely social nor purely formal, neither purely local nor purely global. Architecture, all architecture, is here *and* there, specific *and* abstract, social *and* formal, local *and* global. It is only a question of how and to what degree it attempts to enact this here and thereness, this specificity and abstraction, this socialness and formalness, this localness and globalness, in the work itself, in form and in content.

There is so much to say on these matters in such a short time that I will only be able to make a few small points, these points being points from some earlier themes of my work that resonate, in canny and uncanny ways, with the topic under discussion here.

I will begin at the beginning, from my first substantial essay, 'Spatial Narratives',[1] to speak to the title *Building Dwelling Drifting*, the conference's and the collection's play on Martin Heidegger's title for his 1951 essay 'Building Dwelling Thinking', an essay in which he celebrates all the homely, the *heimlich*, the canny aspects of dwelling – while repressing the unhomely, the *unheimlich*, the uncanny aspects. Take, for example, Heidegger's etymological derivations, his sleight of hand as he moves from word to word ('building', 'neighbour', 'peace'), from Old English to High German to Old Saxon to Gothic, until he gathers up what he was already looking for, a *heimlich* definition as follows: 'To dwell, to be set at peace, means to remain at peace within the free, the preserve, the free sphere that safeguards each thing in its nature. *The fundamental character of dwelling is this sparing and preserving*' (original emphasis).[2]

Well, as the title *Building Dwelling Drifting* suggests, there is already some drift here, some drift not only in his method, not only in his conclusion, but in the etymological derivations themselves, or perhaps it would be better to say: there is the attempt to repress any drift. As I discussed in my essay, the English verb 'to dwell' is derived from the Middle English *dwellen* (from the Old English *dwellan*), which means 'to lead astray, hinder', related to the Middle Dutch *dwellen,* which means 'to stun', as well as indeed the Old High German *twellan* and the Old Norse *dvelja,* which mean 'to delay, to deceive'. The derivation of all these words is from the Indo-European base *dh(e)wel* – which means 'to mislead, to deceive, to obscure, to make dull'.[3] A parallel uncanny confluence can be found among the Madagascar Sakalava tribes, where the word *mody,* meaning 'at home' or 'heading home' also means 'to pretend what one is not'.[4]

Now Heidegger's etymological repressions are just one manifestation of his later repressions of his earlier work, in this case, the repression of his earlier examinations of the concept of *Unheimlichkeit* in his *Prolegomena to the History of the Concept of Time*, his Marburg University lectures from 1925, which led to *Being and Time* of 1927, as David Krell has well noted:

In *Being and Time* and in his Marburg lecture courses that led up to it, Heidegger defined human existence itself in terms of being *not-at-home* […]. Section 30 of his 1925 *Prolegomena to the History of the Concept of Time* declares that human existence (Dasein) has essentially nothing to do with homely homes, that its very being is *Unheimlichkeit*, 'uncanniness', 'unhomelikeness'. Our being in the world, the world that serves as our only home, is marked by the uncanny discovery that we are *not* at home in it. *Dasein*, or being-there, when it is truly there, is an absentee; it is stamped and typed by *Unzuhause*, the not-at-home, the nobody-home.[5]

This returns us to Sigmund Freud's seminal 1919 essay 'The Uncanny' ('*Das Unheimliche*') in which Freud states that 'we are tempted to conclude that what is 'uncanny' is frightening precisely because it is *not* known and familiar'. But Freud's own etymological research reveals other meanings for what should be the homely and canny meanings of the word *heimlich*: '… concealed, kept from sight, so that others do not get to know about it … to behave *heimlich*, as though there were something to conceal … *heimlich* places (which good manners oblige us to conceal)'. Thus, Freud concludes, the 'uncanny is in reality nothing new or foreign, but something familiar … which has been estranged only by the process of repression'.[6]

So let us say, then, between my staged sleight-of-hand here (emphasising what is *unheimlich*) and the later Heidegger's sleight-of-hand there (emphasising what is *heimlich*), that it is the oscillation and migration between these states, the hybrid condition, as Freud and the earlier Heidegger suggest, that may provide the more relevant and productive model for the relations of dwelling. This now brings us to Homi Bhabha, whose own scholarly hybridity on the topic of hybridity seems to me of seminal importance in thinking about the relation of dwelling and migrancy.

Let us start first with the issue of dwelling, in a passage, say, from his essay 'Halfway House': 'Home may be a place of estrangement that becomes *the* necessary space of engagement; it may represent a desire for accommodation marked by an attitude of deep ambivalence towards one's location … home is territory of both disorientation and relocation.'[7]

Bhabha succinctly demarcates dwelling as a connecting of what is generally perceived as two opposite poles (estrangement and engagement, accommodation and ambivalence, disorientation and relocation), but these are no more opposite than the *heimlich* and the *unheimlich*, the here and the there. In this forever mixing of the one in the other, there remains only a question of, let us say, proportion, or rather of the concept of proportion in the title, but not in the text of the essay 'Halfway House'. Halfway? – I would say: no. Not half, not 1/3, not 2/3, but as he reaffirms in many penetrating ways through this essay, a constantly adjusting and readjusting measure, a hybridising, an intermixing, the one in and of the other.

Bhabha carries this analysis forward to address these forms of relations between the local and the global, native culture and migrant culture:

What it does suggest is that we have overemphasised, even fetishised, the relation between culture and national identity, or traditional, customary community. There is, of course a link between territory, tradition, and 'peoples' that serves certain functions of state and governance and bestows an important sense of belonging. But the strong, *nationalist* version of this relationship can lead to a limiting collusion that returns us to the dominant sociological paradigms of the nineteenth century. To be overly focused on the authenticity of national identity leads to an 'authoritarian' or 'paternalist' gaze – however well-meant – towards those who are part of the great history of migration. Authenticity unleashes a restrictive sense of indigenous or native 'belonging' ... these questions of home, identity, belonging are always open to negotiations, to be posed again from elsewhere, to become iterative, interrogative processes rather than imperative, identitarian designations.[8]

This great history of migration (which includes but is not restricted to the current situations of migrancy),[9] as Bhabha says, has already changed our sense of what it is to be native and national, and thus how those architectural categories of vernacular, regionalist, nationalist and internationalist might need to be totally rethought, given the great history of migration of individuals and ideas in architecture (Palladianism in English architecture, Miesianism in American architecture, internationalism in the neo-vernaculars of Murcutt and Mockbee).

But if all aesthetic objects are already inherently hybrid, then how might an aesthetic object enact this condition of hybridity rather than merely represent it,

265

within the object, as an object, not just as an inadvertent representative of a cultural and historical condition? Here is what Bhabha suggests:

Might this hybrid, culturally diverse landscape then make visible the rough edges, the complex negotiations of aesthetic values that find themselves not only 'outside' the artwork in the social problematic of its production but 'inside' the work itself, both formally and affectively? Cultural contradictions, disjunctive historical spaces, identifications created on the crossroads – these are the issues that the arts of cultural hybridization seek to embody and enact rather than 'transcend.' It is an art that is no less valuable because it takes what is unresolved, ambivalent, even antagonistic, and performs it in the work, underlining the struggle for translation.[10]

In a number of his other essays, Bhabha has already suggested one set of tactics – drawn from certain historical resistances to certain colonial authorities – that an aesthetic hybridity might utilise, that is mimicry, sly civility: 'a discursive process by which the excess or slippage produced by the *ambivalence* of mimicry (almost the same, *but not quite*) does not merely 'rupture' the discourse, but becomes transformed into an uncertainty which fixes the colonial subject as a "partial" presence. By partial I mean both "incomplete" and "virtual".'[11] The subject is incomplete and virtual because it is put into a set of 'conflictual, fantastic and discriminatory "identity-effects",' so that its location (its position) within its locale (its place) is revealed to be problematic, simultaneously located and dislocated, simultaneously localised and delocalised, simultaneously here and there. It is this question (and questioning) of identity through mimicry that Bhabha draws from Lacan, and thus Bhabha's essay 'On Mimicry and Man' opens with the following quote:

Mimicry reveals something in so far as it is distinct from what might be called an itself that is behind. The effect of mimicry is camouflage ... It is not a question of

harmonising with the background but, against a mottled background, of becoming mottled – exactly like the technique of camouflage practiced in human warfare.[12]

Returning to the dictionary once again to look up 'mimicry' will not result in as dramatic a surprise as with 'dwelling', but will be useful nonetheless. Now in the *Oxford Dictionary*, 'mimicry' is defined in a somewhat broader manner, as: 'ridicule by imitation (person, manner, etc); copy minutely or servilely; (of thing); resemble closely'. The latter definition indicates the close relation between mimicry and mimesis, but for now, before we return to the potentially transgressive aspect of what it could mean to 'resemble closely', let us concentrate on the second half of the second definition: to copy servilely.

Architecture is always a mimic to itself, all architecture is already mimetic, is already mimicking what has been previously stated, constructed, even the most 'extreme' avant-garde projects maintain the mimicry of social and cultural programming. When a client comes to you and asks you to design a house, you don't say: what's a house? You say: how many bedrooms would you like? You say: do you need a separate dining room? You say: what sort of appliances do you want in your kitchen, and so forth. Ditto a conference centre. Ditto a library. Ditto an art museum. Ditto an office building. This is architecture's and society's compulsion to repeat, which is its defence against actively questioning the constitutive motivations and attributes of its forms. This is the whole cultural and ideological force of architecture practice, from the most conventional practices (with their Professional Pattern books and Professional Standards books and Building Type books and Manufacturer's Catalogues) to the most avant-garde practices (which use the exact same books and references but bend the walls and roofs around a bit). I am, in case you are wondering, not exempting myself, as an architect, here: this is the cultural transmission that one inevitably has to engage with.

We should not forget that Roger Caillois, whose essay on biological mimicry so influenced Lacan's ideas of

identification, spoke primarily of mimicry as a 'renunciation', 'a depersonalisation by assimilation to space', a 'temptation of space', in other words, as a potential trap.[13] How
might one escape this trap, this spatial assimilation, this
compulsion to repeat the environment as already given,
whether one's homeland or awayland or new-homeland?
Precisely by enacting it as a temptation, as a trap, as a compulsion to repeat, as Freud suggested, by using the compulsion to repeat against itself: 'We render it harmless, and
even make use of it, by according it the right to assert itself
within certain limits ... to display before us all the pathogenic impulses ... only by living through them in this way
will the patient be convinced of their power and existence'.[14]

Not servilely but with sly civility: Bhabha's concept of
mimicry and sly civility is close to the Greek idea of *mêtis*
(or cunning intelligence), which is less about ridicule than
about how the 'only way to triumph over an adversary
endowed with *mêtis* is to turn its own weapons against it',
like 'the feint employed in wrestling (*palaisma*) of eluding
the grasp of the adversary and then, by reversing one's
body, turning against him the force of his own thrust':[15]

**Why does *mêtis* appear thus, as multiple (pantoie), many-
coloured (*poikile*), shifting (*aiole*)? Because its field of application is the world of movement, of multiplicity and of
ambiguity. It bears on fluid situations which are constantly
changing and which at every moment combine contrary
forces that are opposed to each other ... In order to domi-
nate a changing situation full of contrasts it must become
even more supple, even more shifting, more polymorphic
... It is this way of conniving with reality which ensures
its efficacity.[16]**

To be 'almost the same, but not quite', to be 'both
against the rules and within them',[17] as Bhabha suggests, is
to reveal the rules of the game, the rules of social construction, which once revealed might be seen no more as absolute, essential, matters of fact, and might then be possible to
change. This alternation between the 'almost the same, but

not quite', between being 'both against the rules and within them', parallels Brecht's 'alienation effect': 'a representation that alienates is one which allows us to recognise its subject, but at the same time makes it seem unfamiliar' – for the same reason – 'to free socially conditioned phenomena from that stamp of familiarity which protects them against our grasp today'.[18]

Thus, just as one does not have to introduce drift into dwelling (it is already there), one does not have to introduce mimicry into conventional modes of discourse or representation, (servile) mimicry is precisely what conventional forms already are. One just has to operate on these conditions to reveal these conditions at work – at the scale of the site, the programme, the individual spaces, the tectonic elements – to find the unfamiliar within familiarity, to find mannerisms in the manner, the mannerisms of form and content, mannerism being the irresoluble enfolding of the here and the there, the convention and its swerve, straight up with a twist, 'almost the same, but not quite'.

Thus the architectural question is not answered merely by choosing whether forms have either the appearance of mobility *or* stasis, nor whether they have the appearance of being either specifically localised *or* generalised. To localise an architectural event is not to root it in some essential and proper place, some irreducible form of dwelling, but to find it enmeshed, enfolded, in a field of non-localised relations. In design or discourse, the specific, the here, is only interesting to the extent it draws forth the general, the there, and the general is only interesting to the extent it can be conveyed in and through specific occasions.

This perpetually alternating here and there is already evident in Lacan's concept of the mirror-stage, where (and when) you, the subject, in front of a mirror, around the age of 18 months, become aware of yourself as a self as *here*, as a whole image rather than all those disjunctive fragmentary bodily sensations that were your perception of 'self' up to that moment. But this image, your image, is not located in you, it is located elsewhere, in front of you, *there* in the mirror, in advance of you, and henceforth your identity will always circulate between internal and external, specific and general, attempts and acts of identification.[19]

In Lacan's essay on the mirror-stage (the essay where Caillois' concept of mimicry makes its first appearance), he refers to 'the spatial captation manifested in the mirror-stage' (*'la captation spatiale que manifeste le stade du miroir'*), but to find the word 'captation' you would have to reach for the bigger *Oxford* with the smaller print (at the same time reaching for the accompanying magnifying glass out of its drawer in the double-volume slipcase). This *Oxford* says the word is 'obsolete', which is probably why the otherwise welcome new translation of *Écrits* renders this phrase as 'the spatial capture',[20] but the often passive and finished sense of capture misses the more active and desirous sense of captation: 'a catching at, an endeavour to get', a seeking after identity, or as the newer double-volume version of *Oxford* (which no longer designates the word as obsolete) has it, 'an attempt to acquire something', as in the sense of *ad captandum*, something '(designed) to appeal to the emotions',[21] or as my French dictionary translates it, an 'inveigling'. We are always tempted to catch, to endeavour for, to acquire, to inveigle these identities, as they always give the appearance of being, as insides and outsides, home-lands and awaylands (even if for the migrant, homeland is now the one that is away), here-lands and there-lands. But you don't capture your identity in the space of the mirror, it is in this seeking after your identity that you are forever in the act of being captured, captured in the space between yourself and the mirror, in these spatial temptations of identity circulating between your inner and outer world, your 'self' and your 'environs.'

This seeking to acquire something that will never be acquirable as a fixed entity (but will always be alternating), this appealing to (alternating) emotions, is further played out, within and between selves, in the *fort-da* 'game' of Freud's grandson: that repeated enunciation of the alternating absence (*fort*) and presence (*da*) of some small *object* (the little bobbin) that the child – in response to the presence then departure of his mother (Freud's daughter) – enacts for and in himself, by making his object become absent, throwing it to where he cannot see it, uttering '*fort*' (gone) and then pulling it back into view with a '*da*' (here). Freud: 'I eventually realised that it was a game and that the only use he made of any of his toys was to play "gone" with them.' As in Lacan's mirror-stage, Freud's grandson is in fact 18 months old at the time of these observations: as in the mirror-stage, the subject makes of himself the object of his own operation *and* observation: a piece of himself (*his* toy) is repeatedly tossed away or hidden and then retrieved – peek-a-*boo* – in order that the 'here' (what is 'present') is not separate from, is not opposed to, but already enfolded in, the 'there' (what is 'absent'), and it is this perpetually enfolded relationship that the child enacts.[22]

This enactment of absence and presence may take place on a psychological and a social level, in relation say, to the mother *or* the motherland – playing gone with them – enacting the desire *and* the fear, the appeal, the endeavour, for both separation and belonging, independence and association – personally, culturally. So if various migrant populations still – as Stephen Cairns stated in his original outline for this *Building Dwelling Drifting* collection – 'manage to throw up new tactics of attachment … through the projection of a hyper-stable architecture, an architecture that announces fixity, permanence', then this very hyperness already anticipates his 'yet' that follows, anticipates an equally hyper enactment of separation: 'Yet, in turn, this fixity and permanence is itself constituted through memory and the experience of a profound mobility.' Experienced, that is, through an alternating of separation and the need to draw what is now there, here.

But why should we be surprised at that, any more than we should be surprised that even the most avant-garde of houses maintain whole areas and categories of homeliness? Why not just weave this hybridity into the story of our architecture, rather than repress it, why not work off and through it?

If dwelling had no drift, then this alternation of absence and presence might be understood as an attempt to resolve and master this splitting, as some have suggested about the *fort-da* scene. But as Lacan observed, already noting in 1964 the Heideggerian postwar (why not put a name on it) tendency (or need or desire) to contain the alienating effects of absence and drift:

There can be no *fort* without *da* and, one might say, without *Dasein*. But, contrary to the whole tendency of the phenomenology of *Daseinanalyse*, there is no *Dasein* with the *fort*. That is to say, there is no choice ... The function of the exercise with this object refers to an alienation, and not to some supposed mastery, which is difficult to imagine being increased in an endless repetition, whereas the endless repetition that is in question reveals the radical vacillation of the subject.[23]

It is these various radical vacillations that, as Bhabha says, 'the arts of cultural hybridisation seek to embody and enact rather than "transcend".' They do so by performing their own hybridity within the aesthetic object, their own mimicry of close (but not too close) resemblance, to return to that last dictionary definition at last.

This dialogue of resemblance is a form of comparative double-description. As Gregory Bateson said, it doesn't take one to know one, it takes *two* to know one. As in binocular vision, which is a lie that tells a deeper truth. Each eye sees the same thing, more or less, but between that more and that less, between that shift and overlap, is the deeper depth of perception. Binoculars, the mechanical ones, are like having another set of eyes, allowing you both close attention and distance from the object of your attention. The way the group of children I met my first day in Nakuru, looking through my binoculars, shaking their heads and clicking their tongues in disbelief and belief, would point first far and then draw that pointing finger back near to themselves. This same kind of reaction occurs when the young Andrea in Brecht's play *Life of Galileo* first looks through a telescope – 'Holy Mary! Everything comes close. The bells of the campanile are right here.' Bringing the there and the here into relation. And binoculars, even when they are drawing what's near even nearer, give you some distance on it, so you can see it anew, in its familiarity and unfamiliarity. The degree to which this seemingly insignificant process of drawing near and far things into new relations can result in major ideological battles and shifts is precisely the subject of *Galileo* – the astronomical and clerical propositions of how the universe is structured by positing what revolves around what's located where and what structures what).

Unlike human binocular vision, which achieves depth at the cost of resolving difference, aesthetic binocular operations most productively achieve depth by putting into play sameness and difference, not by resolving but by exaggerating samenesses and differences, both collapsing *and* keeping some distance, keeping two almost similar conditions apart in order to draw them deeper into relation and depth. Exposing the desire for resolution even as it reveals the impossibility of resolution.

This is why Bhabha insists on the necessity to avoid the easy resolution of (cultural) difference – 'Hybridity … is not a third term that resolves the tension between two cultures'[24] – on the necessity to see how they are both separated from and tied up with each other, or as he says, 'less than one *and* double'.[25] Less than one because the dominant identity has lost its unified status through the difference revealed by multiple description: not unified because multiplied. But perhaps it would be more precise to say not doubled, at least not, as the dictionary definition goes, copied servilely. Not copied exactly, but playing at resemblances, thus copied slyly. Almost doubled, but not quite. Less than one and not *exactly* double. Less than one and slyly doubled.

The hybrid play of resemblances is a 'process of classificatory confusion' that Bhabha has described as 'the metonymy of the substitutive chain of ethical and cultural discourse'.[26] This play is metonymic because ethical and cultural discourse is already *within* the social circumstance, just as architecture is already within the architectural circumstance: the building. Architecture of course is articulating its ethical and cultural discourse all the time, but it mainly does so as rote repetition (of fixed classifications of building types, programme spaces, elements), as a compulsion to repeat, as servile mimicry. The possibility and ability to draw this ethical and cultural discourse forth in order to rearticulate it – so we can see it in the act of its act – is precisely what architecture may yet find a way to do, in its own becoming hybrid in and through itself, in and through its own aesthetic operations: by being less than one and slyly doubled.

'Less Aesthetics, More Ethics': this was the theme, the provocation, of the 2000 Venice Biennale, and my response to this provocation (in the Biennale competition *Città: Terzo Millennio/The City: Third Millennium*), as in my earlier response to the title of Bhabha's 'Halfway House', was this: let's not play the percentages, let's not play at totalising proportions if it becomes a matter of re-apportioning, if more of one aspect always results in less of another (that was always the problem of colonialism and of migrancy). Proportion is more productively understood as an enfolding, as an entanglement, as relations, not as definitive allotments. So if more ethics is what you're after in architecture, then you'll need *more* not less aesthetics. Ethics, by definition, is not that which is morally proper, but the *discussion* of what might be considered to be – at any given historical moment – society's moral relations. Ethics means a field of discussion, not of prescription, and for a good discussion, an articulate discussion, you need more (not less) articulation and re-articulation. All architecture is ethical, just as all architecture is social – in that all architecture is entangled in the ethical and social conditions of its time and culture. So if architecture is to be more ethical then that can only mean it needs to be more articulate of its ethics, and so it needs more aesthetics to be more articulate – but an aesthetics that recognises and articulates, enacts, its own and our own entanglements.

Michel Foucault has already suggested this entanglement of ethics and aesthetics in his tracing of the genealogy of ethics from its development in Antiquity as an 'aesthetics of existence': 'This art of the self involves the ways individuals constitute themselves and are constituted as ethical subjects in relation to the rules and values that are operative in a given society or group, the agencies or mechanisms of constraint that enforce them, the forms they take in their multifariousness, their divergences and their contradictions.'[27] Earlier in his work Foucault had examined another aesthetics: the development of politics as an aesthetics of the state in Europe during the seventeenth and eighteenth centuries. This marked the beginning of the political rationality of those systems of 'rules and values that are operative in … society', as the state involved itself 'as agency and mechanism' in the demarcation and numeric regulation of time as schedule and location as address, as well as in the development and administration of infrastructural networks of transportation and communication for the distribution and regulation of individuals and goods (in public interventions such as urban development and welfare management).[28]

That the personal and the political are entangled, that ethics is a form of aesthetics and that aesthetics is a form of ethics, the spatial circumstances of migrancy makes abundantly clear, from the level of the city to the level of an individual domestic shrine. The ways in which migrants occupy space, from local housing to urban contexts, have often put into question some of the most fundamental architectural categories of the host architectural culture: ideas of proper one-to-one correspondences of rooms to familial domestic use are reconceived in relation to the multiplicity of extended families, the proper delimitation of the public and private edge of commercial use (the strict demarcation of the storefront) is put into question by the opening and extension of the store into the sidewalk and street.

These uncanny doublings of spatialised cultures, almost the same, *but not quite*, bear the marks and connections that Bhabha charted in 'Halfway House': estrangement and engagement, accommodation and ambivalence, disorientation and relocation. These occur in and through architectural and sub-architectural elements: sidewalks, storefronts, doorways, windows, walls, storage and display areas, enacting as these do the constitution of self and community through the engaged and conflictual interactions of public and private, domestic and urban, identities. Therein lies a great many binocular lessons for those of us, architects, trying to learn from the issues of migrancy, even if, or especially because, we may never have the occasion to design specifically for those circumstances. In these matters architects still have much to consider from Krzysztof Wodiczko's multimedia 'industrial designs' for immigrants that mimic the walking staff and backpack of the wanderer, his *Alien Staff* and *Ægis: Equipment for a City of Strangers*, all to allow for the collection and commentary of memories and memorabilia, with their visual and audio recordings of the user's migrancy stories and places to display artefacts related to those stories, allowing both closeness and distance for the user from their own travails, a binocular ability of the object and the user to both inhabit and stand outside of these stories of location and dislocation.[29]

This sly doubling 'results in the *splitting* of colonial discourse so that two attitudes towards external reality persist: one takes reality into consideration while the other disavows it and replaces it by a product of desire that repeats, rearticulates 'reality' as 'mimicry'.[30] This close attention to repeat yet rearticulate reality, to draw forth new relations from and through conditions of authority, is a metonymic rather than a metaphoric operation,[31] in that it finds from within the object, and what is contingent to the object, the material to export, to rearticulate, rather than completely replacing it with some totally foreign imported material – it works the relations between the native *and* the foreign, between the exported *and* the imported. Which is why, looking from the other way around, if we architects do import lessons from migrant cultures into non-migrant projects, we still have to find within our own architectural and critical culture the basic material to export, to rearticulate, from within our own objects.

Importing and exporting, from here to there: some years back, in the late 1980s, I read an interview with the

Japanese Butoh dancer, Kazuo Ohno, conducted with the assistance of the performance team of Eiko and Koma. Ohno's most famous performance is entitled 'Admiring La Argentina', which he created at the age of 71 as a homage to 'La Argentina', Antonia Merce, the Spanish dancer famous for adopting and developing the dances of the Gypsies (certainly one personification of migrancy), whom he saw perform at the Imperial Theatre in Tokyo in 1929, when he was 23. Ohno credits this experience as the one that instigated his desire to become a dancer, and his performance is a remembrance of that moment and that dancer. Like all homages, this one involves a certain form of mimicry, a certain bittersweetness of time and place and circumstance now past, and thus Ohno performs this work dressed in 'a long yellowed dress and a withered flower hat'. As the final question in the interview, Ohno was asked what it was like to go from everyday life as a (then, in the late 1980s) 80-year-old Japanese man to a stage performance enacting the dance of a (then, in 1929) 43-year-old Spanish woman. His response, as conveyed by Eiko and Koma: 'He says he doesn't commute.'

If there is a widespread interest today in the work of Shigeru Ban – I'll just restrict my comments here to one architect who is involved in some form of practice immediately related to certain forms of migration – it is due to the fact that his work on refugee shelters following the Kobe earthquake and the Rwanda crisis (both from 1994) are not unrelated to his work for his most affluent clients. In other words, the degree of interest in his work, in the long run, will match the degree to which he doesn't commute but circulates between equally significant inhabitations of his practice. From the fixity of his temporary material (cardboard tube) shelters in Kobe, say, to the temporariness of position of his mobile rooms in his house in Kawagoe. From here to there:

Even in disaster areas, as an architect, I want to create beautiful buildings, to move people and to improve people's lives. If I did not feel that way, it would not be

possible to create works of architecture and to make a contribution to society at the same time.[32]

And from there to here:

Architects are generally very egotistic, including me, I'd like to build my monument, too; there's no doubt about that. But it's not the only thing I want to do. I wanted to use my skills and knowledge for society. The reason I worked for Kobe and Rwanda is, obviously, the humanitarian feeling, but also to develop my ideas further and apply them at the same time, as long as I'm satisfying the humanitarian need. The two things are mixed together.[33]

This mixing is never simple, never without consequences, never always successful, but nevertheless it happens, here and there, and it is from here that questions about the architectural articulation of this migration may be asked.

Ban's work is rightfully well known for its purity, its exquisite elegance, but this purity, this exquisiteness threatens to conceal some of his more intriguing projects, no less elegant, but with greater conceptual depth and play, mannerist play, subtle mimicries, of his deepest inspiration, Ludwig Mies van der Rohe.[34] For example: in his aforementioned Kawagoe House with its 'universal space', but with cores and not just partitions now mobile. Or his Curtain Wall House, with its two-storey external tent sheet that plays off the idea of the curtain wall Mies was so known for, as well as the domestic curtains Mies was so opposed to, as well as the super-scaled silk curtain Mies once did use in his and Lilly Reich's Silk Exhibit of the *Exposition de la Mode,* as well as Ban's own Shelter1 tents for African refugees. Or his Sagaponac Furniture House, which is a direct play on Mies's unbuilt Brick Country House, only what was there linear 'structural' brick walls is now here a series of lines and cells 'comprised of modular, full-height furniture units which become elements of structural support, spatial division and storage',[35] closets upon closets, this again in relation to Mies, whose love of closets was only matched by his love of curtains and whose clients were known to incredulously ask others 'You mean your architect *lets* you have closets?'

But then Ban's purity reasserts itself again, more minimalist than Mies, more monocular than binocular, for once again the storage units, judging from all the interior photographs of his projects, are there to keep everything '... concealed, kept from sight, so that others do not get to know about it ... to behave *heimlich*, as though there were something to conceal ... *heimlich* places (which good manners oblige us to conceal)'. Whereas all the storage units and curtains, rather than being so mono-, suggest the binocular possibilities of concealing and revealing, *fort* and *da*, given that there are many social stories – canny and uncanny, *heimlich* and *unheimlich*, homeland and awayland – to tell, in the entire range of his work, not just in the affluent houses but especially in the refugee shelters and housing for where the cardboard tubes suggest all manner of possible storage and display, and where the display of what was there may be all the more poignant and needed here.

Now it may seem that we have come a long way from the concerns of this collection, if the most significant migration the owners of the Sagaponac Furniture House will have will be between their city home and this, their country house in the Hamptons, but if Ban's furniture house series (four have been built to date in Japan and China) began as designs for affluent clients, then this series has also included his design for mass housing for the Kobe earthquake survivors, and the lessons learned from any one of these explorations in prefabricated construction may well be useful towards the other, say, towards some future migrant housing. Because if we say one type of use is social architecture and one isn't, then aren't we just ghettoising all over again, with yet another badly thought binary opposition. What might make architecture social is that it critically enacts what is social in its condition, within its architecture, not just in its circumstance, so a Hamptons vacation house may be considered social architecture too. So then, even though the client commutes, the (intentions and attentions of the) architect doesn't (have to). Isn't that what social architecture should be: the exploration of what is social in whatever design one is designing? Which of Ban's projects would fall under that classification? – or by being hybrid might put into play a productive 'process of classificatory confusion?' – are some questions that his work engagingly suggests.

I have to tell you, before I finish, the origin of the title for this essay. It begins in 1989, long before I wrote these words, at another conference in which I was speaking (in fact making my first public presentation of 'Spatial Narratives'), but at this particular moment I was listening, to another speaker. His talk consisted primarily of what he considered to be fundamental propositions on space, all of which I considered to be overly obvious, binarily oppositional, and therefore underthought as propositions. Propositions such as: 'A maze is complex space and an urban retail street is simple space' (you could of course argue quite the opposite: a maze is homogeneous space, and even the simplest street is filled with all kinds of social and architectural complexity) or 'A plaza is public space and a bedroom is private space' (Joan Copjec has brilliantly analysed how in the film *Double Indemnity* the very public-ness of a space might allow for private transaction,[36] and as for the guarantee of the privateness of the bedroom, well, not in over a quarter of the so-called United States where it's still illegal as I am writing these words, if you are gay, to do what's done in a bedroom, and where still in the state of Louisiana any homo or hetero oral or anal is punishable by law). This speaker I am speaking about had a long litany of such oppositional propositions, choreographed with both hands flung to the right for one side of the binary and then to the left for the other side of the binary. It ended at last with what he considered the most obvious opposition of all: 'Either you are here ...' (hands to the right) 'or you are there ...' (hands to the left), and then as if in a fit of pique at how fundamentally fundamental this final fun-damental principle was, he burst out: 'you-can-not-be-here-and-there-at-the-same-time-this-is-clear-no?' (hands right, hands left, hands front with palms raised towards the heavens).

What I hope is clear is this: I didn't believe that then and there and I still don't believe that now and here. Architecture, and you, and I, are neither here nor there, but always here and there at the same time.

After all, there it is, now, years hence, and somehow these words have managed to migrate (to strain this word one last time) here, into your hands and your eyes, wherever and whenever in the world your hands and your eyes may be.

Originally presented at *Building, Dwelling, Drifting: Migrancy & the Limits of Architecture*, the 3rd 'Other Connections' (Forum for Architecture and Urbanism in Decolonization) Conference, University of Melbourne, Australia, June 1997, and published in Stephen Cairns (ed.), *Drifting: Architecture and Migrancy* (London: Routledge, 2004), 99–115.

TECTONIC ACTS OF DESIRE AND DOUBT

NOTES

1. Mark Rakatansky, 'Spatial Narratives', in this volume.

2. Martin Heidegger, 'Building Dwelling Thinking', in Heidegger, *Poetry Language Thought*, trans. Albert Hofstadter (New York: Harper, 1971), 145–61.

3. *The Compact Edition of the Oxford English Dictionary* (New York: Oxford University Press, 1971) and the *Webster's New World Dictionary* (New York: William Collins and World Publishing, 1978). I would like to thank James F. Gramata for pointing out this etymology to me.

4. Peter J. Wilson, *The Domestication of the Human Species* (New Haven: Yale University Press, 1988), 98. Wilson quotes the anthropologist Gillian Feeley-Harnik regarding how among the Sakalava 'no one would refuse another entrance into his house *unless he were hoarding or hiding something*' (emphasis in original).

5. David Farrell Krell, *Architecture: Ecstasies of Space, Time, and the Human Body* (Albany: State University of New York Press, 1997), 93.

6. Sigmund Freud, 'The Uncanny', in Freud, *On Creativity and the Unconscious* (New York: Harpers, 1958), 122–61.

7. Homi K. Bhabha, 'Halfway House', *Artforum* 35:9 (May 1997), 11.

8. Ibid., 125.

9. All nations and peoples have at their heart origin-myths that involve their own great history of migration (Virgil's epic of Aeneas bringing the Trojans to found Rome, all the biblical migrations from Eden to the Flood to the flight from Egypt, the Navajo's sojourn through the Four Worlds), which is why nations are always worried about the next set of immigrants to arrive, who may arrive as they once did, to settle and overtake their new home as their new homeland – one displacement leading to the displacement and replacement of another – that *heimlich* story is all too familiar and thus all too *unheimlich*.

10. Bhabha, 'Halfway House', 125.

11. Homi K. Bhabha, *The Location of Culture* (London: Routledge, 1994), 86.

12. See Jacques Lacan, *The Four Fundamental Concepts of Psycho-Analysis* (New York: Norton, 1977), 99.

13. Roger Caillois, 'Mimicry and Legendary Psychasthenia', *October* 31 (1984), 16–32.

14. Sigmund Freud, 'Further Recommendations in the Technique of Psychoanalysis: Recollection, Repetition and Working Through', in Freud, *Therapy and Technique* (New York: Collier, 1963), 164–65.

15. Marcel Detienne and Jean-Pierre Vernant, *Cunning Intelligence in Greek Culture and Society* (Chicago: University of Chicago Press, 1991), 36.

16. Ibid., 20–21.

17. Bhabha, *The Location of Culture*, 89.

18. Bertolt Brecht, 'A Short Organum for the Theatre', in John Willett, ed, *Brecht on Theatre* (New York: Hill and Wang, 1964), 192.

19. Jacques Lacan, *Écrits: A Selection*, trans. Alan Sheridan (New York: Norton, 1977), 1–7.

20. Jacques Lacan, *Écrits: A Selection*, trans. Bruce Fink (New York: Norton, 2002), 6.

21. When Oxford adds the word *vulgus* in parenthesis after the phrase *ad captandum*, then this appeal becomes an appeal to the emotions of, as it says, 'the rabble', the crowd, just as for all our inner sense of the specialness of ourselves, what appears before us here in the mirror (or in a photograph or in the holiday video) is a common human being, just another face, there, in the crowd.

22. Sigmund Freud, *Beyond the Pleasure Principle* (New York: Norton, 1959), 8–11.

23. Lacan, *The Four Fundamental Concepts of Psycho-Analysis*, 239.

24. Bhabha, *The Location of Culture*, 113.

25. Ibid., 100.

26. Ibid., 91.

27. Michel Foucault, *The Use of Pleasure* (New York: Random House, 1985), 29; see also Foucault, *Ethics: Subjectivity and Truth* (New York: The New Press, 1997).

28. Michel Foucault, 'The Politics of Health in the Eighteenth Century', in *Power/Knowledge* (New York: Pantheon, 1980): 166–82. See also Michel Foucault, 'The Political Technology of Individuals', in *Technologies of the Self*, ed. Luther H. Martin et al (Amherst: University of Massachusetts Press, 1988), 145–62 and Michel Foucault, 'Governmentality', in *The Foucault Effect: Studies in Governmentality*, ed. Graham Burchell et al (Chicago: University of Chicago Press, 1991), 87–104.

29. Krzysztof Wodiczko, 'Alien Staff', *Assemblage* 23 (1994), 6–17, and *Critical Vehicles: Writings, Projects, Interviews* (Cambridge MA: MIT Press, 1999). See also Rosalyn Deutsche, 'Sharing Strangeness: Krzysztof Wodiczko's Ægis and the Question of Hospitality', *Grey Room* 6 (2002), 26–43, and in this volume Mark Rakatansky, 'Krzysztof Wodiczko: Why the Figural'.

30. Bhabha, *The Location of Culture*, 91.

31. Ibid., 120: 'The metonymic strategy produces the signifier of colonial *mimicry* as the affect of hybridity – at once a mode of appropriation and of resistance, from the disciplined to the desiring.'

32. Shigeru Ban, *Archilab Presentation*, 1999, http://www.archilab.org/public/1999/artistes/shig01en.htm

33. Hans-Ulrich Obrist, *Hans-Ulrich Obrist Interviews Shigeru Ban*, Paris May 1999, http://amsterdam.nettime.org/Lists-Archives/nettime-l-9908/msg00079.html

34. 'One of my favourite buildings is the Farnsworth House by Mies van der Rohe. This was a revolutionary work that achieved complete continuity between inside and outside by means of a totally glazed exterior. However there is no physical continuity as in traditional Japanese residential spaces, where various openable screens exist between inside and outside. The "Curtain Wall House" was formed with an authentic exterior curtain wall. Other works are a response to the "Universal Space" proposed by Mies, that is, the idea of a fluid space generated under a large continuous roof by means of furniture-like cores and partitions.' Shigeru Ban, <http://www.archilab.org/public/1999/artistes/shig01en.htm> 1999.

35. Shigeru Ban, <http://www.housesatsagaponac.com/images/ban/architect-own.htm> (2001).

36. Joan Copjec, 'The Phenomenal Nonphenomenal: Private Space in *Film Noir*', in *Shades of Noir*, ed. Copjec (London: Verso, 1993), 167–98.

INDEX

Architecture Words 9
Tectonic Acts of Desire and Doubt
Mark Rakatansky

Series Editor: Brett Steele

AA Managing Editor: Thomas Weaver
AA Publications Editor: Pamela Johnston
AA Art Director: Zak Kyes
Design: Wayne Daly
Series Design: Wayne Daly, Zak Kyes
Editorial Assistant: Clare Barrett

Set in P22 Underground Pro and Palatino

Printed in Belgium by Die Keure

ISBN 978-1-907896-15-6

For a catalogue of AA Publications visit
aaschool.ac.uk/publications
or email publications@aaschool.ac.uk

AA Publications
36 Bedford Square
London WC1B 3ES
T + 44 (0)20 7887 4021
F + 44 (0)20 7414 0783